100 GREAT ARCHAEOLOGICAL DISCOVERIES

Archaeology & Art

Copyright © 2021 Archaeology & Art

On the cover: Floor mosaic, Dionysos on panther (leopard), House of the Masks, c. 120—80 BC, Delos, Greece.

Contact: *archaeoandart@gmail.com* & instagram.com/archaeologyart

All rights reserved.

ISBN: 9798752703744

CONTENTS

MURUJUGA ROCK ART 2
CAVE OF EL CASTILLO 5
LION MAN OF HOHLENSTEIN STADEL 8
CAVE OF ALTAMIRA 10
CHAUVET CAVE 12
VENUS OF WILLENDORF 15
THEOPETRA CAVE 17
LASCAUX CAVE 21
CAVE OF HANDS 25
SHIGIR IDOL 27
TELL ES-SULTAN 32
TELL QARAMEL 35
TASSILI N'AJJER 37
GÖBEKLI TEPE 41
ÇATALHÖYÜK 51
SETTLEMENT AT LEPENSKI VIR 58
GGANTIJA TEMPLES 61
ÖTZI THE ICEMAN 62
SKARA BRAE 67
NARMER PALETTE 69
PRIAM'S TREASURE 70
KHUFU SHIP 72
SEATED SCRIBE 74
EBLA TABLETS 76
ROYAL TOMBS AT UR 77

PALACE OF KNOSSOS	79
HATTUSA: HITTITE CAPITAL	83
HAMMURABI'S LAW CODE	86
NEBRA SKY DISC	89
GREEK POMPEII: AKROTIRI	91
ROCK CARVINGS IN TANUM	96
FORTRESS CITY OF AGAMEMNON	100
THE FIRST ALPHABET	102
THE SUN CHARIOT	103
BUST OF NEFERTITI	105
THE TOMB OF TUTANKHAMUN	108
OLMEC HEADS	117
LIBRARY OF ASHURBANIPAL	119
SANCTUARY OF DELPHI	120
ISHTAR GATE	130
BABYLONIAN MAP OF THE WORLD	134
PERSEPOLIS	136
PAZYRYK RUG	138
SIBERIAN ICE PRINCESS	141
TOMB OF THE DIVER	143
THE RIACE BRONZES	148
TOLLUND MAN	154
PANAGYURISHTE TREASURE	156
LYCURGUS CUP	160
TOMB OF PHILIP II	164
BOXER AT REST	166
DELOS	168

APHRODISIAS	170
MUSEUM HOTEL	173
THE LADY OF ELCHE	176
BAGHDAT BATTERY	180
DEAD SEA SCROLLS	183
THE TERRACOTTA ARMY	184
VICTORY OF SAMOTHRACE	186
THE ROSETTA STONE	189
MAWANGDUI HAN TOMBS	191
VENUS DE MILO	194
ANTIKYTHERA MECHANISM	196
LION OF KNIDOS	203
TREASURES OF BEGRAM	205
THRONE OF GODS: MOUNT NEMRUT	207
NAZCA LINES	210
LAOCOÖN AND HIS SONS	214
BROKEN POT MOUNTAIN	216
ARCHAEOLOGICAL PARK OF BAIA	219
NERO'S GOLDEN PALACE	221
TEMPLE OF GARNI	226
POMPEII	230
THRACIAN CHARIOT OF KARANOVO	236
CARVILIO'S RING	238
OXYRHYNCHUS PAPYRI	240
ANTINOUS AT DELPHI	242
MITHRAEUM	243
APOLLO BELVEDERE	245

FAYUM MUMMY PORTRAITS 247

THE ROYAL TOMBS OF SILLA 251

ROMAN VOODOO DOLL 254

GIRLS IN BIKINI MOSAIC 255

MOGAO CAVES 259

PYRAMID OF THE SUN 263

THE MOZU TOMBS 266

SIGIRIYA PALACE 267

MOSAICS OF HAGIA SOPHIA 269

SUTTON HOO SHIP BURIAL 278

AMERICA'S POMPEII: JOYA DE CERÉN 280

TOMB OF THE PAKAL THE GREAT 285

THE MAYAN CALENDAR 290

TEMPLE OF BOROBUDUR 293

OSEBERG VIKING SHIP 296

EASTER ISLAND 300

ONFIM DRAWINGS 303

SACSAYHUAMÁN 310

MACHU PICCHU 313

THE GRAVE OF RICHARD III 315

AZTEC SUN STONE 320

ACKNOWLEDGMENTS 324

BIBLIOGRAPHY 325

PREFACE

The term archaeology derives from the two Greek words archaios ("ancient") and logos ("knowledge"). In its modern sense, it has come to mean the study of the material remains of the past and is generally restricted to the study of artifacts dating up to the end of the Middle Ages.

Archaeology began as a treasure hunt. In the 1920s, archaeology was all about digging. Digging is still a major part of archaeology. Today archaeologists study every clue to the past to piece together the history of civilization. Even a garbage pit can help to reveal how people lived.

Archaeology is partially about objects but mostly about people. The excitement of archaeology lies in building up a picture of human life thousands of years ago, by making connections between objects found in the ground and the people who left them there long ago. Day by day archaeologists bring to light more of the past. By excavating the things ancient people made and used, they piece together a picture of life in ancient times. Since every fragment that is excavated adds to this picture, a piece of broken pottery can be just as important as gold. For example, finding a treasure in a 5.000-year-old tomb is exciting. Even more exciting is understanding why people put such a treasure there in the first place.

Both the beauty of the things that are found and the clues they give about the past are great pleasures for an archaeologist.

This book introduces you to some of the most impressive and exciting archaeological discoveries that have been made since the 1800s when the study of archaeology began. From Aboriginal rock art to the 10.000-year-old Shigir Idol, from the Göbekli Tepe to the Nazca Lines, the world's 100 greatest discoveries are in this book.

While preparing the book, we took the utmost care to use a simple narrative that anyone interested in archaeology can understand. Our aim was to create a book that would appeal to everyone, not only for professional archaeologists but also for children and adults who have an interest in archaeology and art. We hope that this book will give you new insights into the fascinating world of the past.

Archaeology & Art

MURUJUGA ROCK ART

(Murujuga, Australia, c. 47.000 BC)

Murujuga is located in Western Australia, which covers the Burrup Peninsula. It is an Aboriginal term that is used to define Dampier Archipelago.

Burrup Peninsula is famous for its petroglyphs. It is thought that there are more than one million petroglyphs on the peninsula. You can take a journey in the history of our kind which dates about 47.000 years ago. It will be worth noting that this is also an archaeological record.

Many extinct animal species such as Thylacines and megafauna were depicted in the images together with human figures and images. You can also find a wide range of marine, avian, and land animals. Moreover, there are also arts about the tools that we have used such as fish traps, stone arrangements, ceremonial places, middens, and rock shelters.

Figure 1: The ancient Aboriginal rock art at the Burrup Peninsula is the world's largest and oldest. Humans have lived on the Australian continent for around 50.000 years.

Historians believe that the images in the Burrup Peninsula are connected to each other and provide evidence about the lifestyle of Aboriginal tribes.

Some of these arts also belong to the Yaburrarra community that used to live in the area before they were destroyed by a massacre in the 1860s. Unfortunately, some of Australia's largest factories are located a few kilometers away from the heritage. These polluting facilities have an adverse effect on the living proofs of Aboriginal tribes.

The Burrup Peninsula is also home to the world's largest and oldest Aboriginal rock art. Before Westerners discovered Australia, the continent was home to many Aboriginal tribes for over 50.000 years

Figure 2: Rock art of Burrup Peninsula: Turtles.

Figure 3: Tasmanian Tiger

Murujuga Rock Art

Figure 4: Kangaroo.

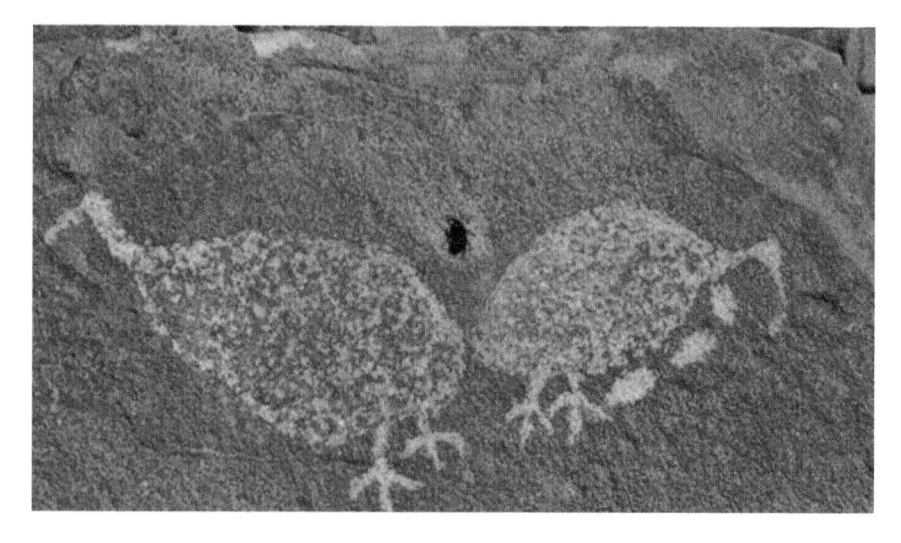

Figure 5: Rock art of Burrup Peninsula.

CAVE OF EL CASTILLO

(Spain, c. 38.800 BC)

Europe's oldest artwork, believed to be at least 40.800 years old, was discovered in the Cave of El Castillo, near the town of Puente Viesgo, about 30 kilometers south of Santander in the Cantabria region of what is today Spain.

The cave inside contains one of the most unique and important environments in Prehistoric Europe, a reference point for history. It's over 275 figures, all dating back to the dawn of the presence of Homo sapiens in Europe, represent an underground passageway through the origins of symbolic thought, the abstract mind and artistic expression.

Figure 6: The 'Corredor de los Puntos' lies within Spain's El Castillo cave. Red disks here have been dated between 34.000 and 36.000 years ago, and elsewhere in the cave to 40.800 years ago, making them examples of Europe's earliest cave art.

The walls contain the actual silhouettes of prehistoric human hands and various representations of animals, including what appears to be a mammoth, in the depths of the cave. The abstraction of these Paleolithic art styles is said to have been an inspiration for the more recent artists such as Picasso and Miro.

Prehistoric artists probably spent years learning and practicing their craft. Many sketches and corrected drawings have been found alongside other surviving prehistoric pictures. This may be evidence that skilled older artists taught younger ones.

For the first 2.5 million years of the archaeological record, the only artifacts of human beings and their hominid precursors were strictly utilitarian: stone tools and perhaps fragments of bone used for simple digging tasks. Then, around 40.000 years ago, at the beginning of a period prehistorians know as the Upper Paleolithic (40.000 to 11.000 years ago), Western Eurasia underwent a major cultural transformation. Where almost no material images had existed before, the people began to paint, to engrave, to sculpt, to make and wear items of personal adornment, and to devise musical instruments. Some of the earliest images that have been found were made by families. They are handprints. Adults and children placed their hands against a greased wall and blew pigment through hollow sticks over them. When they took their hands away, the hand shape was left.

Finger painting Early artists created skillful and realistic images. Pictures of animals found in caves were produced using the most basic tools and equipment. We think that artists applied paint by blowing through hollow sticks or bones. They also used leather pads, feathers, fur, sticks with the ends crunched (or chewed) into a kind of brush or their fingers.

Paints were made by crushing minerals into powder and putting them onto damp surfaces, like a rock. Sometimes the powder was mixed with wax or oil to make it stick to other surfaces, such as hide, wood, or bone. Powdered pigments were kept in hollow bone tubes. Crushed rocks and soil produced browns, yellows, reds, and oranges. Powdered charcoal gave black. Another rock, called manganese, produced violet. Chalk made white. Greens and blues came from crushed rocks, but these rocks were not found everywhere in the world.

Figure 7: Some of the hand stencils, mostly near the front and middle sections of the cave, were painted more than 37.000 years ago, but some of the more recent hand stencils are 24.000 years old.

Paleolithic artists painted the animals they hunted, such as bulls, bison, or mammoths. Many experts think that the artists believed they captured the animal's soul when they painted it. This could be why the images are so lifelike.

If the artists captured the animal's true likeness, they thought they would be sure to capture the real thing during the hunt. Whatever the paintings mean, surely no one would have crawled so deep into these caves to paint unless the pictures had serious meaning. Dark and eerie, the caves were probably sacred places for Paleolithic people, and the art was part of their beliefs.

Modern humans arrived in Europe from Africa some 41.500 years ago. And before 42.000 years ago, the only humans in Europe were Neanderthals, who had been running around Europe for 200.000 or 300.000 years. The oldest drawings in El Castillo Cave are over

40.000 years old. Some scholars claim these drawings could be 42.000 years old. These dates caused great turmoil. Because it is thought that modern humans came to Europe on this date, and Neanderthals (Homo Neanderthalensis) were in this region before this date. Therefore, it is still debated whether the creators of these drawings were a hybrid of our Neanderthal cousins, modern humans, or maybe both.

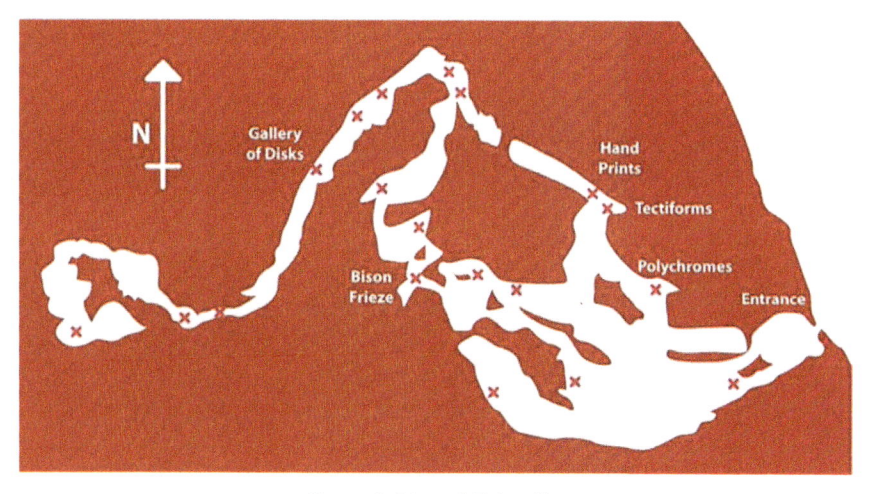

Figure 8: Map of El Castillo.

LION MAN OF HOHLENSTEIN STADEL

(Mount Hohlenstein, Germany, c. 38.000 BC)

The oldest known zoomorphic figure in the world (dating to approximately 38.000 BC), the Lion Man of Hohlenstein Stadel was discovered by archaeologist Robert Wetzel in 1939 in a cave on Mount Hohlenstein in the Swabian Jura in southwest Germany. Due to the outbreak of World War II just a week after the discovery, the finds were never studied and so forgotten.

Pieces that were forgotten for thirty years after the outbreak of the Second World War were rediscovered and partially reassembled by Professor Joachim Hahn of the University of Tübingen in 1969. However, this assembly was not successful due to missing parts. The figurine was restored again in 1987/88. Since 2008, other missing pieces were unearthed in the excavations in the cave, and in 2012 the figurine was separated into separate pieces and new discovered pieces were added together with the old pieces. As a result of the restoration works, nearly 300 pieces of the figurine were completely combined in late 2013.

The Lion Man, 31 centimeters tall, 6.3 cm wide, and 5.9 cm thick, was made from a mammoth tooth, the largest animal of the time. An experiment using the same type of stone tools found in the Ice Age showed that it took more than 380 hours to carve the Lion Man. So, it was a very demanding job.

Figure 9: Lion Man of Hohlenstein Stadel.

Lion Man of Hohlenstein Stadel

Figure 10

The plate standing in the groin area of the Lion Man, part lion and part human, is interpreted as stylized male genitalia. Part of the front part of the Lion Man's body is missing. The posture and muscularity of the shoulders resemble a man standing on his toes and arms at his sides. The head of the figurine is forward facing and directed towards the viewer, with a stimulating gaze emphasized by a strong jawline and erect ears. The details of the Lion Man's face show that he is attentive, watching and listening. The left upper arm is marked with incisions depicting the tattoo or scar. We do not know if this figure depicts a man (perhaps a shaman) wearing a lion's headdress or a legendary being.

Researchers have determined that the Stadel Cave, where the Lion Man is located, was not a suitable place to live 40.000 years ago due to its north facing position and position in the sun. For this reason, it is likely that the cave was a gathering place for rituals. In 2017, UNESCO declared Stadel Cave and other Swabian sites World Heritage. The Lion Man statue is exhibited in the Ulmer Museum in Germany today.

CAVE OF ALTAMIRA

(Altamira, Santander, Spain, c. 34.000 BC)

Near Santillana del Mar in Cantabria, Spain, the Cave of Altamira is located, which is famous for cave art with charcoal drawings and polychrome paintings depicting human hands and plants.

A hunter accidentally discovered the caves in 1869. They were first explored by an archaeologist, Marcellino Sanz de Sautuola, in 1875, and four years later, he discovered the underground chambers containing the paintings.

Cave paintings of Altamira date back between 36.000 and 15.000 years. The colorful ceiling paintings depict wild animals in motion and at rest, including deer, wild horse, and wild boar in addition to bison; they represent a high point of Ice Age cave art (rock paintings).

Figure 11: A bison painted onto the wall of the Altamira cave. The artists used natural minerals such as ocher to make their paints, which they often put on the walls with their hands, or with a stick or a brush made from animal hair.

The authenticity of the pictures was disputed for a long time because of the freshness of the colors and the lack of comparison. It was only after the

Cave of Altamira

discovery of other caves with similar depictions in southern France (1902) that Altamira came back into the public eye. In the following decades, the cave was thoroughly explored. In 1979 it was closed to visitors for conservation reasons. Since the summer of 2001, they have been able to visit an exact replica (Neocueva, "New Cave") in Santillana del Mar. The Deutsches Museum in Munich houses a true-to-scale reproduction of the ceiling paintings. Altamira has been declared a World Heritage Site by UNESCO.

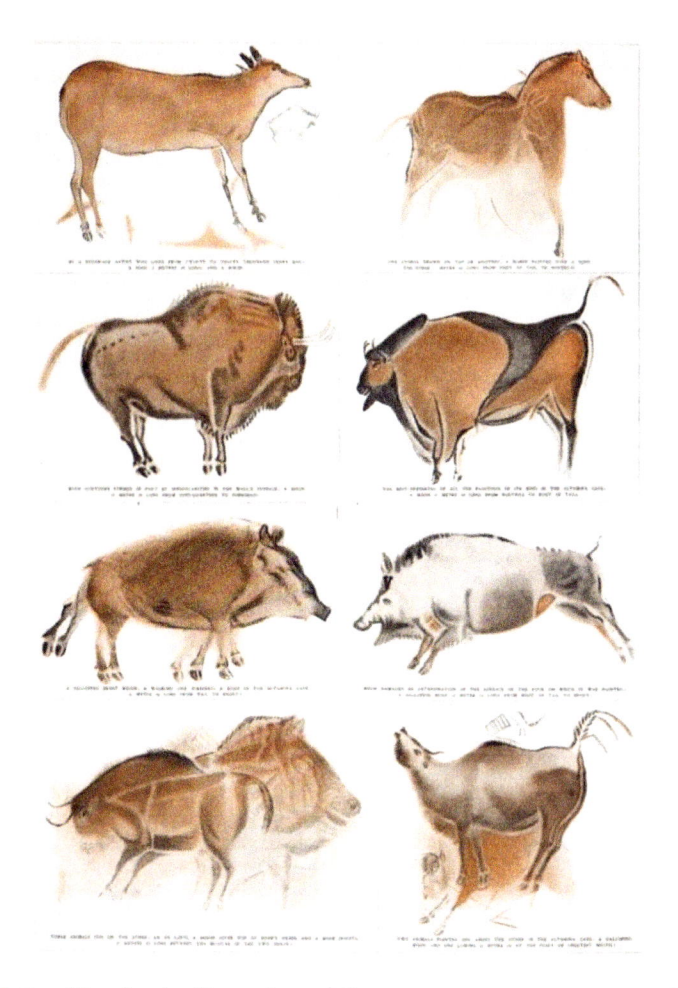

Figure 12: Henri Breuil, color illustrations of Altamira Cave paintings, 1906. In- Illustrated London News, 1912.

CHAUVET CAVE

(Ardèche, France, c. 33.000 BC)

On Christmas Eve, 1994, three spelunkers -Jean-Marie Chauvet and his friends Elitte Brune and Christian Hillaire- made one of the greatest archaeological discoveries ever inside a cave near Pont-d'Arc in the Ardéche region of southern France. Some paintings are 35.000 years old.

Figure 13: Lion Panel, Chauvet Cave.

The paintings in the Chauvet Cave complex include images of herds of hooked- horned aurochs (wild oxen), ibex, running deer, charging wooly rhinoceros, prowling lions, rearing thick-maned horses, wooly mammoths, open-mouthed bears, owl, and animals that are usually associated with Africa, not Europe. In all, there are 442 animals created over thousands of years, using nearly 400.000 square feet of cave surface.

Some animals are solitary or concealed but most are in groups, some of which look like great mosaics or multiple movie frames.

Unlike other caves in France and Spain, which show mostly hunted animals such as bison and oxen, the animals in Chauvet Cave are large, powerful animals that generally weren't eaten for food: lions, cave bears, rhinos. The cave has been sealed off to the public since 1994.

Chauvet Cave

Caverne du Pont-d'Arc, a facsimile of Chauvet Cave on the model of the so-called "Faux Lascaux", was opened to the public on 25 April 2015.

Figure 14: Oldest owl engraving in the world. c. 33.000 years ago. This owl, circa 45cm in height, is found in the second section of the cave. The official cave website describes the Chauvet owl image as follows: "This finger tracing represents an owl. The position of the wings shows that its head is turned 180 degrees relative to its posterior face. The anatomical characteristics of the animal permit its attribution to Moyen Duc [Long-eared Owl] (Asio otus). This drawing was realized on the soft outer layer of the cave wall. In the background we see traces that show the wall surface was scraped before the drawing was made."

Figure 15: Female rhinoceros head, Chauvet Cave.

Figure 16: Oldest known image of a leopard, c. 30.000 BC, Chauvet Cave.

Figure 17: Red Mammoth, Chauvet Cave.

VENUS OF WILLENDORF

(Willendorf, Austria, c. 29.500 BC)

One of the most famous items of prehistoric sculpture, the Venus of Willendorf, dates to between 28.000-30.000 BC, making it one of the oldest and most famous surviving works of art. It was found in 1908 at a paleolithic site near Willendorf, a village in Lower Austria near the town of Krems.

The statuette, carved from limestone decoratively tinged with red ochre, depicts a female nude. Though without a face, the crown of the figure's head is decorated with a repeating motif resembling either a braided hairstyle or a patterned headdress. By about 30.000 years ago, people could spare the time from the endless task of hunting for food to express themselves in art. They painted on the walls of caves and produced simple sculptures.

Figure 18: The Venus of Willendorf was carved from stone. She has hair but no facial features. She measures just under 11.1 cm high (4½") and could fit comfortably in the palm of her hand. She may have been used in rituals to do with finding food or giving thanks for a successful hunt.

Venus of Willendorf

The face of the sculpture is totally abstract, with no attempt to craft features or different planes. The head and face are represented by a sphere, with no neck to speak of. Much of the head of the figurine is covered with a knot-like pattern. The arms and feet of the sculpture are almost non-existent, showing that the artist was not concerned with an accurate depiction of life. The major emphasis is placed on the breasts, belly, thighs, and genitalia of the statuette.

It is a small statue of a woman with huge breasts and thighs, but no real facial features. So, why did the Stone Age artists carve women in such a way? One theory is that these statues represented goddesses of fertility, and their ample figures suggested the richness of the earth. But perhaps women really did look a bit like that in those days.

These statues were carved during the last Ice Age when the winters were so cold that people could not survive unless they developed a large supply of fat in their bodies during the summer.

Figure 19

Today, the Venus Cabinet in Naturhistorisches Museum Vienna houses the famous 29.500-year-old Venus of Willendorf. The Venus Cabinet is bathed in a deep red light designed to recreate the red ochre that would have originally covered the Venus of Willendorf. Furthermore, an animation shows visitors how the area near the Danube where the "Venus" was found looked like 30.000 years ago, in the Ice Age, and how the climate and landscape have changed since then.

THEOPETRA CAVE

(Meteora, Greece, 23.000 years ago)

The Theopetra Cave is an archaeological site located in Meteora, in the central Greek region of Thessaly.

Over the past decades, many prehistoric finds have been unearthed from many different periods of our prehistoric period. Stone tools, burials, animal remains, the oldest known human-made structure, are only a few of them.

According to archaeologists, evidence of human habitation in the cave can be traced without interruption from the Middle Paleolithic to the end of the Neolithic period. Archaeological evidence now indicates that humans occupied the cave during the Middle Paleolithic period, approximately 130.000 years ago.

Figure 20: Theopetra Cave is located at the foot of a 100-meter (330 foot) tall limestone cliff which looms over Theopetra village.

The Theopetra Cave has been the subject of systematic multidisciplinary archaeological excavations conducted since 1987 by Dr. Nina Kyparissi-Apostolika. The excavations continued up until 2007.

Theopetra Cave

In 2009, the Theopetra Cave was officially opened to the public. Objects discovered in the cave include stone tools of the Paleolithic, Mesolithic, and Neolithic periods, as well as Neolithic pottery, bone and shell objects, skeletons from 15.000, 9.000, and 8.000 BC, a stone wall from 23.000 BC, and traces of plants and seeds that reveal dietary habits. Analyzes of skeletons confirmed that the community in the cave mostly lived on grains, hunting large and small animals, but taming animals, including dogs. The Theopetra Cave is thought to have been abandoned at the end of the Stone Age, as water-eroded rocks began to break inland or more communities began to form in open areas.

Figure 21: The wall at Theopetra - possibly the oldest existing human-made structure: c. 23.000 years old. The age of the wall dates to the last ice age. Because of this dating, it is believed that the cave residents built the wall to protect them from the cold outside.

Theopetra Cave

Figure 22: General view of the Theopetra Cave.

Figure 23: General view of the Theopetra Cave.

Figure 24: Skeleton from c. 15.000 BC, Theopetra Cave.

Figure 25: Children's footprints c. 120.000 BC, Theopetra Cave.

LASCAUX CAVE

(Montignac, France, c. 17.000 BC)

Lascaux Cave is a Paleolithic cave situated in southwestern France, near the village of Montignac in the Dordogne region. The Cave of Lascaux is famous for its prehistoric paintings showing various animals, hunts, and wars. Four local boys discovered them on Thursday, 12 September 1940.

Lascaux is often called the Sistine Chapel of Prehistory because of its wealth of pictures. More than 600 paintings – mostly of animals - dot the cave's interior walls in impressive compositions. Horses are the most numerous, but deer, aurochs, ibex, bison, and even some felines can also be found. They have been dated to be 17.000-15.000 B.C.

Figure 26: The paintings in Lascaux Cave in Southwest France are not the oldest examples of art in the world, but they are considered among the most stunning. The pictures, painted approximately 17.000 years ago.

There is a very interesting fact about the drawings: the hunts were drawn on the wall like a comic strip. The story of the hunt goes from the left to the right until the prey is captured. These pictures were obviously used to tell stories. And they may be called the oldest known comic books. Archaeologists believe that the artists painted horses and bulls in hopes of improving their luck in the hunt.

Perhaps the animal images were in movement because they were in flight from hunters.

Throughout the cave, amid the lifelike animal images, are about four hundred signs and symbols. Some of the lines on the walls may represent arrows aimed at the fleeing animals. The strange square symbols may be traps holding the animals' feet.

When Lascaux was opened to the public in 1948, it was an instant success. People from around the world flocked to see the magnificent art. The continuous flow of tourists (1.500 / day) and the carbon dioxide and human respiration began to degrade the prehistoric paintings in the decorated cave. The Lascaux cave was closed to the public in 1963 after it became clear that the many visitors caused, among others, the growth of algae on the cave walls, dealing irreparable damage to the paintings.

Now, the temperature and humidity in the cave are measured constantly. No more than twenty people a week can enter Lascaux after obtaining special permits. They are allowed in groups of no more than five and can stay for only thirty-five minutes.

Figure 27: The strange square symbols may be traps holding the animals' feet.

Lascaux Cave

Figure 28: The Shaft of the Wounded (Dead) Man: A wounded man, aurochs bull, bird and rhino. Dated to the Upper Paleolithic period.

Figure 29: Panel of the Wounded Man, detail.

Lascaux Cave

Figure 30: Hall of the Bulls, Lascaux. One of the great achievements of mankind.

Figure 31: The Great Black Bul

CAVE OF HANDS

(Santa Cruz, Argentina, c. 13.000 BC)

A UNESCO World Heritage site, Cueva de las Manos (or "Cave of the Hands") is a series of rocky overhangs in a remote part of Argentinian Patagonia, containing some of the best ancient cave art to be found anywhere in the world.

The art in the cave dates from 13.000 to 9.000 years ago. The age of the paintings was calculated from the remains of bone-made pipes which were used for spraying the paint on the wall of the cave to create silhouettes of hands. The images are negative painted, that is, stenciled.

Most of the prints are of left hands, which suggests that painters held the spraying pipe with their right hand, or they put the back of their right hand to the wall and held the spraying pipe with their left hand. Aside from handprints, there are also depictions of human beings and animals such as guanacos (a camelid native to South America, closely related to the llama), rheas, and felines, as well geometric shapes, zigzag patterns, sun representations, and hunting scenes.

Figure 32: Stenciled handprints dating back 10.000 years, some of the earliest forms of cave art.

Cave of Hands

The hunting scenes in the cave depict animals and human figures interacting in a dynamic and naturalistic manner.

Different hunting strategies are depicted, with animals being surrounded, ambushed, or attacked by hunters using holds, weighted throwing weapons (called bolas). Some scenes show individual hunters and other groups of ten or more men.

Figure 33: Wall-paintings dating back 10.000 years, some of the earliest forms of cave art.

Figure 34

SHIGIR IDOL

(Yekaterinburg, Russia, c. 10.500 BC)

The great Shigir Idol is an archaeological Ural treasure that humankind has yet to solve. Its age is approximately 12.500 years, and it is the oldest monumental wooden sculpture in the world. Modern studies on the idol started more than twenty years ago, but there are still many unresolved questions.

The middle of the 19th century was the "gold rush" era in the Urals. Due to gold prospecting, the Shigir peat bog was partially drained. Workers found objects made of wood, horns, animal bones, stone, and clay.

Figure 35: Shigir Idol is displayed in the Sverdlovsk Regional Museum of Local Lore in Yekaterinburg, Russia.

The first archaeological discovery of this area was made in 1880 by MV Malakhov. After Malakhov's discovery, many researchers became interested in Shigir peat bog. Thousands of finds were made here (animal figures, arrowheads, knives, shovels, clay pots, wooden skis, etc.). The age of the finds was very different from each other. This area somehow attracted ancient people for thousands of years.

The Shigir discoveries in 1887 aroused great interest at the large Siberian-Ural scientific and industrial exhibition held in Yekaterinburg. However, the most important discovery came three years after this exhibition.

Shigir Idol

On a winter day on January 24, 1890, fragments of a wooden statue that later became the "Great Shigir Idol" were found in the second Kurinsky section of the Shigirskiy peat bog. The wooden idol was lying under a layer of peat four meters deep. The idol was delivered to the Ural Society of Natural Sciences Lovers Association (UOLE).

Dmitry Lobanov, the curator of the UOLE museum, first undertook to rebuild the Shigir Idol in the 1890s. However, his attempt failed. Because Lobanov used only half of the ten pieces. (as in the image below)

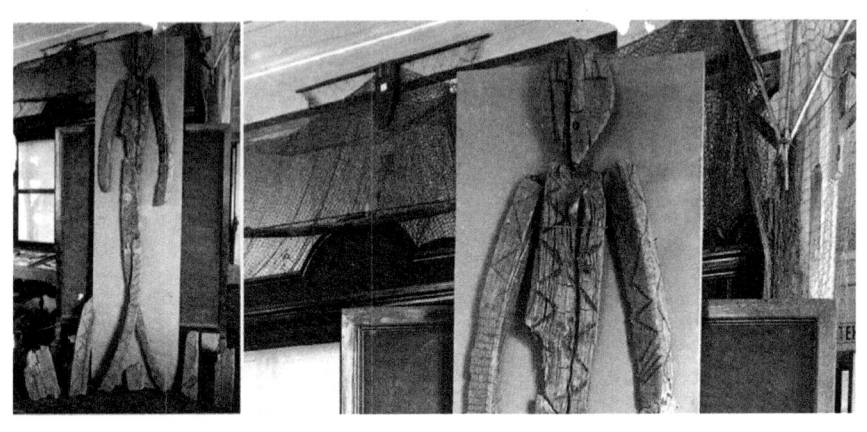

Figure 36: A photo of the Shigir sculpture reconstructed by D. Lobanov in 1890-91. The figure remained displayed in this shape until 1914.

The idol stood in the museum for more than twenty years. The second - most complete - reconstruction of the idol in 1914 was carried out by Russian archaeologist Vladimir Yakovlevich Tolmachev. Tolmachev used all ten tracks. Shigir folded his idol into a tall, narrow figure (about 5.3 m) to match the carved ornament on all of its pieces and detailed the resulting figure from all sides. The Soviet government was not interested in the Shigir Idol and put it in storage. The Shigir Idol remained in the warehouse for about seventy years; during this time, the lower part of this unique archaeological find (about 193 centimeters) has been irreversibly lost. Today we can only see the missing parts of the statue in Tolmachev's drawings. (as in the image below)

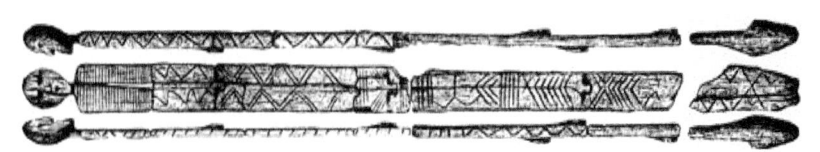

Figure 37: Shigir Idol in Tolmachev's drawings.

Shigir Idol

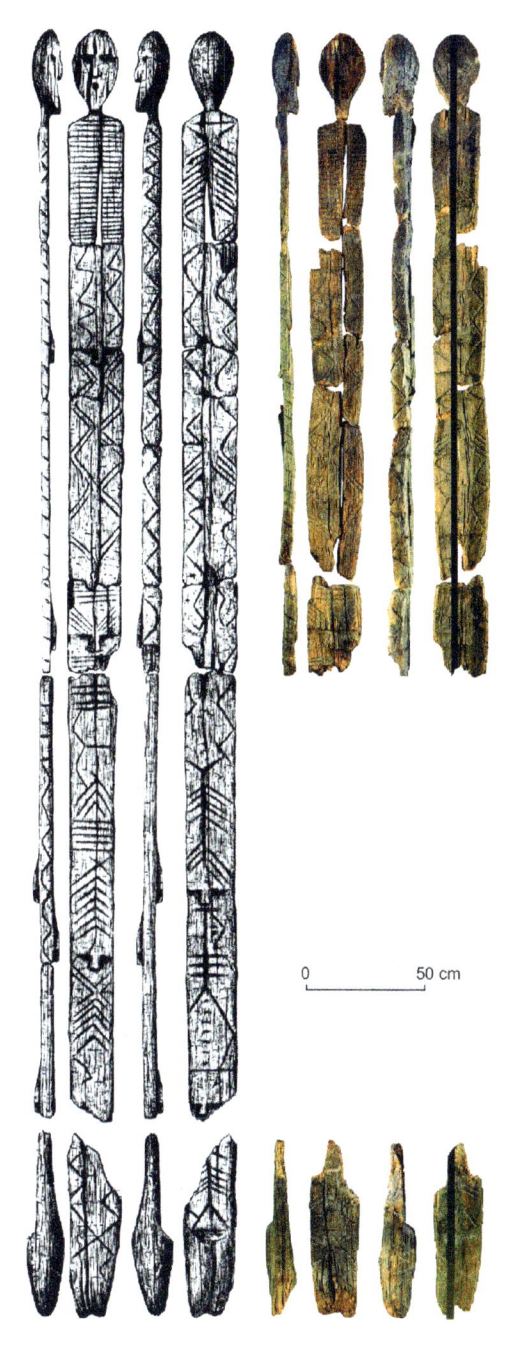

Figure 38-39: Shigir Idol in Tolmachev's drawings and today.

Shigir Idol

Display and research of the idol started again in the 1990s. There was no consensus on dating the Shigir Idol.

For this reason, pieces from the statue were sent to Moscow and St Petersburg in 1997, and as a result of radiocarbon tests, the statue was dated to 7.500 BC. In 2014, scientists from Russia and Germany conducted a second comprehensive radiocarbon study. As a result of this research, the age of Shigir Idol has been determined as 11.600. In March 2021, a study published in Quaternary International has pushed that date back by a further 900 years—making it more than twice as old as Stonehenge or the Egyptian pyramids. Shigir Idol, which was never shown in the Soviet era due to religious prejudices and was kept in storage, began to be displayed in a special hall at the Sverdlovsk Regional Museum of Local Culture.

Figure 40: A Details from Shigir Idol.

A special glass section was created in the museum to protect the Shigir Idol. The idol is displayed in the glass room where it was stored at a constant temperature of 16 degrees. Also, in order to minimize the force of gravity and to minimize the pressure on the parts of the idol, the idol parts are attached to the display case with thin metal brackets. Shigir Idol can be seen today at the Sverdlovsk Regional Museum of Local Culture in Yekaterinburg, Russia.

There are many opinions and debates about how the Shigir Idol survived, what it was erected for, and what the figures on it mean.

Shigir Idol is thought to survive thanks to two factors. First, the idol was just cut and made from a larch tree, about 159 years old. Larch trees are very durable. Secondly, the peat bog where the idol was found provided a natural protective environment for the idol.

Russian archaeologists believe that the Shigir Idol was not dug into the ground like a totem to help it stand upright. The idol was probably standing on a stone plinth because the lower part was flattened by strong pressure and this statue was quite heavy. No supporting beam marks or any other marks were found on the idol. The Shigir idol could be leaning against a tree or a rock.

The Shigir Idol's head is three-dimensional, the nose is chiseled and pinched. Under the nose, double lines are carved. Pupils are marked with depth. The idol's chin is sharpened. The body of the idol is straight and rectangular, and at the approximate level of the ribcage, there are a series of horizontal lines that appear to represent the ribs. The rest of the wood surface is decorated with geometric motifs such as chevrons, herringbone, and other abstract markings.

There is no generally accepted opinion regarding the meaning of figures on the idol. According to archaeologist Mikhail Zhilin of the Russian Academy of Sciences in Moscow: "The shape of the ears and the long nose resembles a wolf or a dog, while the two shallow snouts suggest more of a wild boar. Therefore, the mix of elements may represent a fantasy animal or a mythical creature. The idol may depict local forest spirits or demons."

Today, Göbekli Tepe is the only area outside the Urals where there is evidence of monumental anthropomorphic sculptures and animal representations of the Early Holocene history. Finds from the Shigir peat bog point to the existence of a contemporary, impressive, elaborate art tradition along with Göbekli Tepe.

TELL ES-SULTAN

(Jericho, Palestine, c. 10.000 BC)

The site of Tell es-Sultan (ancient Jericho) is located in the lower plain of the Jordan Valley, approximately 10 kilometers north of the Dead Sea.

The site is the lowest (258 m below sea level) and one of the oldest towns. The Site of Tell es-Sultan is identified with ancient Jericho & is mentioned in the Bible more than one hundred times, often as a symbol of peace and wealth.

The excavations uncovered the cultural history of the site, which stretches over 10.000 years. The earliest settlement at Tell es-Sultan, though probably only seasonal, was during the Natufian period. (circa 10th millennia BC) The cultural material, consisting of flint tools, attests to a hunting Natufian camp near the spring.

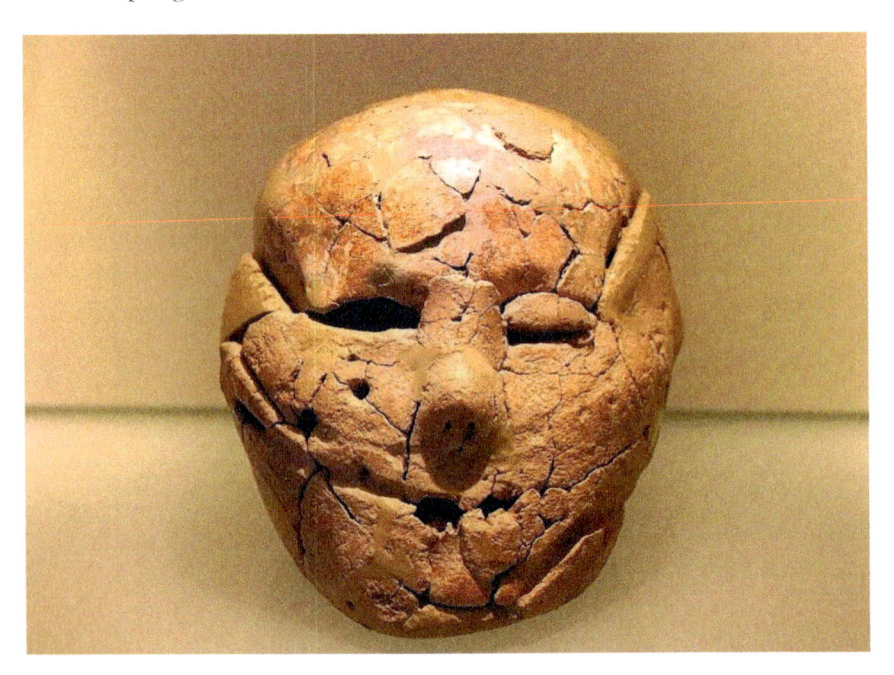

Figure 41: Plastered Skull, Tell es-Sultan, Jericho, c. 9.000 BC, Israel Museum, Jerusalem.

Tell es-Sultan

The Neolithic Period in Tell es-Sultan represents transformations from a prehistoric subsistence model of early human history, based on hunting and gathering, to a new subsistence model based on the domestication of plants and animals in the first settled society.

Tell es-Sultan was deserted in the Late Bronze Age (14th century BC). Archaeological excavations carried out in the mid-20th century evidenced 23 layers of ancient civilizations at the site. The inhabitants of Jericho left behind a mound, averaging 21 meters above the plain, of many strata of human remains.

Figure 42: There is a stone tower (Jericho Tower) built around 8.000 BC. Together with the towers located at Tell Qaramel (today in Aleppo city), it is one of the oldest towers in the world.

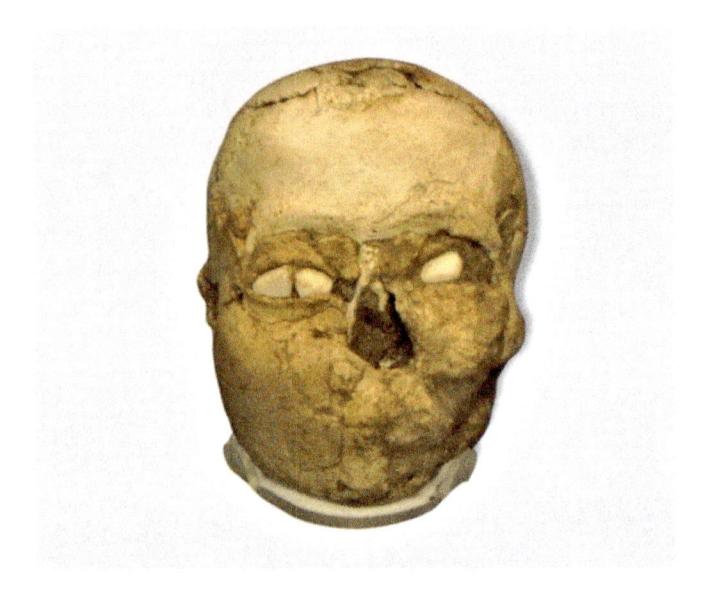

Figure 43: A Neolithic skull which has been covered in plaster, with seashells placed in the eye sockets, and was otherwise adorned to make it look like it's still alive. 17 x 14.6 cm. Now on display at the British Museum.

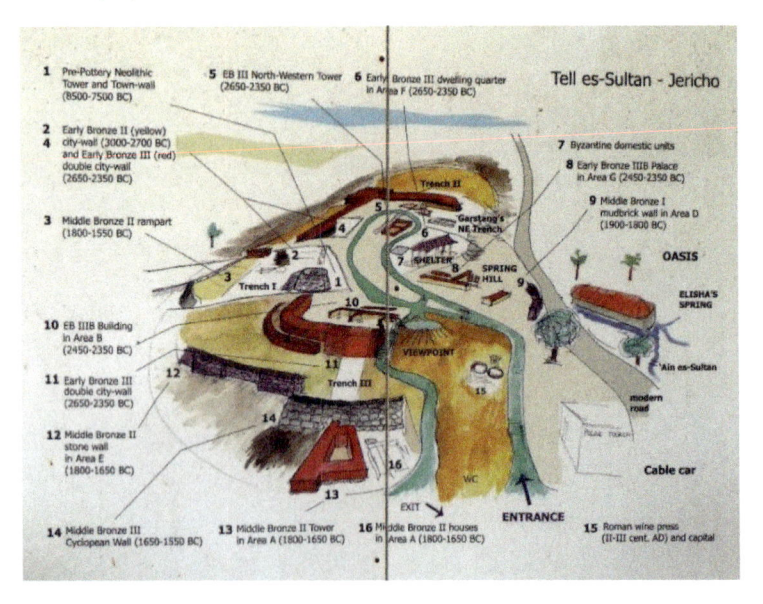

Figure 44: The archaeological site of Tell-es Sultan is a 21-meter-high mound that covers approximately an acre. During excavations, remains were found of the potter, tools, graves, grain storage jars, clay figures, beads, personal belongings, and furniture.

TELL QARAMEL

(Aleppo, Syria, c. 10.000 BC)

Found in the north of present-day Syria, Tell Qaramel dates close in age to Göbekli Tepe (Turkey) 9.130–8.800 BC. Tell Qaramel is a tell, or archaeological mound, located in the north of present-day Syria, 25 km north of Aleppo and about 65 km south of the Taurus mountains, adjacent to the river Quweiq.

In 1999, joint Polish-Syrian research of this area was led by Professor Ryszard F. Mazurowski of Warsaw University. They came up with a number of astonishing discoveries – among them five-round stone towers, each more than 18 feet in diameter with walls over four and a half feet thick. The site has been carbon-dated to between 10.900 and 8.850 BC.

Figure 45: Aerial view of site.

Some 55 charcoal samples were collected during the excavations and dated in the GADAM (Gliwice Absolute Dating Methods) Centre in Gliwice, Poland. The stratigraphy of the settlement and results of radiocarbon dating testify that these are the oldest such constructions in the world, older than the famous and unique tower in Jericho.

Tell Qaramel

Depending on the dates used for the tower at Jericho, the towers in Syria are between a few hundred years and two thousand years earlier. The excavations have revealed a vibrant collection of everyday use of flint, bone, and mostly stone objects, such as decorated chlorite or limestone vessels; shaft straighteners used to stretch wooden arrow shafts, richly decorated in geometrical, zoomorphic, and anthropomorphic patterns; as well as different kinds of stones, querns, mortars, pestles, grinders, polishing plates and celts.

The Discovery of Tell Qaramel is one of a number of discoveries in recent years that take the origins of civilization much farther back in time than previously believed.

These origins now extend back to the last Ice Age, long before archaeologists used to think civilization began.

Figure 46: Towers of Tell Qaramel.

TASSILI N'AJJER

(Sahara Desert, Algeria, c. 10.000 BC)

The Sahara Desert is the home for Tassili n'Ajjer, which is a national part of southeastern Algeria plateaus. This national park is located between Mali, Niger, Libya, and Algeria. It is famous for prehistoric rock arts, which are spread to 80.000 square kilometers in the area. Moreover, it has been preserved by UNESCO since 1982 by taking its place in the World Heritage Site list and accepted as Biosphere Reserve since 1986.

The area was discovered in 1933 and caused a worldwide sensation by hosting thousands of years of prehistoric art forms. Today, more than 15.000 drawings have been discovered in the caves and they are all dated between 10.000 BC and 100 AD. Experts believe that it is a great source and proof for the evolution of our kind. Most of the art depicts animal migrations and the daily lives of the communities.

Sahara was not this dry in the past and there were plenty of water sources running between the mountains, which create the perfect environment for wildlife. The area was also the habitat of hunter-gatherers. Experts also found 11.500 years-old pottery around Aïr Mountains that prove this claim. There are also evidences that mankind started to benefit from domesticated livestock and enjoyed a pastoral lifestyle around 5.000 BC. Moreover, people started to move from the region due to the major climate change in the area around 4.000 BC and took their livestock with them. It was around 3.500 BC when Sahara took its current day form.

Figure 47: African Rock Art in Tassili n'Ajjer, Tamanrasset, Algeria.

Figure 48: The rock paintings show that, among others, giraffe and hippopotamus once lived in the Sahara.

Today, Tassili n'Ajjer is the living proof of the lifestyle and past of Sahara. As of 2021, the oldest discovered art belongs to the Large Wild Fauna Period, which took place between 10.000 and 7.000 BC. Animals that used to live in the area such as rhinos, hippos, giraffes, and elephants can be clearly seen on these paintings.

Besides these animals, there are arts that include human figures and belonging to Round Head Period, which is around 7.500 and 5.000 BC. People in Tassili n'Ajjer were still hunter-gatherers during this period but gradually moved to the Pastoral Period. The pastoral Period took place between 5.000 and 2.000 BC. The next period is called the Horse Period and took place between 1.000 BC and 1 AD.

Tassili n'Ajjer

Since Sahara began to take its current form during this period, our kind gave more importance to long-distance traveling and started to benefit from horses. The last and current period in Sahara is called Camel Period, in which camels started to gain increasing popularity due to changing climate. The youngest art form belonging to this period in the area dates to 200 BC.

Figure 49: About 7.000 years ago, the climate changed again, and the Sahara began to dry up. The animals either died out completely or moved elsewhere. The people were forced to move as well. Some of them went to Egypt where they settled by the banks of the River Nile and became the first Egyptians.

Figure 50

Tassili n' Ajjer

Figure 51: Petroglyph depicting a possibly sleeping antelope, located at Tin Taghirt on the Tassili n'Ajjer in southern Algeria. c. 9.000 BC.

Figure 52: African Rock Art in Tassili n'Ajjer, Tamanrasset, Algeria.

GÖBEKLI TEPE

(Sanliurfa, Turkey c. 9.600 BC)

Göbekli Tepe is located near Örencik Village, 17 km northeast of Sanliurfa in present-day Turkey. Göbekli Tepe, dating to approximately 9.600 BC, is the oldest known monumental structure in the world.

In 1986, a villager named Şavak Yıldız, while plowing his field, found two sculptures, one with a male figure and the other with a reptile relief. Şavak Yıldız took these artifacts to the Sanliurfa Archaeology Museum, 20 km away, on a horse-drawn carriage. However, the official authorities did not understand the importance of these works and put them in a corner in the garden of the museum.

The sculptures caught the attention of German archaeologist Klaus Schmidt, who visited the museum in 1994. Klaus Schmidt asked official museum officials where the artifacts came from. Upon his reply, Prof. Schmidt and his friend Michael Morcsh immediately went to the area where the artifacts were found. After Prof Schmidt discovered one of the T-shaped pillars, they decided to start the excavations.

Göbekli Tepe excavations were initiated in 1995 by Archaeologist Klaus Schmidt with the support of the German Archaeological Institute. Schmidt was the head of the excavations until 2014, when he passed away.

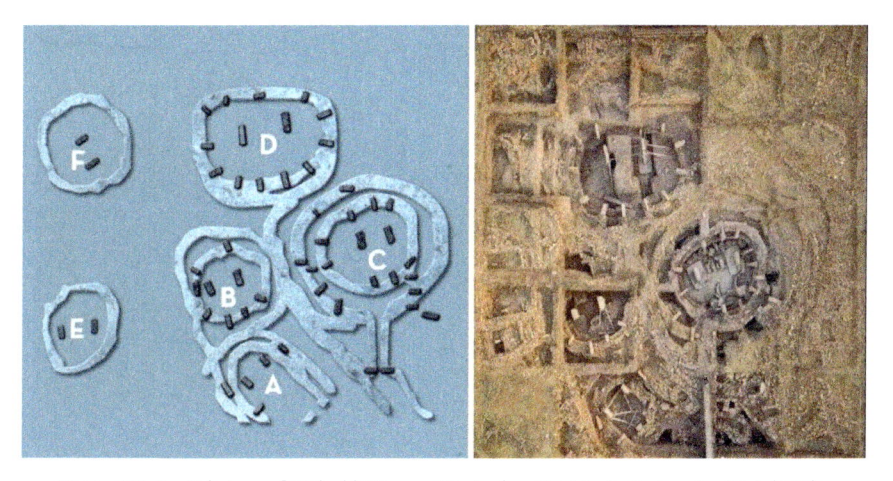

Figure 53: Aerial view of Göbekli Tepe - Deutsches Archäologisches Institut (DAI).

Göbekli Tepe

The excavations continue in cooperation with the German Archaeological Institute and the Scientific Advisory Board consisting of Turkish archaeologists, following Scmidt. In 2018, the site was declared as a UNESCO World Heritage Site.

Figure 54: Göbekli Tepe was discovered by a German archaeologist Klaus Schmidt. (1953-2014)

Göbekli Tepe was built before the agricultural revolution and pottery; it was a place that belonged to the world of hunters and gatherers. The discovery deeply shook and changed everything we learned about the history of humanity, the history of religions and our transition to settled life, our perception of history and our knowledge.

The findings forming the characteristic feature of Göbekli Tepe are large round structures made of T-shaped pillars. Of the 20 known round structures, only 6 have been unearthed so far. There are at least 10 and at most 15 pillars in each round structure; The diameters of the round structures are between 10-20 meters.

Göbekli Tepe

Figure 55: "Göbekli Tepe", illustration by Historic Graphica.

Shaped pillars are distinctly anthropomorphic. The upper part of the pillars represents the head, and the long body represents the body. These pillars were excavated in one piece. So, they are monolithic. They were brought from stone quarries about 2 km away. There are still T-shaped cavities or incompletely extracted T-shaped stones in this quarry.

Figure 56: The findings forming the characteristic feature of Göbekli Tepe are large round structures made of T-shaped pillars.

Göbekli Tepe

In this period when the wheel was not known, the weight of the obelisks around 10 to 20 tons remains a mystery about their construction and transportation.

The fact that the stones were taken out of the quarry and brought to Göbekli Tepe and then shaped and decorated shows that the people of that period reached a certain level of civilization. It is also clear that a certain number of human labor and cooperation is needed to bring such heavy stones from a distance that can be considered too long.

The T-shaped pillars in Göbekli Tepe and the way these pillars are placed have a special architectural form. In the middle of each building there are two pillars larger than the others. The pillars in the center face the entrances of the buildings. Other pillars are arranged in circles or spirals around the central pillars. These pillars are connected to each other by walls and stone benches. None of the buildings have roofs.

Figure 57: Illustration of Göbekli Tepe, Sanliurfa Archaeology Museum, Turkey.

Figure 58: Arm and hand reliefs on the pillars.

It is thought that there is a narrative in the motifs on the pillars. There are many animal depictions in relief on the pillars. The high animal symbolism suggests that this place may have been used for ritual purposes. However, we do not know exactly what these rituals were and how they were performed. The animal motifs depicted on the pillars are fox, lion, snake, wild boar, wild cattle, wild ass, spider, frog, gazelle, vultures, and other bird species.

Figure 59: Animal symbolism in Göbekli Tepe.

Göbekli Tepe

Figure 60: When Göbekli Tepe was built, its surroundings were probably much lusher than it is today and could support a wide variety of wildlife. This was before thousands of years of human habitation and agriculture, what has become the present dusty land.

Especially the vulture reliefs in Göbekli Tepe are striking. Vultures are also characteristic of the iconography of Neolithic sites such as Çatalhöyük and Jericho. In the early Neolithic cultures of Anatolia and the Near East, it is assumed that the deceased were deliberately exposed to the open air by vultures and other predators to extract their meat. The deceased's head was sometimes detached from the body and was kept separate, perhaps as a sign of ancestor worship. This may represent an early form of sky burial, as still practiced today by Buddhists in Tibet and Zoroastrians in India. Perhaps the purpose of the obelisks at Göbekli Tepe was to provide the necessary 'height' for these birds.

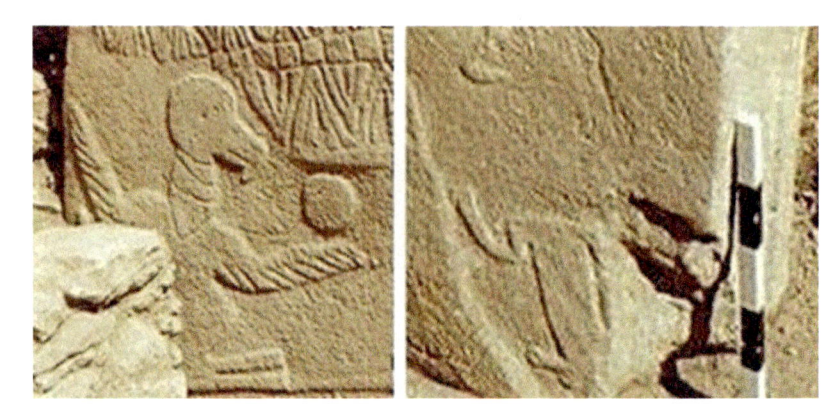

Figure 61: Details from Pillar 43 in Enclosure D, Göbekli Tepe.

Figure 62: Details from Pillar 43 in Enclosure D, Göbekli Tepe.

Along with the structures made of large stone blocks, many animal statues, human statues, stone plaques, arrow and spearheads, stone beads, grinding stones and figurines were discovered in Göbekli Tepe.

To date, 84 animal sculptures belonging to the fauna of the region have been found in Göbekli Tepe. In animal sculptures, animals with visible teeth are usually expressed. It is thought that the animal sculptures, which are expressed in an aggressive way, were made for protective purposes for the place where they were found. There are also snake, arrow, animal, bird and tree branch-like motifs on the stone plates. In addition to the animal sculptures, 43 human sculptures, some of which are close to life size, were found inside the round structures.

Göbekli Tepe

Figure 63: In animal sculptures, animals with visible teeth are usually expressed.

Figure 64

There are no mythological animals or surrealistic creatures. All animal depictions found are animals naturally found around the site.

Therefore, it can be said that Göbekli Tepe is a special place that hosts religious rituals, but sufficient evidence has not yet been obtained to mention that it is a place of worship or temple for worshiping the gods. Residue analyzes of stone vessels with a volume of 160 liters at Göbekli Tepe revealed the presence of alcoholic beverages. In addition, the remains of large amounts of hunting animals (such as gazelle, wild cattle, red deer and wild boar) indicate the existence of large-scale social events in Göbekli Tepe, where large amounts of meat and alcoholic beverages are consumed. Periodic feasts are a necessity that serve the purposes of hunter-gatherer societies to exchange and strengthen bonds.

Göbekli Tepe

Figure 65: A stone slab from Göbekli Tepe (c. 10.000 - 8.000 BC), with a carving depicting a woman in a birth giving position.

The explorer of Göbekli Tepe, Klaus Schmidt, claimed that rituals related to death were also performed in Göbekli Tepe. However, no human bones were found during the excavations of Prof Schmidt. Schmidt predicted that human bones could be found behind the walls surrounding circular structures; this prediction was confirmed after the death of Prof Schmidt in 2014.

Most of the human bones recovered from Göbekli Tepe are skull bones. Traces of cutting tools and holes were found in some bones. Analysis of the skull bones showed that the heads detached from the human body may have been hung by ropes. Headless human depictions at and archaeological findings regarding skull cults in other Neolithic settlements in the nearby geography indicate that there was a skull cult there.

Göbekli Tepe

Activities at Göbekli Tepe stopped completely around 8.200 BC and Göbekli Tepe was buried with soil and abandoned. Burying it must have been a very laborious task because thousands of cubic meters of heavy soil were required for them to be transported here. Why Göbekli Tepe was deliberately buried is still a mystery today.

Göbekli Tepe is referred to as the first temple, the first religious center or the first place of worship in many sources. It is clear that it is a religious cult, but it is not clear how and why it was used. As Prof Schmidt said, "Göbekli Tepe may be the first to show the power of belief, but it would be tooe xaggerated to say that it is the birthplace of belief." If excavations at Göbekli Tepe are not interrupted, it is estimated that it will take 30 or more years to uncover all of the structures. As we finish our short article, we respectfully commemorate Klaus Schmidt, who discovered Göbekli Tepe and passed away in 2014. We would also like to thank the staff of the Deutsches Archäologisches Institut, especially Oliver Dietrich, Laura Dietrich and Jens Notroff.

Figure 66: German archaeologist Klaus Schmidt. (1953-2014

ÇATALHÖYÜK

(Konya, Turkey, c. 7.400 BC)

Çatalhöyük is a large Neolithic "town" with a history of 9.400 years and home to approximately 8.000 people. In this big town without streets, people were walking around on the roofs and entering their homes through the openings in the roofs. These people created wonderful works of art, as can be seen from the murals, reliefs and sculptures inside their homes that have survived thousands of years ago. The works of art found in Çatalhöyük shed light on the early periods when the people of Asia Minor began to live in the city.

Çatalhöyük was first discovered in 1958 by British archaeologists James Mellaart (1925-2012) and David French. The first excavations were carried out by the British Archaeological Institute between 1961 and 1965. It consists of two mounds side by side in east and west directions; On the eastern mound, there are 18 layers of neolithic settlements dated between 7.400 BC and 6200 BC. On the western mound, there are Chalcolithic layers dated between 6.200 BC and 5.200 BC.

Figure 67: Illustration of Çatalhöyük. Çatalhöyük Archaeological Site, Konya, Turkey.

Thousands of people lived in Çatalhöyük, one of the oldest towns in history. Although the city has a regular structure, the existence of a central system or administration that keeps this population together is unknown. In addition, during the archaeological excavations, no structures were found as fortifications that limit and protect Çatalhöyük.

Çatalhöyük

This shows us that the area has not been attacked and that the people living here are not concerned about "defense".

Figure 68: Mud-brick houses were clustered together and there were no outside doors. People went in and out of the houses through openings in the rooms.

Figure 69: Çatalhöyük after the early excavations by James Mellaart and his team. It became a trading center and its craftworkers produced a range of goods, such as weapons, textiles, clay figures and metal trinkets, which they exchanged for raw materials.

In Çatalhöyük, families lived in small adobe houses located in a dense urban fabric.

Çatalhöyük

The people living in Çatalhöyük used their homes much differently than we do now. The houses were planned separately, and one house was built next to the other. Each house had its own walls, and there were no streets in Çatalhöyük because of the adjacent walls of the houses. Walking on flat roofs was the only way to get around.

The entrance to the houses was by going down a portable ladder through an opening in the roof. Daily life was probably spent both on roofs and inside houses, despite poor light and ventilation conditions. Each house had a room and a warehouse. Inside the rooms, there are platforms (benches) slightly raised from the ground and niches on the walls. They used these platforms for sleeping, sitting, and doing their daily work. They buried their dead together with their grave gifts under the platforms.

Tools and jewelry made of seashells, bones and stones have been discovered as burial gifts. The vultures and headless human figures seen in some wall paintings are also thought to be related to burial customs.

Figure 70: A reconstruction of one of four Çatalhöyük houses. On the wall are frescoes of what look like vultures, some scholars believe that dead bodies were subject to excarnation which means that their flesh was stripped from the body to leave the skeleton.

Çatalhöyük

The walls of the houses in Çatalhöyük were plastered, and after the plaster was painted white, wall paintings were made in red, black, and yellow tones. These paintings are a continuation of the tradition started by the Paleolithic man who painted on the cave walls. Among the depictions painted on the walls, geometric motifs, handprints, human and animal figures (vulture, leopard, wild deer), hunting and dance scenes that may have been made for good hunting, and wall paintings reflecting the natural environment come to the forefront.

Figure 71: Painted leopard reliefs from ÇatalHöyük, c. 6.500-6.000 BC, now on display in the Museum of Anatolian Civilizations, Ankara, Turkey.

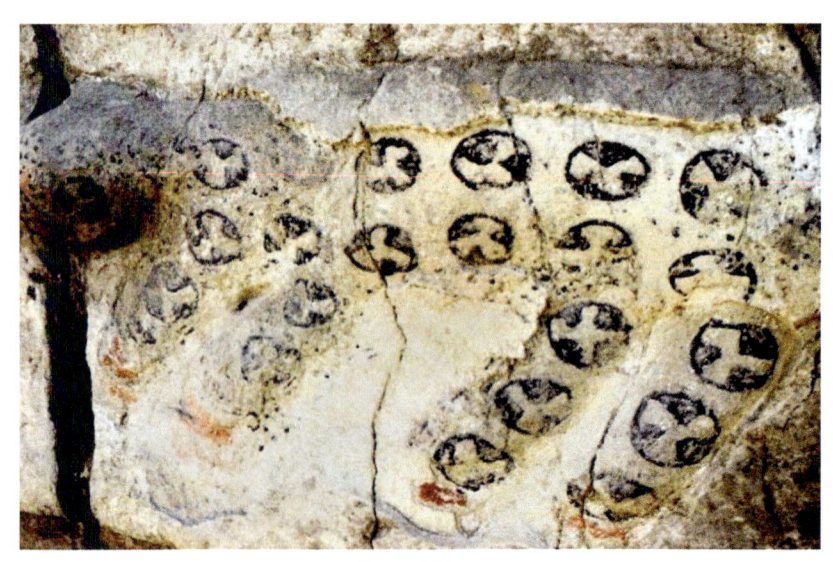

Figure 72

Figure 73

Figure 74: Çatalhöyük, Mural painting of a red bull chased by hunters. (c. 7.500 - 5.000 BC)

Çatalhöyük

Figure 75: Reconstructed fresco of an original hunting scene found at Çatalhöyük. Reconstructed houses, Çatalhöyük Archaeological Site, Konya, Turkey.

Another type of decoration used apart from the paintings is the depictions made in relief and the bull heads and horns placed on the platforms in the buildings. There are reliefs made by plastering real bull heads with clay on the walls of many houses. In buildings that are thought to be sacred places, bull heads are found in denser and sometimes in rows arranged one after the other. In the archaeological excavations, it was determined that the heads of the bulls, which were plastered with clay, were painted with red ocher.

Çatalhöyük

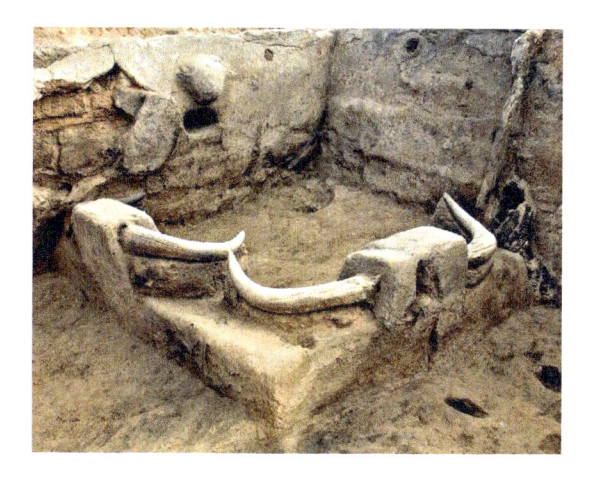

Figure 76: Bull bucrania, corner installation in Building 77, Çatalhöyük.

Small figurines found in Çatalhöyük excavations give us important information about the beginning of the cult of the Mother Goddess and the religious beliefs of the period. These small statues made of baked clay and stone are 5-15 cm high.

Female figures are fat and plump, with big hips. They are sometimes depicted as giving birth. These figurines are thought to represent abundance and fertility. Stone or clay axes, plates, figurines of the goddess of fertility, bracelets and necklaces, sharp tools made of bones, arrows and spearheads made of obsidian are other objects found at Çatalhöyük.

Figure 77: Neolithic stone sculpture representing Mother Goddess (?), or Goddess of Fertility(?), from the site of Çatalhöyük, Museum of Anatolian Civilizations, Ankara, Turkey

SETTLEMENT AT LEPENSKI VIR

(Boljetin, Serbia, c. 6.300 BC)

In the 1960s, Serbian archaeologists discovered a Mesolithic fishing village nestled in the cliffs of the Danube, near one of the river's narrowest points. The area, called Lepenski Vir was a Mesolithic village consisting of a series of residences located on the Serbian coast of the Iron Gates gorge above the Danube River, on the high sandy terrace of the Danube River. This village was a settlement that existed from 6.300 BC until 4.900 BC and was occupied at least six times.

This locality, which was named after the Danube whirl, was the center of one of the most important and most complex cultures of pre-history. Seven terraces and 136 buildings were discovered during archaeological excavations. The settlement is built on terraces of clay and sandy loam overlooking the Danube, the river that gives them life, as well is divine and admirable.

Figure 78: Settlement at Lepenski Vir.

Several key things set Lepenski Vir apart from other prehistoric cultures. It was continuously inhabited for about 2.000 years, and during that time, its people traveled the evolutionary path from hunters and fruit gatherers to an organized socio-economic community. Three stages are seen in Lepenski Vir; the first two are the remnants of a complex hunter-gatherer foraging society, and the third stage represents an established farming community.

Settlement at Lepenski Vir

Because the settlement is a permanent and planned structure, architect Hristivoje Pavlović described Lepenski Vir as "the first city in Europe" with organized human life.

During archaeological excavations, settlements built according to a plan were discovered, making it the first urban settlement discovered in Europe. The peculiarity of this settlement was houses with trapezoid bases with primitive wooden structures arranged in a horseshoe shape. The buildings surrounded an open space. The interior of each house contained a fireplace made from large rectangular stone blocks. The fireplaces were further expanded with the stone block to create a small shrine behind the house. These shrines were decorated with sculptures carved from huge round river stones.

Figure 79: Quartz sandstone sculptures from 6.300-5.900 BC. on display at the Museum Lepenski Vir.

Settlement at Lepenski Vir

These statues are thought to represent river gods or ancestors. Their size is 16-60 cm.and they represent human heads with protruding eyes and lips or complete figures with a fish's body. The sculptures of Lepenski Vir can be separated into two distinct categories, one with simple geometric patterns and the other representing humanoid figures. Many fish-like traits can be noticed in both categories. The humanoid figures are realistically modeled with only the head, face, eyebrow arches, a long nose and fish-like mouth.

Lepenski Vir, with his Natural Environment, is included as a part of Djerdap Gorge and National Park in UNESCO Global Geoparks List from 10th July 2020.

Figure 80: Settlement at Lepenski Vir.

Figure 81: Lepenski Vir Collection contains items from the site of Lepenski Vir, covering the chronological span from the 10th till the 6th millennium BC., that is the Mesolithic and Neolithic Period.

GGANTIJA TEMPLES

(Malta, c. 3.600 BC)

The Ggantija Temples are famous for being one of the oldest standing stone monuments and located in Xaghra, Gozo. Archaeologists estimate that the monument was built between 3.600 and 3.200 BC. This also makes Ggantija Temples the oldest manmade religious building in the world after Göbekli Tepe located in Turkey.

The mighty megalith in the monument is longer than 5 meters and some of them weigh over 50 tons. According to the tales, the monument was built by giants, and this is why they are called Ggantija Temples.

Ggantija Temples are older than many famous monuments such as Egyptian pyramids in Egypt and Stonehenge in the United Kingdom.

The construction technique is still a mystery, but experts believe that builders rolled the massive blocks from a distance to create these monuments. Spherical stones may have been used to transport these blocks. However, this is just a guess made by some experts and no evidence was found about how they were built.

Figure 82: Aerial view of the Ggantija Temples.

The Ggantija Temples is the home of many female statues and figurines, most of which were discovered in 1826. The abundant number of female statues and figurines led experts to believe that the complex was dedicated to fertility gods. This theory is also supported by the architectural plan of the temple, which has a fat woman shape.

ÖTZI THE ICEMAN

(Ötztal Alps, Italy, c. 3.300 BC)

The natural mummy now known as Ötzi was first discovered in 1991 by German tourists hiking in the Ötztal Alps, a mountain range in Austria and Italy. While returning to a mountain hut after tackling the summit of Finailspitze mountain, they made their discovery the top part of a body sticking out of the ice. They did not know that the body had been there for 5.300 years.

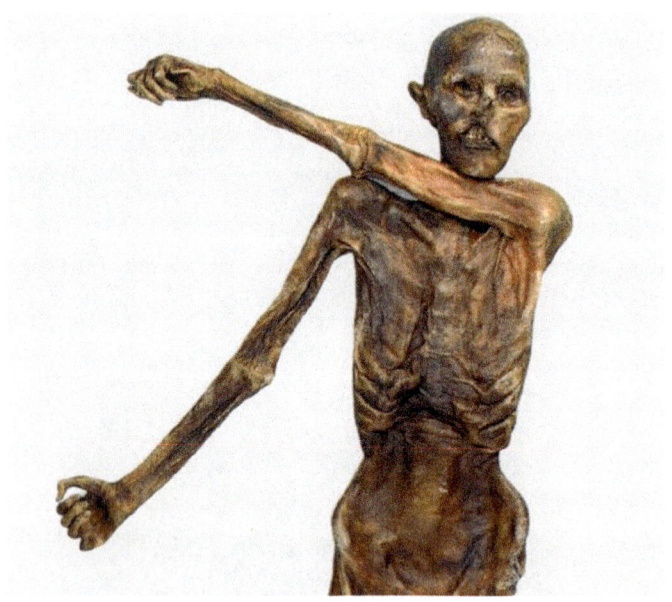

Figure 83: Ötzi.

The age and significance of the discovery were not immediately understood. A number of people visited the site to see the body before it was recovered. They stepped on the fragile objects and removed artifacts before their locations were noted. This was very unfortunate and led to the destruction of important evidence on the site.

When the Austrian archaeologist Konrad Spindler saw the copper ax found with Ötzi, he immediately understood that this was not a recent glacier body, but that it had to be at least 5.000 years old. Radiocarbon-dated to 3.300 BC, the body is that of a man aged 40 to 45 who had been about 1.6 meters tall and had weighed about 50 kg.

Ötzi the Iceman

Several different items were found along with the corpse. One of the most important items was a copper blade ax capable of cutting down an entire tree without sharpening in just 35 minutes. Also found on the remains of Ötzi's clothing were two pieces of birch fungus threaded onto narrow strips of hiding.

Sixty-one different tattoos were found on the body, all made with fine incisions and were rubbed with charcoal, probably for pain relief. Today, it is assumed that tattoos served therapeutic purposes. The places they were located are thought to have had illnesses on his body. Another proof of this idea is that acupuncture lines we still use today are in similar places on the body.

The ice not only froze Ötzi where he had died, but the high humidity of the ice also kept his organs and skin largely intact. In this way, researchers were able to analyze a portion of Ötzi's stomach and lower intestine to reveal the last meals he ate before his death.

About eight hours before his death, they discovered that he had consumed a meal of dried ibex meat and fat, red deer, einkorn wheat, and traces of toxic fern. The Ice Mummy died in late spring or early summer. This was confirmed by different types of pollens that were discovered in Ötzi's stomach. These pollens came in from the food he ate, and the water he drank.

Figure 84: Until the discovery of Ötzi and his beautifully preserved copper axe, it was assumed that humanity in 3.500 B.C. had not yet mastered the technology to forge such tools.

Figure 85: One of the dozens of tattoos discovered on the Iceman. The current belief is that Ötzi may have had them for therapeutic reasons. South Tyrol Museum of Archaeology, Italy.

Figure 86: One of the many items found on the Iceman's clothing was this rudimentary 'bracket fungi' medicine kit. South Tyrol Museum of Archaeology, Italy.

Ötzi the Iceman

At first, it was thought that Ötzi had died in an accident in the mountains. The 2001 discovery of a stone arrowhead embedded in his shoulder, and later evidence of a possible trauma to the head, has turned Ötzi from a victim of hypothermia into a murder victim. The arrow had been shot from behind and from a considerable distance. It penetrated the left shoulder blade but was stopped by tissue just short of the left lung.

Ötzi lost a great deal of blood. His wound was agonizingly painful, and his left arm was probably paralyzed. Ötzi pulled out the arrow shaft but the head remained stuck in his shoulder. He reached the top of the mountains but was now exhausted and weakened from bleeding. He could go no further, lay down, and died.

No trace of the culprit has been found. A few days before his death, he was involved in hand-to-hand combat and had received a deep cut to his right hand.

Apparently, there are many questions to be solved. The identity of the murderer is one of them. Besides, we couldn't understand the reason for the murder- revenge, jealousy, or greed, etc. Looking at the equipment which had a great price left on his body after the attack, what was the motive of this action? Why was Ötzi on that glacier at that time? The answers to all these questions are still a mystery.

There are a few mummies in the world as old as Ötzi, but none so well preserved. Since 1998, Otzi and his artifacts have been on display at the South Tyrol Museum of Archaeology in Bolzano, Italy.

Figure 87

Ötzi the Iceman

Figure 88

Figure 89: Naturalistic reconstruction of Ötzi using forensic methods, exhibited in the South Tyrol Museum of Archaeology, Italy.

SKARA BRAE

(Scotland, c. 3.180 BC)

Situated in the grounds of Skaill House is Europe's best-preserved Neolithic site, the world-famous Skara Brae. This "British Pompeii", one of the most famous prehistoric settlements in Europe, was preserved by being buried by sand in a storm - the occupants clearly left in a hurry. In 1850 another storm revealed the ruins of the best- preserved Neolithic village in Europe.

Skara Brae presents a remarkable picture of life 5.000 years ago. Of particular interest at Skara Brae is that the vestiges of Stone Age interior fittings and furniture have been preserved. The site was never large and consisted of about 10-15 houses that, in total, probably housed no more than 100 inhabitants at any one time. The houses of Skara Brae lay under a thick layer of sand until 1850 and were only uncovered thanks to a storm.

Figure 90: A house at Skara Brae. In the middle of the room is the hearth, surrounded by stones to keep the fire in. The people slept on stone box beds, like the one on the right. Stone slabs around the beds kept out the cold night air. At the back is a storage unit.

Each house was roughly square but with rounded corners, entered through a single doorway, and contained a stone dresser facing the door and two beds flanking the central hearth.

Skara Brae

The walls were up to 3m. high. The roof was probably of turf supported on rafters of timber or whalebone. Archaeologists found that the houses usually had one large stone dresser that typically had three shelves divided into two bays. The houses even had open areas with drains that would likely have been used as prehistoric toilets.

The people who lived at Skara Brae were farmers and fishers as well as hunters. They used tools of stone, bone, and wood. Their diet contained many foods which would be regarded as luxuries today: Venison from deer imported to Orkney, meat, and eggs from seabirds like the Great Auk; Oysters, crabs, cockles, and mussels, as well as giant cod and saithe from the sea. Strangely, no fishing equipment was discovered when the village was excavated, but water-tight tanks on the floor of each house were probably designed to hold limpets for fish bait.

Researchers think that these Stone Age people left their villages after (or during) a natural disaster. Only the skeletons of a young boy and an old man have been discovered. The most important of the finds are now on display in the National Museum of Antiquities in Edinburgh. Skara Brae appears to have been abandoned about 2.500 BC, but the reason remains a mystery. The strange thing is that the abandoned houses at Skara Brae were then filled with garbage, such as shells and animal bones, which had been arranged in layers. This may have been some sort of religious ritual, but we do not know what it means.

Figure 91: Aerial view of the site.

NARMER PALETTE

(Komel-Ahmer, Egypt, circa 3.100 BC)

The Narmer Palette is one of the most famous artifacts of Ancient Egypt. It was found with a collection of other objects used for ceremonial purposes and then ritually buried within the temple at Hierakonpolis. The palette is so important because it shows the development of early Egyptian hieroglyphics. It features some of the earliest hieroglyphics found in Ancient Egypt and dates to circa 3.200-3.100 BC.

Figure 92: The Narmer Palette.

The Narmer Palette is carved of a single piece of siltstone, commonly used for ceremonial tablets in the First Dynastic Period of Ancient Egypt. There may have been kings before the First Dynasty, which began with Na'rmer's reign. There is some evidence of a king called Scorpion who may have ruled over Upper Egypt before Na'rmer: But we cannot be sure as there is no written evidence.

The fact that the Narmer Palette is carved on both sides means it was created for ceremonial, not practical purposes. Everyday pallets were decorated only on one side. The Narmer Palette is intricately carved to tell the story of King Narmer's victory in battle and the approval of the gods at the unification of Ancient Egypt.

Although the Narmer Palette dates to the Early Dynastic Period, it conforms to the artistic formality of later Ancient Egyptian art and shows that both the hieroglyphic language and symbolic art were already well developed at this early stage.

PRIAM'S TREASURE

(Troy, Asia Minor, Turkey, c. 2.750 BC)

Ancient city Troy is one of the most famous archaeological sites in the world with its 4.000 years of history. In 1826, Scottish journalist and geologist Charles Maclaren was the first one who argued that Hisarlik Hill was a possible site of Homeric Troy, but in 1870 German archaeologist Heinrich Schliemann undertook the first excavations at the site. Priam's Treasure is a collection of gold diadems, necklaces, bracelets, rings, assorted gold, bronze vessels, and other artifacts discovered by amateur German archaeologist Heinrich Schliemann.

Schliemann claimed the site to be that of ancient Troy and assigned the artifacts to the Homeric king Priam. In reality, all of the objects date to the first half of the third millennium BC, i.e., at least 1.500 years before the Trojan War, but the name that Schliemann gave to the treasure has not changed.

Immediately after their discovery, Schliemann stole them from the Ottoman Empire, their rightful owner, to Germany. In 1877, the 'Treasure of Priam' made its first public display in Victoria and Albert Museum. After being displayed for several years in London, the 'Treasure of Priam' was then moved to Berlin in 1881.

Figure 93: Sophia Schliemann wearing the "Jewels of Helen" excavated by her husband, Heinrich Schliemann, in Hisarlik, modern-day Turkey. (Photograph taken ca. 1874)

Priam's Treasure

Between 1882 and 1885, the artifacts were temporarily displayed in the Kunstgewerbe Museum before being transferred to the newly built Ethnological Museum. During World War II, the treasure was hidden in a secret bunker and disappeared entirely until 1996, when 259 pieces were exhibited in this museum. They had been stolen by the Red Army and brought to Soviet Russia along with 440 other objects.

In the early '90s, it was discovered that the treasure was secretly taken to Moscow after the war and held in the vault of the Pushkin Museum of Fine Arts. The German government demanded the return of the treasure claiming that it belongs to them. The Russian government declined the request, saying that they were keeping it as compensation for the great damage and destruction their country suffered during the war started by the Nazis. Most of the artifacts are currently in the Pushkin Museum in Moscow.

Figure 94

Figure 95

KHUFU SHIP

(Giza, Egypt, c. 2.540 BC)

Khufu's Ship is a largely intact and incredibly well-preserved boat dating back more than 4.600 years.

During the Fourth Dynasty of the Old Kingdom of Egypt, the three famous pyramids were built at Giza by three successive Pharaos: Khufu, who ruled from 2.589 to 2.566 BC, Khafre and Menkaure.

The largest of the pyramids was the Great Pyramid, built by the Pharaoh Khufu (Cheops). Khufu reigned for 23 years. it is estimated that during every year of his reign, 100.000 stone blocks were quarried, shaped, and taken to the site at Giza to be added to his massive pyramid. No one knows exactly how the blocks were moved into position on the site. Near the base of the great pyramid are five underground chambers. In each of these chambers, the ancient Egyptians placed a dismantled boats for the Pharaoh's use in the afterlife. Khufu's Ship was buried in the 26th century BC., very carefully, in a carved stone pit directly beneath the museum where it now rests.

Figure 96: Khufu Ship.

Khufu Ship

Discovered on 26 May 1954 by Egyptian archaeologist Kamal el-Mallakh, the beautiful boat is believed to have been built for the Egyptian Pharaoh Khufu. It measures 43.6 m long and 5.9 m wide.

According to ancient Egyptian mythology, Khufu's Ship had a religious function – it was placed inside Khufu's burial chamber to allow him, as a deceased king, to sail across the heavens with Ra, the sun god. It is alternatively believed that the boat could have been used to transport the body of Khufu to his place in the pyramid.

Figure 97

Figure 98

SEATED SCRIBE

(Saqqara, Egypt, c 2.500 BC)

The Seated Scribe statue is one of the masterworks of Ancient Egypt. Egyptologist Auguste Mariette discovered the scribe in 1850 at Saqqara, an ancient burial ground in Egypt, serving as the necropolis for the Ancient Egyptian capital, Memphis. The sculpture was dated to the period of the Old Kingdom, circa 2.620–2.500 BC. It is now in the Louvre Museum in Paris.

The scribe is sitting cross-legged, his right leg crossed in front of his left. The white kilt, stretched over his knees, serves as a support. He is holding a partially rolled papyrus scroll in his left hand. His right hand must have held a brush, now missing. His right hand eternally poised to write.

Figure 99: The Seated Scribe.

Seated Scribe

The Seated Scribe statue is a painted limestone statue. The most striking aspect of this sculpture is the face, particularly the elaborately inlaid eyes made of rock crystal. On the back of the eye is a layer of organic material that creates the color of the iris. A line of black paint defines the eyebrows. His chest is broad, and the nipples are marked by two wooden dowels.

The particular care given to this sculpture suggests that it is a very high dignitary of the Old Kingdom (c. 2.686-2.181 BC). The scribe's name and prestigious titles were likely carved on the statue's missing base.

Since the base of the statue is missing, we know nothing about the person portrayed: neither his name nor title.

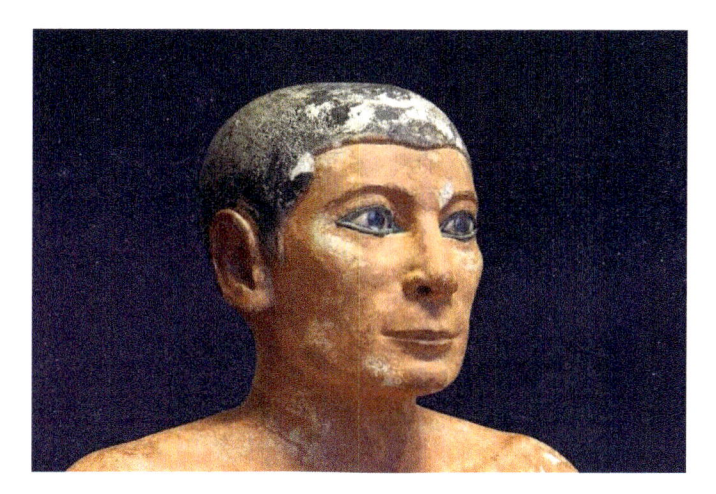

Figure 100

Figure 101: Detail, the Seated Scribe.

EBLA TABLETS

(Syria, c. 2.500 BC)

In 1974, Italian archaeologist Paolo Matthiae from the University of Rome La Sapienza and his team discovered up to 1.800 cuneiform tablets and 4.750 fragments, and many thousand minor chips representing the palace archives of the ancient city of Ebla, Syria.

About 85% of the tablets are written using the usual Sumerian combination of logograms and phonetic signs, while the others exhibited an innovative, purely phonetic representation using Sumerian cuneiform of a previously unknown Semitic language, which was called Eblaite. Bilingual Sumerian/Eblaite vocabulary lists were found among the tablets, allowing them to be translated.

In one room of the palace, archaeologists found a scribe's equipment for writing on the tablets. There was a bone style for making the symbols, and a stone eraser for removing mistakes.

Figure 102

Once scholars could read them, they found that the tablets formed a library of information about Ebla-the city's history, trade, and much more- giving insight into life in Syria 4.500 years ago.

The Ebla tablets are preserved in Syrian museums in Aleppo, Damascus, and Idlib.

ROYAL TOMBS AT UR

(Tell al Muqayyar, Iraq, c. 2.500 BC)

Archaeologists have discovered an amazing deal of proof about the Mesopotamian ancient culture since the 19th century. George Smith announced that he found the remaining of the world's oldest literary work during the Society of Biblical Archaeology meeting in 1872. These were clay tablets found in Nineveh and they were all about the Epic of Gilgamesh.

This discovery became a huge sensation and there was great interest in the Mesopotamian era. Every year more and more reputable United States, German, British and French universities, and museums funded archaeological expeditions in areas where Babylonia, Assyria, and Sumer civilizations started and developed. The most popular one among these regions was Tell al Muqayyar, which we all know as Ur today.

British diplomat J. E. Taylor was already in the area in 1853 and working on some basic excavations. However, it took about 70 years for a full excavation of the ancient city. British Museum and Penn Museum funded a joint excavation plan and program, and this effort was led by Leonard Woolley.

Figure 103: Known as the Standard of Ur, this box is held at the British Museum. It depicts scenes of peace on one side (above) and war on the other. It was found in a royal tomb near the body of a sacrificed man.

Royal Tombs at Ur

Just like many ancient civilizations, Sumerians also prepared mighty graves for their rules, and these were called death pits.

16 large tombs and Leonard Woolley worked in the area between 1922 and 1934 and bring the ancient Sumerian city of Ur to light. This excavation helped us to understand the daily life in the area, which dates to 4.500 BC as a small settlement area next to River Euphrates in Mesopotamia. After 2.000 years from its first settlement, the city became the capital of Sumer with its full richness.

1840 graves were discovered in the city. The interesting thing about the Sumerians' burial traditions is kings and queens used to be buried together with their servants and courtiers. The tomb of Queen Shub-ad is one of the popular ones and she was buried with her maiden holding her harp and 74 more servants.

These tombs helped us a lot to understand the rituals of one of the ancient Mesopotamian civilizations. The skill and artistry level of the objects buried with the rulers are astonishing. This discovery changed the perception of Mesopotamia and its culture. Woolley completed this duty at Ur in 1934 and he devoted his life to Ur. He published many studies and books about his memories, experiences, and things that he learned during the excavations.

Figure 104: The Golden Lyre of Ur in the National Museum of Iraq, Baghdad.

PALACE OF KNOSSOS

(Knossos, Crete, Greece, c. 1.900 BC)

The island of Crete lies at the southern end of the Aegean Sea. By 2.500 BC, it had become the home of the Minoan civilization. The Minoans named after their legendary king, Minos-were peaceful people who loved art and beauty, and also built-up trade links around the Mediterranean.

The Palace of Knossos is located just south of modern-day Heraklion near the north coast of Crete. The palace is over 20.000 square meters and the largest of all Minoan palatial structures. It was built of ashlar blocks, had many floors, and was decorated with magnificent frescoes.

The palace consisted of about 1.000 chambers surrounding the central courtyard and was equipped with a sewage system. One of the most gorgeous was the Throne Room. It consisted of a large chair built into the wall, facing several benches. In addition, this room included a tank, which archaeologists believe was an aquarium. On the south wall is a fresco depicting mythical beasts called griffins, with a lion's body and an eagle's head. In the west wing, there were shrines, official rooms, and a huge warehouse, while in the east, there were ruler's apartments and workshops.

Figure 105: Excavated ruins of the nearly 4.000-year-old palace of Knossos on the Greek Island of Crete. Built by the Minoan culture, considered the oldest advanced culture in Europe.

Palace of Knossos

Figure 106: Throne Room, Knossos Palace, Greece.

Figure 107: A detail of the griffin fresco from the throne room, palace of Knossos, Crete.

Knossos Palace is also well-known for its beautiful wall frescoes. These frescoes portrayed a non-militaristic society, one whose activities included fishing, athletic games, and ceremonies such as acrobatics on the back of a charging bull.

Palace of Knossos

The old palace was built around 1.900 BC but was destroyed by an earthquake around 1.700 BC. The newer, more complex palace was built almost immediately after the first one was destroyed. In the middle of the 15th Century BC, the Achaeans took over the island of Crete and settled in the palace. Once again, the palace was destroyed by fire in the middle of the 14th Century B.C and henceforth ceased to function as a palatial center.

Figure 108: Bull Jumping, fresco wall painting, Knossos, Crete 1.700 BC. -1.500 BC.

Figure 109: Dolphin Fresco in the Queen's Megaron (detail) circa 1.600 BC.

Palace of Knossos

Figure 110: Reconstruction sketch of Knossos Palace

Figure 111: Detail, frescoes.

HATTUSA: HITTITE CAPITAL

(Çorum, Central Anatolia, Turkey, c. 1.800 BC)

Hattusa is an ancient site located near modern Boğazkale in the Çorum Province of Turkey. Hattusa was discovered in 1834 by Charles Texier (1802-1871), and after the discovery of a clay tablet with Babylonian cuneiform writing, was visited in 1905 by Hugo Winckler (1863- 1913) and Theodoros Makridi Bey. In 1906-12, they excavated numerous clay tablets there and recognized the site as the site of the Hittite capital. Archaeological excavations in Hattusa have been going on since 1931.

This ancient site once served as the capital of the Great Hittite Empire, one of the superpowers of the ancient world. Hattusa was inhabited as early as the 3rd millennium BC., and in the 18th century BC was a walled city where Assyrian merchants had their establishments. The site was made the capital of the Hittite Empire by Hattusili I around 1.650 BC.

Figure 112: Lion Gate, Hattusa, Turkey.

This gate is situated at the south-west of the city fortifications. It is flanked by two towers and has an inner and an outer doorway, both parabola-shaped and once furnished with pairs of wooden doors that opened to the interior of the monument.

The foreparts of two lions are carved from the huge stone blocks on either side of the outer entrance. The open mouth and staring eyes, the latter originally inlaid with different materials, have a protective function, a motif well known in Hittite and Mesopotamian architecture. Above and to the left of the broken head of the lion on the left (as seen from the outside) are several hieroglyphic signs, most easily detected around noon. The upper blocks of the facade of the left tower are unsmoothed, showing that the gate, although in use, never received the final touch.

Figure 113: Reconstruction of Lion Gate.

The Hittites were an Ancient Anatolian people, who established an empire covering Anatolia, northern Levant, and Upper Mesopotamia and the population of Asia Minor with the oldest known Indo-European language. They founded the kingdom of Hatti in central Anatolia in the 1st half of the 2nd millennium BC., which continued until about 1.200 BC.

Hattusa exerted a dominating influence upon the civilizations in the thirteenth century BC in Anatolia and northern Syria. The palaces, temples, trading quarters, and necropolis of this political and religious metropolis provide a comprehensive picture of a capital city and bear unique testimony to the vanished Hittite civilization.

Hattusa: Hittite Capital

The city's fortifications, along with the Lion Gate, the royal Gate and the Yazilikaya rupestrian ensemble with its sculptured friezes, represent unique artistic achievements as monuments.

Inside the walls, the city is built on two levels. To the northwest is the lower town with its great temple, dedicated to the god of storms and the goddess of the Sun, Arinna. Thousands of cuneiform tablets were found in this area.

The remains of Hattusa are now accessible as an open-air archaeological museum (the center of a national historical park). The site has been declared a World Heritage Site by UNESCO. The cuneiform archives are on the UNESCO Memory of the World list.

Figure 114: Twelve Hittite gods of the Underworld in the nearby Yazilikaya, a sanctuary of Hattusa.

Figure 115: The Sword God in Chamber B at the Hittite Rock Sanctuary of Yazilikaya, Hattusas, Bogazkale, Turkey

HAMMURABI'S LAW CODE

(Iraq, c. 1.754 BC)

Hammurabi was the oldest son of Sin-Muballit and did not inherit much from his father. But by the time of his death, his empire came to dominate all of Mesopotamia. Hammurabi also established a set of laws that is today called the Code of Hammurabi. One of the most influential codifications of law in ancient history, the text provides a concrete example of the expanding influence of centralized government on the personal and professional lives of the general population. Despite Hammurabi's stupendous success as a conqueror and king, he is best remembered for his accomplishments beyond the battlefield, and among these, as the father of legislation.

The code set fines and punishments to meet the requirements of justice and governed the people living in Hammurabi's fast-growing empire. At the time of Hammurabi, Babylon had become a large city with crowded streets.

Hammurabi's Law had to rule over nomads, Assyrian merchants, aristocratic Babylonians, Elamite slaves, and Sumerian housewives. By the time of Hammurabi's death, his empire included modern-day Iraq, extending from the Persian Gulf along the Tigris and Euphrates rivers.

The Code consisted of 282 laws, with punishments based on social status (slaves, free men, and property owners). There were three social classes: the amelu (the elite), the mushkenu (free men) and ardu (slave). Women had limited rights and were mostly based around marriage contracts and divorce rights.

Figure 116

Hammurabi's Law Code

Scribes wrote these laws on 12 tablets. The code consists of rules and punishments for if those rules were broken. The structure of the code is very detailed: each offense receiving a particular punishment. Hammurabi's Law Code contains some important ideas like having people provide evidence of a crime, innocent until proven guilty, and protection for the weak.

Figure 117: One of the best surviving examples of the code is written on the "diorite stele". Today it can be found in the Louvre Museum in Paris, France. The stele was found at the site of Susa, in modern-day Iran. Historians believe that it was brought to Susa in the 12th century BC. by an Elamite ruler who conquered Babylon and then who erased a portion of the text in preparation for creating his inscriptions. The stele is in two parts: in the upper part you can see two figures in relief, and in the lower part the text of the laws. The upright figure on the left is Hammurabi himself, symbolically receiving the laws from the sun god Shamash, the patron of Justice, recognizable by the flames behind him.

Hammurabi's Law Code

EXAMPLES OF THE LAWS

Laws Concerning Social Structures

141. If a free man's wife wishes to divorce him, the man may divorce her and give her no settlement. If the man does not wish to divorce her, he may marry another woman and keep his first wife in his house as a slave.

143. If she has committed adultery, then she shall be executed by being thrown into the water.

129. If the wife of a free man is caught lying with another man, they shall both be tied up and drowned in the water; but if the husband decides to let his wife live, then the king shall let the man live.

Laws Concerning Economic Structures

122. If a free person wishes to pawn anything, that person is responsible for drawing up a contract signed by witnesses before completing the transaction.

233. If a builder builds a house for a man and does not make its construction sound, and a wall cracks, that builder shall strengthen that wall at his own expense.

Laws Concerning the Operation of the Judicial System

5. If a judge delivers a written verdict and later changes it, that judge shall pay twelve times the amount of the damages awarded in the verdict. Then the judge shall be publicly expelled from office.

Laws Concerning Trade

88. A merchant may collect interest of thirty-three and one-third percent on a loan of grain, and twenty percent interest may be charged on a loan of silver.

108. If a wine seller does not take grain for the price of a drink but takes money by the large weight, or if she makes the measure of drink smaller than the measure of grain, they shall call that wine seller to account and throw her into the water.

NEBRA SKY DISC

(Nebra, Germany c. 1.600 BC)

The Nebra Sky Disc is a decorated bronze plate with gold symbols, like the Sun, the crescent-shaped Moon, and 32 stars. The symbols are made of gold and didn't corrode. Being dated to the end of the Early Bronze Age around 1.600 BC, the Sky Disc is the world's oldest representation of the cosmos.

Found by treasure hunters in 1999, it's been named the "Nebra Sky Disc" after the town of Nebra, Germany, near the site where the disc was found. Following its discovery in 1999, the disc spent over three years on the black market until authorities seized the relic in a February 2002 sting operation.

Figure 118: Nebra Treasure.

The artifact measures about 30 centimeters wide and weighs 2,2 kilograms. A series of 39 to 40 tiny holes were made along the perimeter. Color-wise, the disc has a bluish-green backdrop punctuated by golden symbols. The Nebra Sky Disc shows representations of the sun, moon, Pleiades and three other crescents; two presumed to be horizon lines and the other a possible 'Solar Barge' at the bottom. These representations on disc conceal a wealth of information: the endpoints of the horizon arcs are aligned to the winter solstice and summer solstice, while the Pleiades, in combination with sun and full and crescent moon, signal the important dates for sowing and harvesting in the farming year.

Nebra Sky Disc

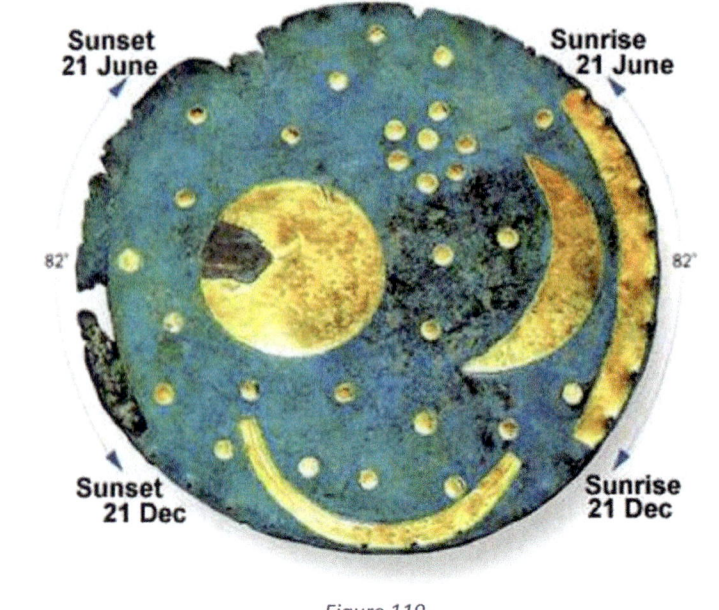

Figure 119

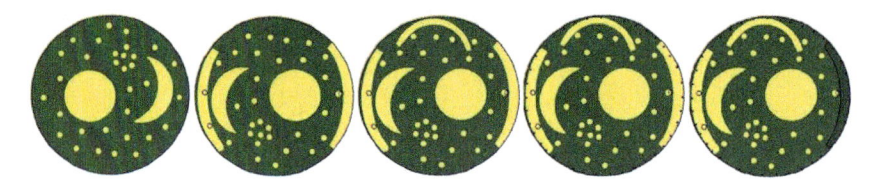

Figure 120: The Phases of the Sky Disc.

Radiocarbon dating of birch bark found on one of the swords in the hoard dates to between 1.600 BC - 1.560 BC. The Nebra Sky Disc was created in four phases. Initially, the disk had the Sun, the crescent moon, and thirty-two small round gold circles representing stars. At a later date, the two side arcs were added, and this was determined by chemical analysis of the gold. At least several generations had likely used the disk before being buried so that it may be much older.

Until the discovery of Sky Disc, no one thought prehistoric people capable of such precise astronomical knowledge. In June 2013, the Nebra Sky Disc was included in the UNESCO Memory of the World Register and termed "one of the most important archaeological finds of the twentieth century.

GREEK POMPEII: AKROTIRI

(Santorini Island, Greece, c. 1.600 BC)

Akrotiri is a Bronze Age settlement located in the southwest of the island of Santorini (Thera) in the Greek Cyclades Islands. In the 1.600s BC, one of the largest volcanic eruptions that humanity has ever seen occurred on the Aegean Island of Thera (now Santorini). Volcanic ash preserved the remains of buildings, streets, frescoes, and many artifacts and works of art. The explosion is estimated to equal 50.000 times the atomic bomb dropped on Hiroshima.

In 1866, the first traces of an ancient Minoan settlement were accidentally uncovered during attempts to extract volcanic soil from Santorini to isolate the Suez Canal Bridge. Excavations in Akrotiri were initiated in the early 1870s by the French School of Archaeology of Athens. Systematic excavations began in 1967 by archaeologist Spyridon Marinatos, supported by the Archaeological Society of Athens.

Figure 121: Streets of Akrotiri Thera.

Spyridon Marinatos began uncovering the ruins of the ancient city shortly after the excavations began, but his job was not easy. Because the buildings were two or even three floors, the thickness of the ash layer covering the ancient city reached up to 40 meters in places, and the structures were heavily damaged by fires and earthquakes caused by the volcano eruption. Therefore, it was necessary to proceed slowly and carefully.

Greek Pompeii: Akrotiri

Professor Christos Doumas took over the excavations after Spyridon Marinatos passed away in 1974. As a result of the archaeological excavations that have been going on for more than 40 years; An elaborate sewage system, two- and three- story buildings covered with walls, incredible wall frescoes, furniture, and household items were found.

Items from the Greek mainland and Crete and other Greek islands, as well as Syria and Egypt were even found inside the buildings.

Figure 122: Houses of Akrotiri Thera.

Since the original name of the discovered city is unknown, the archaeological site took its name from the present-day village of Akrotiri, located on a hill. Akrotiri was a simple fishing and farming village that grew olives and grain in the early days. However, being located on the trade route between Europe and the Middle East, it prospered and became a large, prosperous port city. People lived in two- and three-story houses with balconies, underfloor heating, hot and cold-water systems, and some of the first indoor toilets. The Minoans decorated their homes with frescoes and made their own furniture, pots, and sculptures. This situation is surprising when we consider it was during the Bronze Age when people in many parts of the world still lived in huts and built stone flats.

Greek Pompeii: Akrotiri

Figure 123: Details from frecoes.

It is even said that Akrotiri was Plato's inspiration for the city of Atlantis. It is perhaps this level of complexity that has led scholars and historians to believe that Akrotiri was Plato's inspiration for the city of Atlantis.

In Plato, Timaios and Kritias dialogues, he spoke of an island with "a great and wonderful empire" and suddenly collapsing. "Severe earthquakes and floods occurred; and in one unfortunate day and night, all your warrior men in one body sank to the ground, " Plato wrote," and the island of Atlantis also disappeared in the depths of the sea. Some scholars have suggested that Plato's description of the sudden disappearance of Atlantis is a reference to the explosion of Thera and the subsequent destruction of Akrotiri.

"Akrotiri" is a modern name given to the settlement after the nearby town of the same name. There is no way of knowing what the original inhabitants called this city - perhaps Akrotiri's real name was "Atlantis", who knows?

Figure 124

Greek Pompeii: Akrotiri

Akrotiri is also often compared with the Roman city of Pompeii, which suffered the same fate in 79 AD and is therefore called "Pompeii in Greek". However, unlike the Roman Pompeii, no human remains, and precious jewels have been found in Akrotiri. This situation shows us that the residents of the city have enough time to escape. However, we do not know exactly where the people who left ancient Akrotiri went and how long before the explosion left the island.

Figure 125: The Spring Fresco, c. 17th c. BC, National Archaeology Museum of Athens.

This is only wall painting of Akrotiri found in situ, covering three walls of the same room. It depicts the rocky Theran landscape before the volcanic eruption: clusters of red lilies with yellow stems dominate the red and gray formations, while swallows swoop above, alone or flirtatious pairs, animating the scene and symbolically announcing nature's annual rebirth. The abundant use of colors - black, white, red, yellow and blue- and the lively movement created by the lillies dancing in the wind and swallows allow for the attribution of this composition to the painter of the "Saffron Gatherers" fresco. The room had a shelf high on the wall and an opening for communicating with a smaller room to its north.

Figure 126: Details from the Spring Fresco.

Figure 127: Saffron Gatherers Fresco, c. 17th c. BC, National Archaeology Museum of Athens.

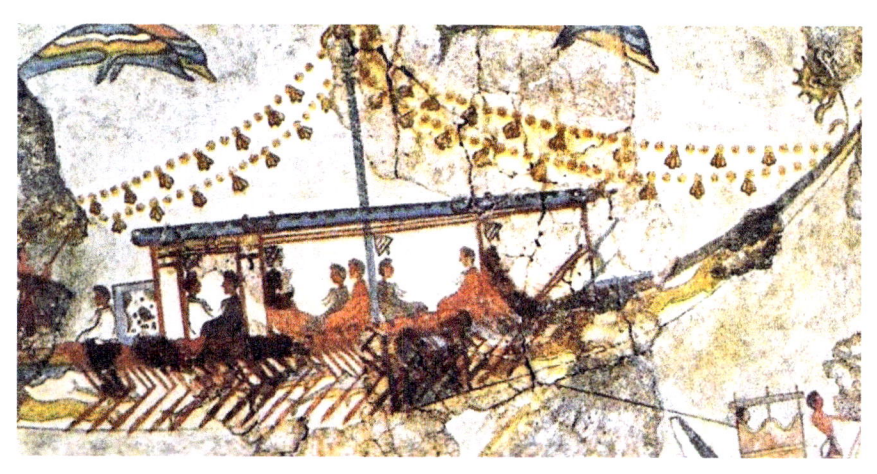

Figure 128: Fresco of a ship procession - Room 5 of the West House, c. 17th c. BC, National Archaeology Museum of Athens.

ROCK CARVINGS IN TANUM

(Tanum, Bohuslän, Sweden c. 1.500 BC)

In Tanum, close to Norway's border, there is a prehistoric diary that is incomparable and has eternal value: Tanum's Rock Carvings - the most important rock drawings from the Bronze Age in all of Europe. They are messages carved in stone, consist only of pictures. The outstanding artistic qualities and vivid scenic compositions of Tanum's rock art make it a unique expression of Bronze Age existence. The elaborate motifs illustrate everyday life, warfare, and culture.

The carvings vary from 1 mm deep to as much as 0,30 or 0,40 mm. It is suggested that the more deeply engraved figures were of greater symbolic significance and therefore required to be visible to larger gatherings of people. At the time of their creation, the carvings were located directly on the sea; due to the Scandinavian land uplift, they are now 25-30 meters higher.

Figure 129: Rock Carvings in Tanum.

In Tanum, as in the rest of Scandinavia, figures at selected rock carving sites have been repeatedly painted since their granitic environment can make them difficult to distinguish. Today, exposed panels are painted with non-destructive paint by trained specialists.

Rock Carvings in Tanum

Figure 130: Fossum Rock Carving - Tanum.

Fossum is a rock carving situated at a higher level, unlike most of the other carved rocks in the World Heritage Area and it has never been in contact with the Bronze Age Sea. The rock depicts circa 200 figures of different types in what appears to be a conscious cohesive composition with images of people, ships, foot soles, animals, and cup marks. The figures are stylistically very similar and were produced with the same skillful carving technique. The Fossum carvings must have been carried out by someone who laid down a great deal of effort not only in the production but also in the design. The artistic formulation is of a very high standard. Details of the weaponry discerned from the depictions date the carving to 700-600 BC, namely, the Late Bronze Age.

Figure 131: c. 3.000 years old rock carving from the bronze age, showing a man running away from a snake, Tanum, Sweden.

Rock Carvings in Tanum

Figure 132: The most frequently visited rock art site in the Tanum World Heritage area is the Vitlycke panel.

The Vitlycke rock is unique in containing imagery relating to love, power and magic. Most of the figures can be dated to the Later Bronze Age, 1000-500 BC. The last carved images are from the beginning of the Iron Age, c. 500 BC-AD 1. The best known of the images at Vitlycke is the Bridal Couple showing a man and a woman standing close together and accompanied by another man with a raised ax to the pair's left. Perhaps this is a picture of a prehistoric ritual wedding that perhaps took place every year to bring good harvests and healthy livestock. The man with the ax on the left could then be a ritual leader who conducts the ceremony and blesses the couple with his ax. Description Credit: Vitlycke Museum, Sweden.

Figure 133: Petropglyph depicting a blue whale or an ard from Vitlycke Panel.

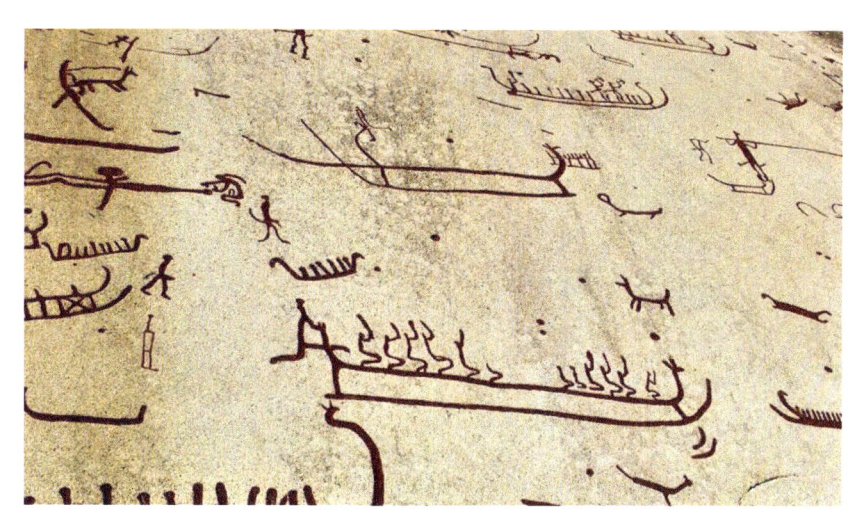

Figure 134: Vitlycke Panel, detail.

Figure 135: A round disc with fork-like sunbeams. The disc is held by two female figures, Aspebérget. The carvings at Aspebérget include images of bulls, warriors and ships. Aspebérget provides a rich pictorial treasure with its mass of images and fascinating activities.

FORTRESS CITY OF AGAMEMNON

(Mycenae, Greece, c. 1.400 BC)

In the late nineteenth century, a German archaeologist, Heinrich Schliemann, set out to find the Mycenaean fortress, which Homer had talked about in his epic poem, the Odyssey. He arrived at Mycenae in 1876. He used the text of Pausanias, the second- century A.D. Roman traveler, as his guide.

The site was already well-known, but he was the first to dig systematically at the site. When Schliemann excavated the royal tombs at Mycenae, he found amazing quantities of gold. In it, he discovered a series of death masks. Upon allegedly finding a particularly fine mask, he wired back to newspapers in Europe: "I have looked on the face of Agamemnon." Agamemnon was the King of Mycenae in Greek mythology, the most powerful ruler of ancient Greece, the leader of the Greek troops in the Trojan War, one of the main heroes of the ancient Greek epic poem "Iliad" by Homer. King Agamemnon was famous for his nobility, courage, and his infinite riches.

Figure 136: The mask of Agamemnon.

Fortress City of Agamemnon

The mask of Agamemnon is made of a thick gold plate and depicts the face of an elderly bearded man of the European race: thin nose, close-set eyes, and large mouth. There were holes in the gold mask for the threads with which it was attached to the face.

During the research of the mask, modern archaeologists had concluded that it refers to circa 1.500 BC and does not correspond to the period when Agamemnon lived. The mighty monarch of Mycenae ruled circa three centuries earlier. However, the golden mask retains the name Schliemann gave him.

So who were the Mycenaeans? The first Greek-speaking peoples began to invade what is now the Greek mainland in about 2.000 BC. The archaeological sites of Mycenae and Tiryns are the imposing ruins of the two greatest cities of the Mycenaean civilization, which dominated the eastern Mediterranean world from the fifteenth to the twelfth centuries BC and played a vital role in the development of classical Greek culture.

Figure 137: Schliemann and visitors at the Lion Gate of Mycenae, 1876 - Deutsches Archäologisches Institut. The Lion Gate was the main entrance of the Bronze Age citadel of Mycenae, southern Greece. It was erected during the 13th century BC, around 1.250 BC in the northwest side of the acropolis and is named after the relief sculpture of two lionesses or lions in a heraldic pose that stands above the entrance.

THE FIRST ALPHABET

(Ugarit, Syria, c. 1.400 BC)

Cuneiform and hieroglyphics wedges which were the writing systems with pictographic symbols were used before the first alphabet. They were made by pressing on the clay. Those techniques needed a plethora of symbols to identify each and every word; writing was difficult and limited to a small group of scribes.

The writing was invented to keep records of trading and business accounts. The earliest forms have been found in Mesopotamia, Syria, and ancient Persia.

In about 1.400 BC, an alphabet using only thirty symbols was devised. Evidence of this alphabet has been found in Ugarit in Syria. As far as we know, this was the first alphabet to be used. Alphabets were later adopted for the writing of Hebrew, Phoenician, and Greek. The Roman alphabet developed from these scripts.

The Ugaritic alphabetic writing system was among the first of simplified forms, reducing the number of signs, hence facilitating the freedom of expression. This innovation was completed in Byblos, three centuries later, by the abandonment of cuneiform and the adoption of the Phoenician script. The Phoenicians benefited from popularizing the alphabet by adapting it to lighter media, such as papyrus, and allowing the substitution of clay and stone tablets.

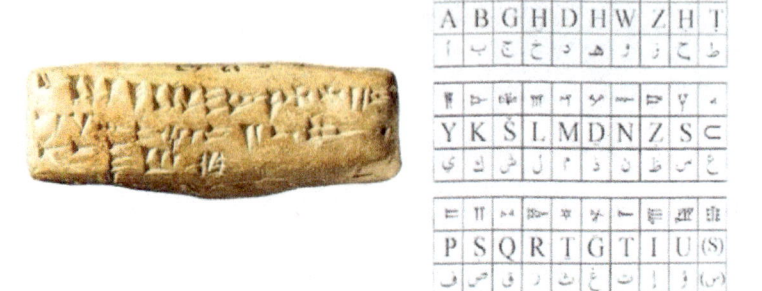

Figure 138: The Ugaritic alphabet is a cuneiform script used in the 15th century BC. As with most Semitic writing systems, each symbol represented a consonant and vowels were not used in the alphabet.

THE SUN CHARIOT

(Trundholm, Denmark, c. 1.400 BC)

The Sun Chariot is the oldest known Danish artwork. It was made in the early Nordic Bronze Age, circa 1.400 BC.

In September 1902, a farmer plowing a peat bog on the Trundholm moor on the northwest of the island of Zealand, south Denmark, spotted a small horse lying in the mud. Thinking he had stumbled on an old toy, he brought it to his home for his children. Ninety-six years after the initial discovery, archaeologists returned to the original findspot and discovered other additional parts of the Sun Chariot.

The Sun Chariot illustrates the idea that the sun was drawn on its eternal journey by a divine horse. The chariot is about 54 centimeters long and consists of cast bronze parts and gold sheets. Probably, the Sun Chariot is a miniature of a larger cult chariot.

Figure 139: The Sun Chariot was probably an object of worship dedicated to a sun god. Original Sun Chariot is on display at the National Museum in Copenhagen and is considered to be one of the most famous Danish national treasures. The symbolism and attraction of the sun is endlessly strong. In the history of art going back several millennia, countless works feature the sun as the main figure.

The right side of the sun chariot is coated with pure gold. The left side is dark - that was how the sun was at night. This corresponds to the sun's course across the northern hemisphere sky.

The Sun Chariot

The sun chariot shows that long ago, people were intensively concerned with the movement of the sun. Ancient people were very aware of how the sun rose each day in the east and moved in an arc across the sky to sink below the horizon in the west. Since the Earth's rotation or the law of gravity were still unknown, many cultures saw the sun as a divine object that traveled across the sky on a chariot day in and day out.

After restoration and the addition of newly discovered parts, the Sun Chariot has been on display since 2002 in the National Museum in Copenhagen.

Figure 140: The Sun Chariot was plowed up from the Trundholm bog in 1902 by this plow.

BUST OF NEFERTITI

(Amarna, Egypt, c. 1.340 BC)

The bust of Nefertiti is one of the finds dating back to ancient Egypt, best known in the world.

Nefertiti was the wife of Akhenaten, the infamous pharaoh who introduced a new monotheistic religion of the sun god that supplanted the worship of all other gods. He portrayed himself as the incarnation of the sun god. Nefertiti served as his queen from the 1.350s-1.330s BC (almost 3.5 thousand years ago). The royal couple lived in Akhenaten's new capital Amarna, about halfway between Cairo and Luxor.

On December 6, 1912, German archaeologist Ludwig Borchardt excavated in the ruins of an old house in Amarna. The house had been identified as belonging to a sculptor named Thutmose. In one of the rooms came to light more than twenty plaster molds incomplete or barely sketched, stone heads completed and others still to be finished. They saw a "skin-colored neck" in the rubble. The excavators put aside their tools and with their hands revealed first the lower part of the bust and then the blue headdress. The portrait of Nefertiti was almost intact. Ludwig Borchardt noted that the colors were still so bright that they appeared to be "freshly painted."

Figure 141: Bust of Nefertiti, Neues Museum, Berlin, Germany.

Bust of Nefertiti

Missing parts of the ear were searched for and discovered; the missing eye was also searched for but never found. Only later, Borchardt wrote, did he realize that this eye had never been put in its place; thus, the bust had never been completed. It is believed that the bust was placed on a wooden shelf and fell because of a collapse but remained almost intact and was later preserved by the rubble above. Ludwig Borchardt was unable to continue working at the site after the outbreak of World War I in 1914.

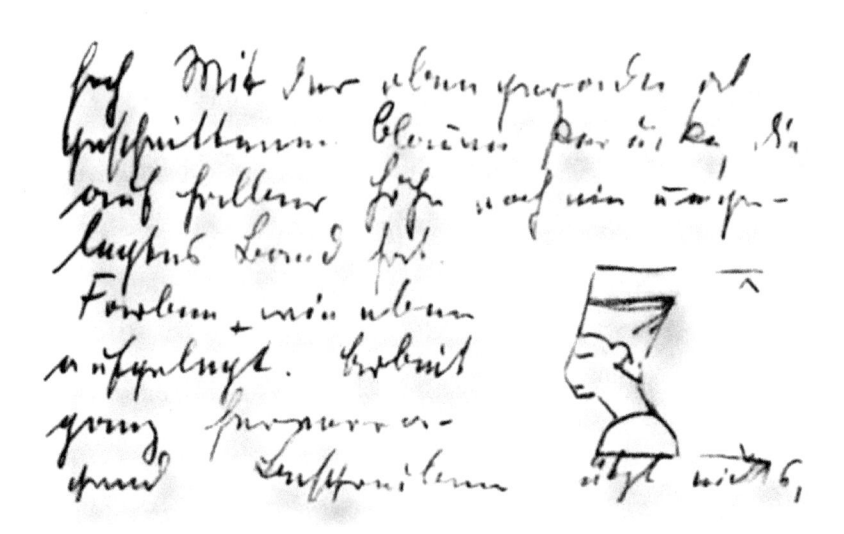

Figure 142: A copy of handwritten note by Ludwig Borchardt on the discovery of the bust. Aside from a quick sketch, it contains the remark "No use describing it, you have to see it." - Original note located at the Ägyptisches Museum und Papyrussammlung, Berlin.

Made around 1.340 BC, or in the last years of the reign of Akhenaton, the bust, 47 cm high, is made of limestone, is entirely covered with painted plaster, and does not show any hieroglyphic inscription. The right eye is made of limestone with rock crystal included for the pupil and iris finely worked in order to give expressiveness to the face. It is instead missing the left eye, for the lack of which were proposed several theories, from the use of the bust as a model to the loss of the artifact during excavations.

Nefertiti is, unquestionably, beautiful: slightly almond-shaped eyes, high cheekbones, thin nose, fleshy mouth with sensual lips, long and elegant neck. The face, perfectly symmetrical, appears made up according to the fashion of the period. Egyptian women, as well as men, applied around the eyes a line of kajal (also called kohl), a mineral-based compound mixed with animal fat; ochre, mixed with oils and fats, acted as a lipstick, while powder was used as a blush.

Bust of Nefertiti

The bust of the queen is then completed by a sumptuous crown with a golden band at the height of the forehead and a central diadem that goes around the headdress.

As per the agreements of the period with the Egyptian authorities, the find was taken by the financier of the excavations, James Simon, who donated it in 1920 to the Prussian state and was exposed to the public for the first time in 1924. The bust of Nefertiti is now preserved in the Neues Museum in Berlin.

Figure 143: Bust of Nefertiti, side view.

THE TOMB OF TUTANKHAMUN

(Valley of the Kings, Egypt, c. 1.323 BC)

On 4 November 1922, British archaeologist & Egyptologist Howard Carter who had been working in Egypt for 31 years, discovered the steps of the entrance to the tomb of Pharaoh Tutankhamun in the Valley of the Kings – a royal burial ground.

The discovery was indeed made by a waterboy who noticed the first step of the entrance which was beneath the mud brick houses of the workmen. They cleared the sand and found the stairway to a sealed door.

After the first discovery, Carter shared the news with Lord Carnarvon, who had been giving fund to Carter since 1917. (After 5 years of excavation Lord decided to stop funding. Carter persuaded him for another last one.) Lord and his daughter arrived in Luxor and were amazed to see the discovery.

Who was Tutankhamun?

Tutankhamun became pharaoh at the age of nine. Then he married to his sister. Because of his parents were closely related, he had genetic disorders. The reason of his death is unknown but when his well-hidden body was analyzed, it was seen that there was an infection above his knee that didn't heal when he died at the age of 19. The next pharaoh was Ay who was one of his advisors and also married to Tut's widowed wife.

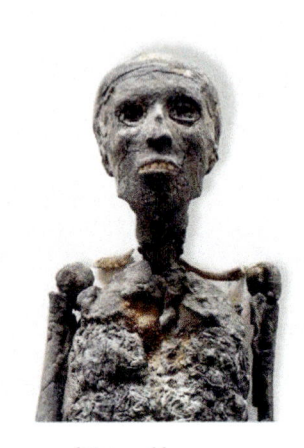

Figure 144: Golden Mask and Mummy of Tutan khamun.

The Tomb of Tutankhamun

The Burial Site

After clearing out the stairways, Carter and his team found the door of the entrance to the tomb, which still bore the Anubis symbol of the royal. There was an evidence that the tomb bad been raided several times before. On November 26, they opened the second doorway leading to the antechamber.

Inside the antechamber were 3 animal-shaped couches, cups, cases, royal chariots and about 700 objects all scattered around. Even a bunch of flowers and leaves were laid by the doorway and a smell of perfume still in the air.

The objects had to be removed with utmost care, so they used bandages, gauze to protect it for removal and celluloid sprays for immediate treatment. It took seven weeks to clean the antechamber. It also contained 7 oars to help the king get across the waters of the underworld.

On the right wall stood 2 life-size statues of the king, facing each other as if to protect the sealed door of the burial chamber in which 4 gilded shrines were found to open. On this sealed door Carter noticed that the hole wasn't resealed unlike the other.

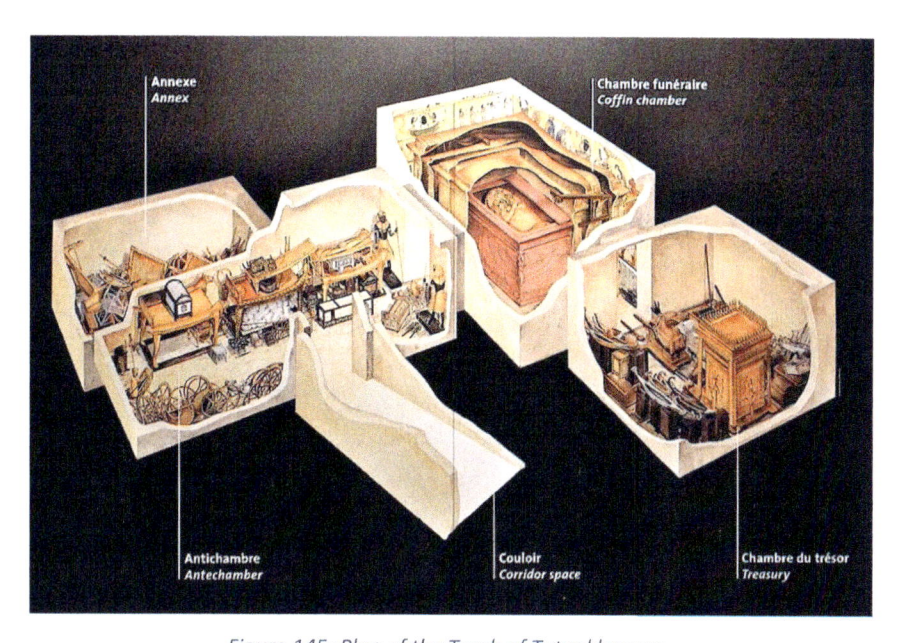

Figure 145: Plan of the Tomb of Tutankhamun.

The Annex

In the annex household items, clothing, tools, and things that the king might need in the afterworld were found. It gives us clues about the everyday life of Egypt in antiquity.

The Burial Chamber

From the sealed door of Antechamber Carter saw a wall of gold which turned out to be the one wall of a gilded shrine that filled the Burial Chamber. Its walls were made of gilded wood. The room that contained the sarcophagus had yellow walls with funeral scenes painted on it.

There were 4 shrines, one inside the other. The inner shrine covered a sarcophagus carved from a block of quartzite. The golden mummy shaped coffin in it was made of solid gold with inlay of enamel and semiprecious stones. He holds the crook and frail on his hands and a cobra his forehead.

There was a death mask in the coffin. It wears striped nemes headdress and a false beard. The back of the mask is covered with a spell from the Book of the Dead.

Figure 146: Burial Chamber.

The Treasury

Inside the burial chamber stood a statue of a wild black wood dog on the entrance to the treasury as if to guard the treasures. The room was filled with boxes, and a gilded canopic shrine which held the single block of calcite. In this canopic chest were the 4 canopic jars, containing the embalmed organs of the kings. Lots of jewelry & statues of the servants and two small coffins which belong to the king's premature babies were found in the room.

It took Carter 10 years to document & clear out Tut's tomb. Its body now rests in his tomb in the Valley of the Kings which is on the west back of the Nile River. Nearly all the things – about 3.000 items all in all – Room in the burial site were taken to the Egyptian Museum in Cairo.

People believed that the curse caught the discoveries when Lord died 6 months later because of blood poisoning after a mosquito bite and Carter's canary at his home was eaten by a cobra.

Figure 147: Howard Carter and associates opening the shrine doors in the burial chamber 1924 reconstruction of the 1923 event.

The Tomb of Tutankhamun

Figure 148: Ongoing excavation efforts at the tomb site of Tutankhamun (1922), photography by Harry Burton.

Figure 149: Carter (left) and Lord Carnarvon together in the tomb.

The Tomb of Tutankhamun

Figure 150: 29-30 October 1925 - Carter and an Egyptian workman examine the third innermost coffin made of solid gold inside the case of the second coffin.

Figure 151: A ceremonial bed in the shape of the Celestial Cow, surrounded by provisions and other objects in the antechamber of the tomb.

Figure 152: Under the lion bed in the antechamber are several boxes and chests, and an ebony and ivory chair which Tutankhamun used as a child.

Figure 153: Unbroken Seal on the Third Shrine of Tutankhamun's tomb November 1922. Photographer: Harry Burton.

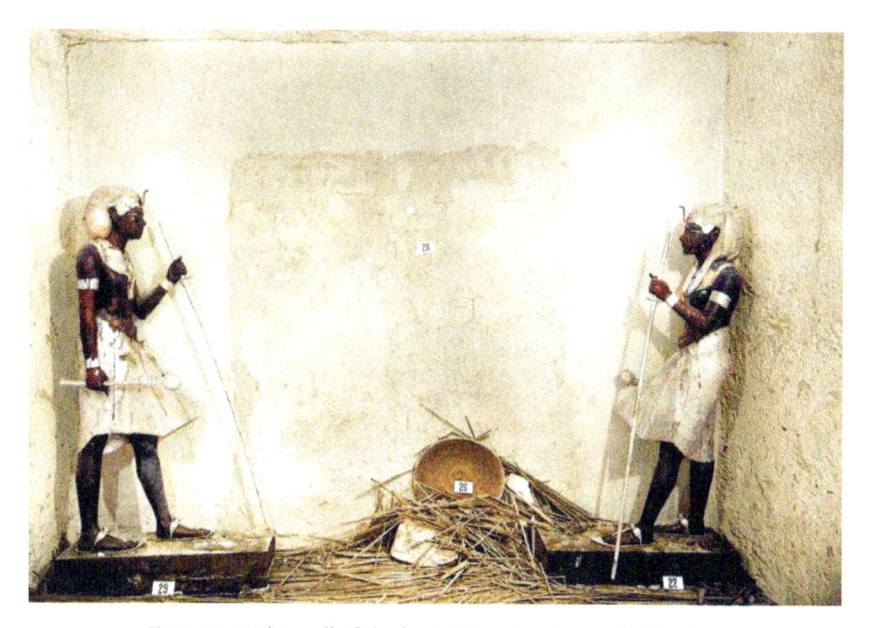

Figure 154: The wall of the burial chamber is guarded by statues.

Figure 155: The Anubis shrine on the threshold of the Treasury.

The Tomb of Tutankhamun

Figure 156: Objects in the tomb's antechamber shortly after its discovery.

Figure 157: Howard Carter in the King Tutankhamun's Tomb. circa 1925. Photographer: Harry Burton.

OLMEC HEADS

(San Lorenzo, Mexico, 1.250-900 BC)

Olmecs are people of unknown origin who created the first advanced civilization in Mesoamerica. They spread over large areas of Mesoamerica. The core area of Olmecs Civilization extended from eastern Mexico through southern Veracruz and northern Tabasco. The main centers were San Lorenzo, Tenochtitlán, and La Venta.

The most remarkable art left behind by this culture is the Olmec colossal heads. To date, seventeen of these colossal stone heads have been unearthed. The people of the Gulf Coast were masters in the art of sculpting hard stone. Olmecs left behind the enormous basalt heads, for which they are famous, and which probably represent priestly princes, together with massive altars, weighing up to 50 tons, stelae, ceramics, and the most delicately carved jade figurines.

The heads date from before 900 BC and are a distinctive feature of the Olmec civilization. San Lorenzo, one of the oldest Olmec sites, was occupied by circa 1.500 BC. Olmec-style ceramics and potteries were found from the earliest period, but the monumental, huge stone sculptures for which the Olmecs are known were not made until around 1.250 BC. For a period of some 350 years, the massive heads and other monuments were carved from basalt, which was floated on huge rafts and then dragged from the Tuxtla Mountains. Around 900 BC, this activity ended, and all of the great stone-heads were intentionally buried.

Figure 158

Olmec Heads

These heads rest on stone foundations and have neither body nor neck. They are up to 2.85 m high, weigh 15-50 tons and have a circumference of up to 6 m. The facial type of these heads shows large eyes with indicated irises, multiple shaggy eyebrows, sometimes appearing like flames, a broad nose, and a half-open, well-defined mouth with bulging lips and downturned corners of the mouth. None of the heads are alike, and each boasts a unique headdress, which suggests they represent specific individuals.

After 400 BC, the Olmec culture was gradually absorbed into the successor cultures: Tres Zapotes and Izapa reveal the transition to Mayan culture. Beyond their core area, the Olmecs influenced all later cultures of Mesoamerica in many ways.

Figure 159: Among the most mysterious and magnificent works of the Olmec civilization are the huge heads that most likely depict rulers. Some of these heads weighed around 30 tons and had to be moved uphill over considerable distances. The heads were hand-carved using hard stones and are likely to have been originally painted in bright colors.

LIBRARY OF ASHURBANIPAL

(Nineveh, Iraq, c. 7th century BC)

The library that once belonged to Ashurbanipal, King of Assyria (668-c. 630 BC), is one of most remarkable and fascinating archaeological discoveries ever made.

Ashurbanipal (668-627 BC) was the last of the great kings of Assyria. During this period, the Neo-Assyrian Empire underwent its greatest territorial expansion, and the areas under Ashurbanipal's rule included Babylon, Persia, Syria, and Egypt. He established his famous library at Nineveh. The library included considerably more than 30.000 volumes, including fired clay cuneiform tablets, stone prisms, and cylinder seals, and waxed wooden writing boards called diptych.

The king's library contained texts from such areas of knowledge as medicine, mythology, lexical, epics, magic, science, and geography. One of the best-known documents from this library is the Epic of Gilgamesh, which is often regarded as the earliest surviving great work of literature.

Nineveh was conquered in 612 BC, and the libraries were looted, and the buildings destroyed. When the buildings collapsed, the ceiling of the library was damaged, and when archaeologists got to Nineveh in the early 20th century, they saw that all the tablets and writing boards on the floors were broken deeply.

Figure 160: Library of Ashurbanipal - Mesopotamia, British Museum, London. The Ashurbanipal Library Project was set up in 2002 as a long-term co-operation with the University of Mosul, in Iraq. British Museum aims to bring Ashurbanipal's astonishing library back to life

SANCTUARY OF DELPHI

(Archaeological Site of Delphi, Greece, c. 600 BC.)

Delphi, in central Greece, is the sanctuary (sacred location) of the god Apollo. A temple there contains the Delphic Oracle, the most famous of the Greek world's oracles (priestly fortune-tellers). Delphi in the sixth century BC was the religious center and symbol of unity of the ancient Greek world.

Delphi is not one of the seven wonders of the ancient world. However, in terms of status and importance, few places were as powerful as Delphi, a two-and-a-half-hour drive from Athens. For a thousand years, rich and poor, kings and peasants came across the to visit the sanctuary of Apollo and pay homage to the god. His oracle was the spiritual center of their world.

According to mythology, Zeus (the king of all other gods and men) sent out two eagles, one to the east and the other to the west, to find the navel of the world. The eagles met at the Delphi — Zeus marked the spot with a sacred stone called the omphalos (meaning navel), which was later held at the sanctuary of Apollo.

Figure 161: Temple of Delphic Apollo, Delphi.

From the second millennium BC to the Mycenaean period, Gaia or Ge, the mother of the gods, was the first to give oracles on the site. Her daughter Themis succeeded her, followed by her sister Phoebe who called Apollo Phoebus the day of his birth on the island of Delos. Then Apollo, son of Leto and Zeus, replaced them shortly after.

Sanctuary of Delphi

According to a Homeric hymn of the 8th century BC, Apollo built his first temple in Delphi after having killed Python, the dreaded serpent guardian of the sanctuary of Gaia. Respecting the law that he himself had established, Apollo was exiled for eight years to atone for his crime. Then he returned as absolute master of the place, becoming Apollo Pythian whose oracles were interpreted by a woman selected for her virtue and chastity, the Pythia.

The Oracle of Apollo at Delphi was one of the most famous in the ancient world and became one of the more prestigious pilgrimage centers of the times.

Whoever wished to obtain information from Apollo had to offer a sacrifice to the god before entering the sanctuary. For this purpose, a sheep or a goat was sacrificed in front of the altar, which was always outside in Greek temples. Then one had to turn to the priests of Apollo. To them, the person seeking advice presented his question to the god, written down on a lead tablet. During excavations in Delphi, archaeologists have discovered many such tablets. After the priests had examined the question, they presented it to the main person in the oracle of Delphi. This was the Pythia. This was the name of the priestess responsible for receiving the divine message in Delphi.

Figure 162: German Illustration, The Oracle of Delphi. Illustrator: Heinrich Leutemann, 1865.

Sanctuary of Delphi

"Pythia" was not a proper name but a title. All women who held this function in those centuries in which the oracle site of Delphi was in operation bore this designation. There were fixed rules for the selection of the Pythia.

She had to be a peasant woman from the surroundings of Delphi, and she could not be younger than 50 years. The Pythia's activity as a liaison between the god Apollo and the people seeking advice took place in the Adyton. This was a room completely inside the temple. Before she could start to receive the answers of the god, she purified herself in a spring, drank from this spring, and ate a laurel leaf. Only then had she achieved that cultic purity with which she was allowed to appear before the god Apollo. After that, she took a seat on a tripod, which was built over a crevice in the earth. Mysterious vapors emanated from this crevice. To this day, it is not clear exactly which substances were involved. But it was clear that vapors had a kind of trance function. Then she was ready, as an extended arm of Apollo, to answer the questions that the priests handed her.

Figure 163: The Pythia on her tripod giving an oracle on a kylix in the Altes Museum in Berlin.

Sanctuary of Delphi

Only the priests could understand the words. To outsiders, they must have seemed like an incomprehensible murmur. The priest on duty had the task of translating the words of Pythia into understandable Greek.

The questioners did not always leave Delphi in a satisfied mood. This was true both for those who had come for political advice as representatives of a king or a state and for people who had been on private business. A specialty of the oracle of Delphi was that the Pythia or the priests interpreting it often gave ambiguous answers. This was not incompetence, but there was a clear intention behind it.

The oracle of Delphi did not want to lose its good reputation through false predictions. Thus, the Pythia gave answers that could always be interpreted as correct and accurate in case of doubt. Also, visiting Delphi was very costly.

Although the information was in principle given free of charge, visitors were expected to reciprocate with generous donations and gifts. The treasuries of Delphi were always well filled for this reason. If Delphi had gotten a reputation for misreading the future and giving bad advice, there would have been financial repercussions. It was better to keep room for maneuver in the answers.

Figure 164: Priestess of Delphi (1891) by John Collier, showing the Pythia sitting on a tripod with vapor rising from a crack in the earth beneath her. (right) - Pythia, the Delphi Oracle . J. Augustus Knap (left)

The Kroisos Example

The classic example of ambiguous information from the Oracle of Delphi was King Kroisos. This was the real name of that fabulously rich ruler who is commonly better known as "Croesus".

Kroisos was the 6th century BC king of Lydia, countryside in the west of present- day Turkey. At that time, the Persians, who were then the eastern neighbors of the Lydians, began to spread westward. Thus, Lydia also came into the sights of the Persian conquerors. Kroisos was not sure how to act. Should he wait for the Persians and then try to stop them? Or should he risk going out to meet them? In his distress, he turned to the oracle at Delphi. The Pythia gave him the answer that if he crossed the Halys, he would destroy a great empire. The Halys was the border river between Lydia and Persia. Kroisos was delighted because he thought that the great empire, he was going to destroy was the empire of the Persians. He crossed the Halys with his army, fought the Persians, and suffered a crushing defeat. The new rulers in Lydia were now the Persians.

Kroisos then sent messengers to Delphi, who complained vehemently that the god and the Pythia had given them false information. But the priests gave him to understand that Kroisos had misinterpreted the oracle. For the great empire that he would destroy in a campaign against the Persians was, of course, not the empire of the Persians but his own kingdom.

Figure 165: This coin was minted depicting Antiochus Hierax of the Seleucid Empire from the mint in Sardis. The reverse side depicts Apollo sitting on the omphalos.

For over 1000 years, the oracle of Delphi was significant. Even the Romans, who took over the rule in Greece from the 2nd century BC, liked to ask the Pythia.

Even Emperor Nero, who ruled from 54 to 68, once sought information about his future. "The number 73 indicates the time of your fall," Pythia told Emperor Nero. Nero took this saying to mean that he would die in his 73rd year. Since he had been born in 37 A.D., he would have had until 110 A.D. in this case. But already in 68 A.D., when Nero was just 30 years old, he was forced to commit suicide by his political opponents. His successor was the 73-year-old Galba.

The end came for the Oracle of Delphi at the end of the 4th century A.D. The Roman emperor elevated Christianity to the state religion and banned all other cults. Since the Oracle of Delphi was a sanctuary of the god Apollo, it was closed.

A Christian city was then established on the site of the sanctuary before disappearing in the 7th or 8th century AD. Modern excavations commenced on the site in 1892 and have since revealed a wealth of invaluable information. The archaeological site of Delphi is situated today about 100 miles northwest of Athens, above the Gulf of Corinth, on the main route EO48.

The Archaeological Site of Delphi includes:

The Temple of Delphic Apollo: The Temple of Delphic Apollo, as it survives, dates only to the fourth century BC, but the foundation is original to an earlier version from the sixth century, which replaces an even older seventh-century version. The temple was home to the Oracle of Apollo. Inside was the seat of the Pythia, the priestess who presided over the Oracle and delivered the prophesies inspired by Apollo. Delphi was the most important oracle in the Greek world.

Altar of the Chians: On the east side of the Temple of Apollo located the Great Altar, or the Altar of the Chians, dedicated by the people of the island of Chios, in the 5th century B.C., after their successful stand against the Persians.

The Athenian Treasury: A small building in Doric order, built by the Athenians at the end of the sixth century BC to house their offerings and other votive objects to Apollo.

Sanctuary of Delphi

Figure 166: The Temple of Delphic Apollo

Figure 167: The Athenian Treasury, Delphi.

Sanctuary of Delphi

Stoa of the Athenians: The Stoa of the Athenians is an ancient portico in the Delphic Sanctuary, Greece, located south of the Temple of Apollo. Built-in the Ionic order, it has seven fluted columns, each made from a single stone. According to an inscription, it was dedicated by the Athenians after the Persian Wars.

Theatre: Originally built in the fourth century BC, its visible ruins actually date from the Roman imperial period. The singing of hymns to Apollo was an ancient tradition at Delphi, and the area occupied by the present theatre most likely served as the place where these musical competitions were traditionally held.

Stadium: The stadium of Delphi is one of the best-preserved monuments of Delphi. It is situated northwest of the theatre, above the sanctuary of Apollo, in the highest part of the Delphi. Constructed in the fifth century BC and remodeled in the second century AD. The Pan-Hellenic Pythian Games, one of the forerunners of the Olympic Games, took place in this stadium. Its track is 177.55 m long, and 25.50 m wide.

Tholos: The Tholos is a circular building within the sanctuary of Athena Pronaia, built by the architect Theodore the Phocaean in 380-360 BC. The Tholos of Delphi may have sheltered an important statue, although the exact purpose of the structure is unknown. It had 20 Doric columns on the circular colonnade and 10 or 13 Corinthian semi-columns in the interior of the cella.

Figure 168: Theatre, Delphi.

Sanctuary of Delphi

Figure 169: Stadium, Delphi.

Figure 170: Tholos, Delphi.

Sanctuary of Delphi

Figure 171: Albert Tournaire's recreation of Apollo's Temple at Delphi and the Sacred Way leading up to it.

Figure 172: The Omphalos, or the navel stone of the earth, in the Archaeological Museum of Delphi

ISHTAR GATE

(Babylon, Iraq, c. 6th century BC)

Ishtar is the counterpart of Aphrodite in ancient Greece and is remembered with love and beauty just like him. It is possible to see Ishtar in Babylon and in Assyrian and Sumerian civilizations (Inanna in these civilizations is the equivalent of Ishtar).

The giant brick door, consisting of two monumental entrances separated by an inner courtyard, opening to the main street called "Ceremonial Road" on the walls of the ancient city of Babylon in today's Iraq. It was built in 575 as the eighth gate of the town, connecting the inner and outer fortifications of Babylon, the capital of the New Babylonian State.

Figure 173: Ishtar Gate.

The door was slightly higher than 12 m, and the relief was covered with glazed bricks with dragon and bull figures. The gate consisted of two consecutive entrances, and there was a wide landing on the south side.

There were terracotta lion statues with one foot raised on both sides of the stone and brick-paved Ceremonial Road, which started behind the door and can be viewed more than 800 meters today.

Ishtar Gate

It is thought that there are 120 lion statues on the street and 575 dragon and bull figures in 13 rows on the front of the door.

When German archaeologists began excavating in 1899, the approximately 2.500- year-old city stood in almost all its glory, including its gate. The Ishtar Gate, which was seen as the main symbol of Babylon's glory during excavations, was found in 1902. This gate was one of the eight gates built in different periods of the city. Most of the 12-meter-high walls were still standing.

Finds from this excavation were later used to create a full-size structure of the Ishtar Gate, considered one of the most spectacular reconstructions in archaeology history. In the 1900s, more than 200 local workers excavated the area and extracted tons of soil. Archaeologists have collected tens of thousands of fragments from the door, enough to fill 900 boxes. The aim was to restore the animal figures based on the best-preserved brick fragments. Only when a certain piece of tile was missing would it be replaced with a modern replica. Thousands of enamel pieces of the Ishtar Gate were laid on workbenches at the Old Near East Museum in Berlin.

Figure 174

Archaeologists managed to complete 30 lions, 26 bulls, and 17 dragons and some of the various palace facades within two years. Partial reconstructions of the Ceremonial Road and Ishtar Gate were opened at the Pergamon Museum in 1930. The museum can only display the front of the door (the second, larger door is in the museum's warehouse).

Ishtar Gate

Visitors can still see them today and share their experiences of what it might be like to approach Nebuchadnezzar's grand entrance to Babylon 2.600 years ago. Several items from the Ceremonial Path have been sold to other museums and can be seen in 11 museums around the world. (Istanbul Archaeology Museums, Detroit Art Institute, Royal Ontario Museum, Louvre, Munich State Museum of Egyptian Art, New York Metropolitan Museum of Art, Oriental Institute of Chicago, and others.)

After World War II, large-scale excavations were carried out by Italians. A smaller reconstruction of the Ishtar Gate was made in Iraq as a museum entrance under Saddam Hussein. However, this reconstruction was never completed due to the war. Today only the lower parts of the Ishtar Gate are still at the site of the ancient Babylonian city, known today as Babylon.

Figure 175: Lower parts of the Ishtar Gate.

Ishtar Gate

Figure 176: The Ishtar Gate in 1932. Iraq, Babylon. Matson Photograph Collection.

BABYLONIAN MAP OF THE WORLD

(Sippar, Iraq, c. 6th century BC.)

The Babylonian Map of the World, known as the Imago Mundi, is the oldest map of the world that has been found. It is dated around the 6th century BC. This map was discovered at Sippar (modern-day in Iraq), north of Babylon, in 1881 by Assyriologist Hormuzd Rassam. The Babylonian World Map is made on a cuneiform clay tablet, preserved in the British Museum in London.

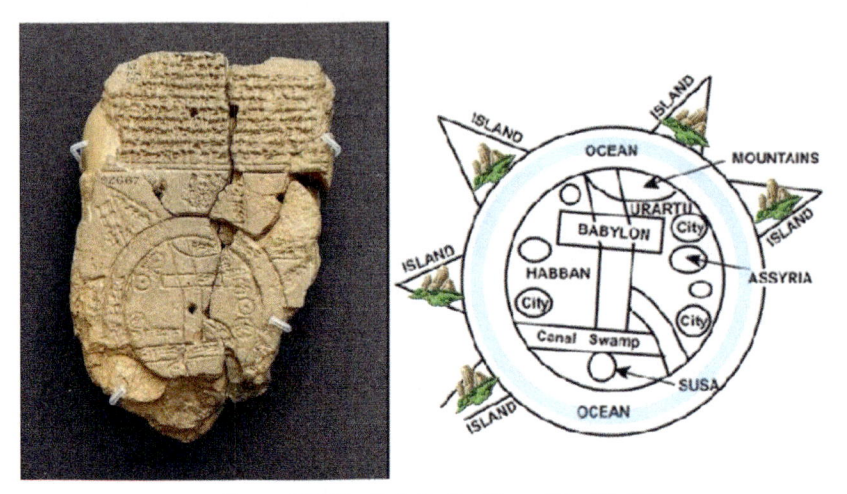

Figure 177: The Babylonian Map of the World.

The Babylonian Map of the World is the aerial representation of the world in a plan. The map has two concentric rings that appear engraved concentric geometric shapes (circles, rectangles, and curved lines); around the outermost circle are drawn eight triangles, of which only five are visible.

This Babylonian map on a clay tablet depicts the Mesopotamian world as a flat disc surrounded by water. Inside, the Euphrates River is depicted in a vertical rectangular shape, Babylon in a central position and a horizontal rectangular shape, and some other less important cities (such as Urartu, Assyria, Der, Susa) with dotted circles on both sides of the Euphrates. The drawing is accompanied by a cuneiform text that runs across the top and back. It describes the composition of the map.

The outer ring represents the marratu (salt sea), an ocean that surrounds the inhabited world, while the outer triangles identify the nagu (regions or provinces) to which are matched distances and exotic animals.

Babylonian Map of the World

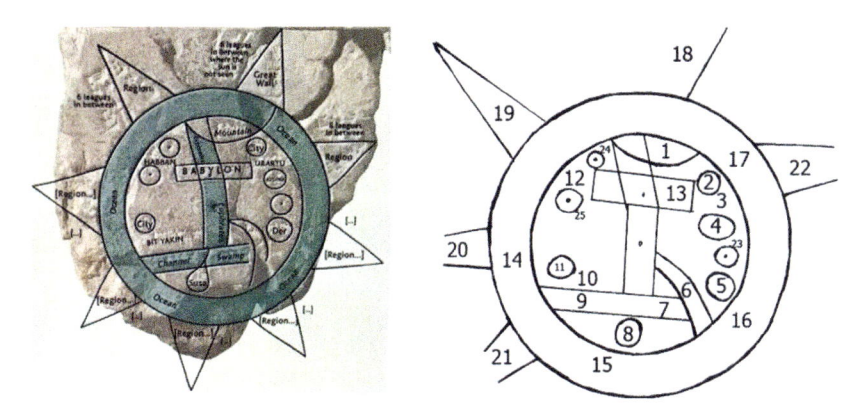

Figure 178: Signs and points on the Babylonian Map.

The interpretation of the signs and points on the map is as follows:
1. "Mountain" (Akkadian: šá-du-ú)
2. "City" (Akkadian: Uru)
3. Urartu (Akkadian: ú-ra-áš-tu)
4. Assyria (Akkadian: kuraš+šurki)
5. Der (Akkadian: dēr)
6. ?
7. Swamp (Akkadian: ap-pa-ru)
8. Elam (Akkadian: šuša)
9. Canal (Akkadian: bit-qu)
10. Bit Yakin (Akkadian: bīt-ia-ʾ-ki-nu)
11. "City" (Akkadian: Uru)
12. Habban (Akkadian: ha-ab-ban)
13. Babylon (Akkadian: tin.tirki), cut by the Euphrates
14 - 17. Ocean (saltwater, Akkadian: idmar-ra-tum)
18 - 22. Mythological objects.

There are different opinions regarding the reading and interpretation of the map. For the ancient Mesopotamian peoples, the place where we identified with the east was the place above (ie, the North) because the place where the sun rises was there.

This situation and other problems with how the map should be read do not give us a full understanding of what its purpose is. But the discovery is truly incredible, as it shows us the first map drawing in history.

PERSEPOLIS

(Iran, c. 515 BC)

The magnificent ruins of Persepolis lie at the foot of Kuh-i-Rahmat (Mountain of Mercy), about 650 km south of the present capital city of Teheran.

Founded by Darius I in 518 BC, Persepolis was the capital of the Achaemenid Empire. Its name comes from the Ancient Greek: Περσέπολις (romanized Perses- polis), a compound of Pérsēs (Πέρσης) and pólis (πόλις), meaning "the Persian city" or "the city of the Persians." But the Persians knew it as Parsa.

It was built on an immense half-artificial and half-natural terrace, where an impressive palace complex was constructed, inspired by ancient Mesopotamian models. Persian King Darius planned this unique complex not only as of the seat of the kingdom but also, and primarily, as a showplace and a spectacular center for the festivals of the Achaemenid kings and their empire. Today, dominating the city is the immense stone terrace (530 m by 330 m), backed against the mountains. The importance and quality of the monumental ruins make it a unique archaeological site.

Figure 179: The stairs at Persepolis were decorated with carved reliefs showing the tribute processions arriving at the palace to celebrate New Year.

Persepolis

Figure 180: Detail, Persepolis.

Figure 181: Detail, Persepolis.

PAZYRYK RUG

(Pazyryk Valley, Siberia, c. 500 BC)

The Pazyryk Rug is one of the oldest carpets in the world, dating around the 5th c. BC. The rug was found in 1949 in the grave of a Scythian nobleman in the Pazyryk Valley of the Altai Mountains in Siberia.

The rug was found in a semi-frozen state near a burial tomb. Water filled the tomb, probably due to the actions of grave robbers, and froze, preventing any of the degradation or decay that would normally occur. It is because of this completely frozen and dark environment, that the Pazyryk Rug was wonderfully preserved for over two and half millenniums. The rug itself, which is almost square, approximately 1.83 x 1.98 m, consists of an inner field and a number of borders. The rug has 36 symmetrical knots per cm^2. (or more than 1.250.000 knots). The pile is hand-knotted and made from hand-spun wool. The dyes are natural.

Figure 182: The Pazyryk Rug.

Pazyryk Rug

The Pazyryk Rug shows a mixture of many styles, including techniques common to motifs found in the Assyrian, Achaemenian, and Scythian regions of the East.

The central field of the rug is occupied by 24 cross-shaped figures, each of which consists of four lotus buds. This composition is framed by a border of griffins, followed by a border of twenty-four fallow deer. The widest border contains representations of workhorses and men.

The creators of the Pazyryk Carpet paid a lot of attention to the details of the figures. For instance, each deer is depicted with its internal organs, including its heart, intestines, urethra, vertebra, and maw.

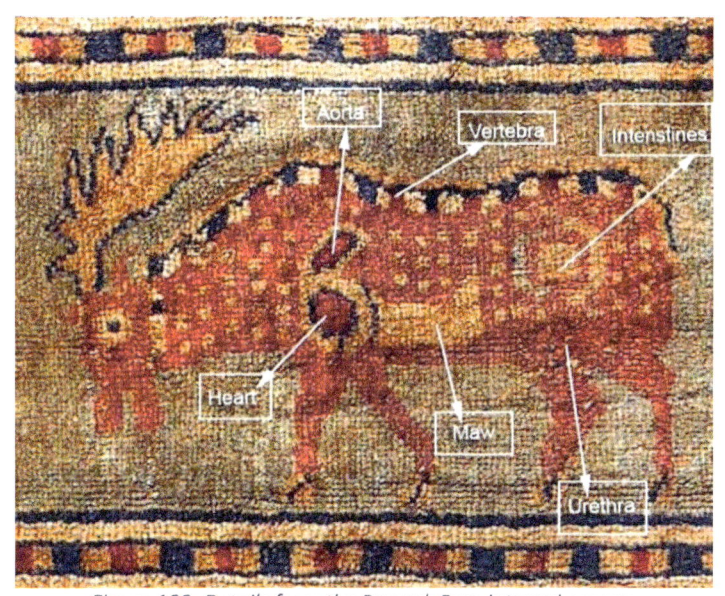

Figure 183: Details from the Pazyryk Rug, internal organs.

Figure 184

Pazyryk Rug

The exact origins of the Pazyryk Rug remain ambiguous to researchers, although the horses depicted on the rug are nearly identical to equestrians on a frieze in the ancient Persian city of Persepolis.

The exact origin of the Pazyryk Rug will remain a mystery. However, its significance and beauty are forever eternal.

The Pazyryk Rug is on display in the State Hermitage Museum in St. Petersburg, Russia.

Figure 185: Detail from the Pazyryk Rug and Relief of Sychtians wearing pointed caps, tribute frieze, Apadana stairway façade, Persepolis.

Figure 186

SIBERIAN ICE PRINCESS

(Ukok Plateau, Siberia, c. 500 BC)

In the summer of 1993, archaeologist Natalia Polosmak discovered the remains of a 5th-century BC Scythian-Siberian woman in the underground burial chambers on the Ukok Plateau of the Autonomous Altai Republic.

The mummy, which is in a dense layer of ice in the underground burial chambers on the Ukok Plateau, could be stored for 2.500 years without damage. As a result of the examinations and research, it was revealed that the mummy belonged to the Pazirik culture peculiar to the Altai Civilization between the 6th and 2nd centuries BC. The mummy, which has been in Russia since 1993, was delivered to the Altai Republic in 2012.

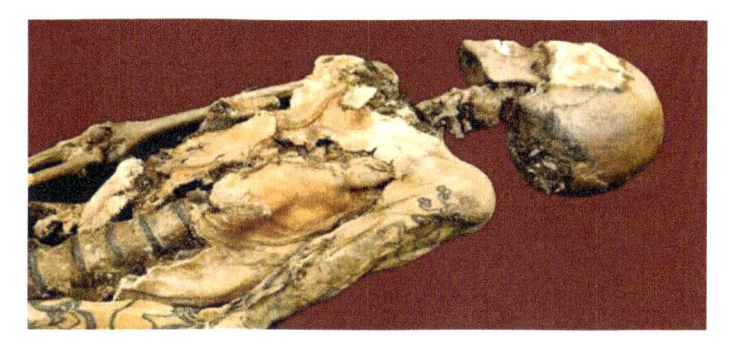

Figure 187

The Ice Princess was buried with six horses that were thought to accompany her in the afterlife. Scientists examining the samples taken from the princess's skin tissue revealed that the princess was buried between the ages of 20-30 and that the cause of death was breast cancer.

The most surprising fact about the princess is her tattoos. The mysterious tattoos on the neck, arm, and leg area have remained intact for 2.500 years! Each of these tattoos featured fantastic animal figures.

The Pazyryk culture had the idea that the body embroidery depicting such fantastic animals would protect people in the afterlife.

The source of the dyes used in tattoos is thought to be burnt plant parts containing a lot of potassium. The most striking of these tattoos was the tattoo on his left shoulder. A deer with a griffon beak and Capricorn antlers were pictured on his left shoulder.

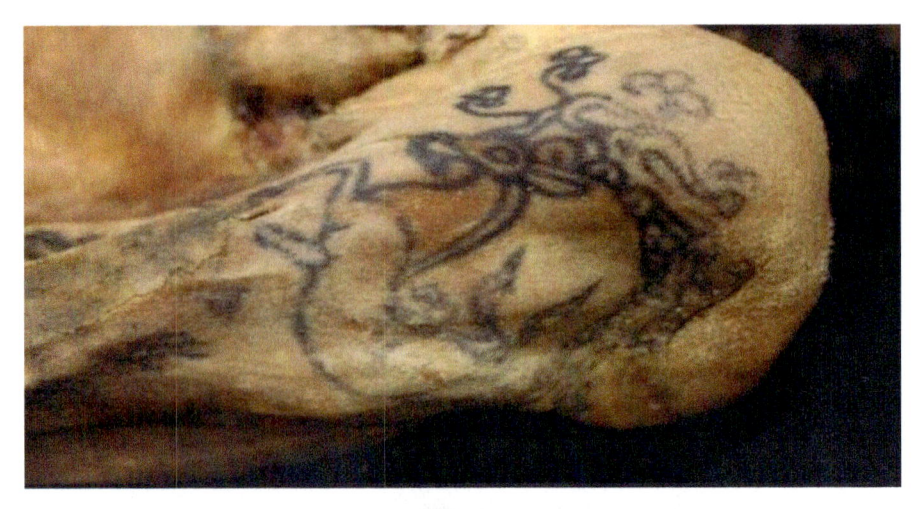

Figure 188: Princess Ukok's shoulder, tattoo of fantastic animal, and a drawing of it made by Siberian scientists

TOMB OF THE DIVER

(Salerno, Italy c. 470 BC)

The Tomb of the Diver in Paestum was found in June 1968 in what used to be known as Magna Graecia, and today is part of the province of Salerno, Italy.

The tomb dates to around 470 BC – the date can be fixed precisely by a Greek vase that was found in the tomb. The tomb is now displayed in the museum at Paestum.

Although a number of other and a number of painted tombs are known from Paestum, they all date to the fourth and third centuries. The tomb of the diver is unique in being dated to the fifth century, the best period of Greek art.

Figure 189: This is the fresco that gave the tomb its name: "a young man diving into the curving waves in the waters."

The Diver's Tomb consists of five limestone slabs, with four sides and a lid, each from a local source. The floor of the tomb was dug into the ground. The limestone slabs are neatly interconnected and form a room about the size of an adult male. All the plates are painted using the 'fresco' technique, but the fresco on the tomb's cover is fascinating.

Tomb of the Diver

This is the fresco that gave the tomb its name: "a young man diving into the curving waves in the waters."

The lateral frescoes surrounding the body depict the symposium scenes of a traditional Ancient Greek banquet: bare-chested young men wearing laurel wreaths lying on sofas, partying, dancing, drinking wine, playing lyre and games, and falling in love.

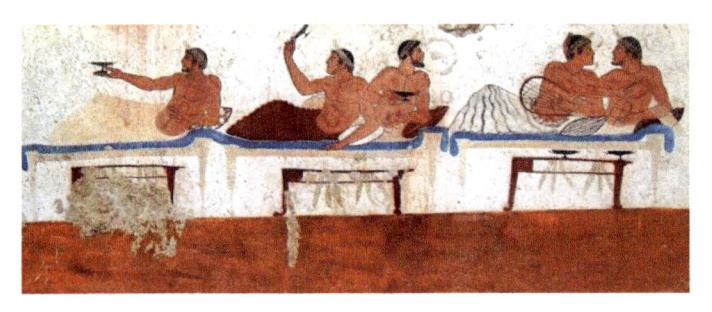

Figure 190: The two long sides of the tomb show scenes from a symposium, a drinking feast. We see homosexual lovers on the right. There are two more men on the sofa in the middle, looking at the couple on the right and the other playing the game called kottabos. To the left, another man is holding a wine glass, possibly preparing to play kottabos.

Figure 191: The scene on this long wall is again from a symposium where homosexuality stands out. The top right is a homosexual couple, the little one (without a beard) playing the flute. The couples in the middle are facing each other. The man on the left is holding a lyre.

Tomb of the Diver

Figure 192: The frescoes below are the small endplates. We see two men watching a woman playing the flute on one plate and a young figure depicted with a large wine bowl on the other.

Figure 193

Tomb of the Diver

The Diver's Tomb is the only surviving example of Greek painting, with figurative scenes from the Orientalizing, Archaic or Classical periods. This is the only tomb decorated with frescoes depicting humans between thousands of Greek tombs (700 - 400 BC) known today.

The diver depicted in this tomb, isolated against the sky, symbolizes the intensity of the moment of death. This man and his leap are the visual metaphor for the transition to eternity from earthly life.

Figure 194: Detail from the diver. The anatomy of the diver is very detailed and fully outlined in black. His genital was very carefully drawn and there is a small growth of hair added to his chin.

Tomb of the Diver

Figure 195: Slabs from The Tomb of the Diver, in their original positions.

Figure 196

147

THE RIACE BRONZES

(Calabria, Italy, c. 450 BC)

The Bronze Statues of Riace, considered among the most significant examples of classical Greek art, are two bronze statues depicting two naked men, originally armed with shield and spear, which became the symbol of the city of Reggio Calabria.

The Bronzes were found in 1972, at the bottom of the Ionian Sea, near the town of Riace Marina, by a passionate diver during a dive about 200 m from the coast and at a depth of 8 m. The divers initially thought they had found the remains of a corpse. Immediately after the discovery, officials were informed, and a police dive team under the supervision of archaeologists lifted the two figures with air balloons. Further exploration of the discovery area in 1972 and 1981 revealed a hull part containing 28 lead rings and two bronze axles, possibly used as part of a ship sail.

Figure 197: Discovery of the Riace Bronzes, 1972. Photographer: unknown.

The Riace Bronzes

Figure 198: The lifting of the Riace warriors from the seabed by Italian police divers on August 16, 1972. It was one of the greatest archaeological moments in the history of underwater archaeology.

Figure 199

Figure 200-201: Diver and Bronzes.

The Riace Bronzes

The Bronzes of Riace are original works of the mid-fifth century BC. The bronzes depict two completely naked men with beards and curly hair, the left arm bent and the right lying along the side. Both wore a helmet, held a spear or sword in their right hand, and held a shield with their left arm, elements that were disassembled at the time of embarkation to allow the statues to be placed on their backs and facilitate transportation.

The two statues are made of bronze, with a very tenuous thickness, except for silver, calcite, and copper details. The statues are commonly referred to as "Statue A" and "Statue B". The 'older' man, known as Riace B, wears a helmet, while the 'younger' Riace A has nothing covering his rippling hair.

The Riace Bronzes are 1.98 (Statue A) and 1.97 (Statue B) meters high and weigh about 160 kg. The bronzes have considerable muscle elasticity being in a position defined as "chiasmus". Bronze A (the young man) appears more nervous and vital, while bronze B (the older man) seems more relaxed. The statues convey a remarkable sense of power, mainly due to the arms being strongly distanced from the body. Bronze B's head is oddly shaped and appears small because it wears a Corinthian helmet. The right arm and the left arm of the B underwent second welding, probably for restoration in antiquity.

Figure 202: Details from Statue A.

The Riace Bronzes

Figure 203: Statue A.

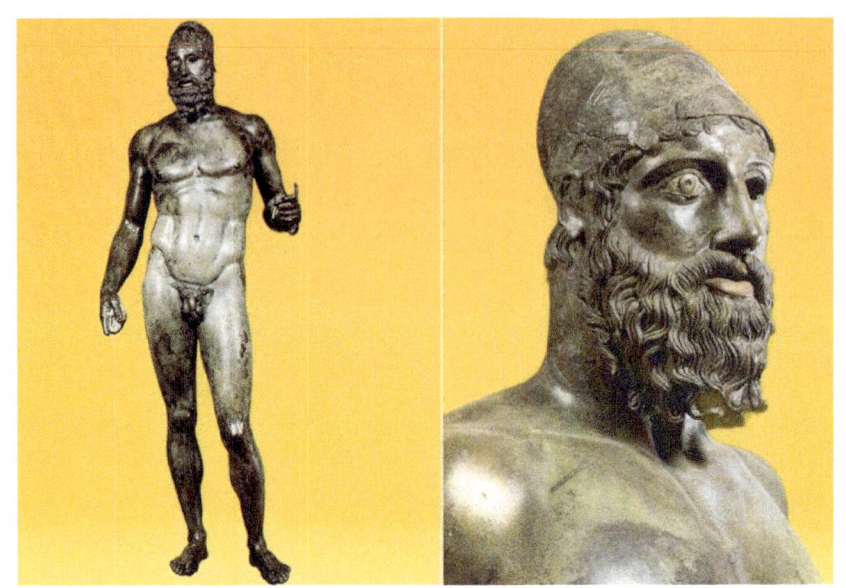

Figure 204: Statue B.

The Riace Bronzes

Figure 205: Reconstruction of Riace Bronzes. "Gods in Color - Golden Edition", The Frankfurt Exhibit, 2020.

The hypotheses on the origin, dating and the authors of the statues are different. It is generally thought that two separate Greek artists created them 30 years apart around the 5th century BC. Dating back probably to the mid-fifth century BC, it is assumed that the Bronze Statues were thrown into the sea during a storm to lighten the ship that carried them or that the boat itself had sunk with the statues. The first restoration was carried out in 1975-80 in Florence. In addition to the total cleaning of the surfaces performed with specially designed instruments, in Florence, the statues were subjected to radiographic analysis, necessary to know the internal structure, the state of preservation, and the metal's thickness.

During the meticulous cleaning, it was discovered some details for which it had been used different material from bronze. The two statues are made of bronze, of very slight thickness, except for some silver, calcite, and copper details. The teeth of Statue A are in silver. In copper are the nipples, lips, and eyelashes of both statues, as well as the traces of a cap on the head of Bronze B. In white calcite is the sclera of the eyes, whose irises were made of glass paste, while the lacrimal caruncle is made of a pink stone.

When the Riace Bronzes first went on display in 1981, a million people came to see them. The statues are now on display at the Archaeological Museum of Reggio Calabria.

TOLLUND MAN

(Tollund Fen, Denmark, c. 405 BC - 380 BC)

On May 6, 1950, the brothers Viggo and Emil, who lived in the small village of Tollund on the Danish Jutland peninsula, were cutting peat in the peat bog. While working, the wife of one of the workers, who helped load the peat into a vehicle, noticed a corpse in the peat layer. He looked so new that those who saw him believed they had recently discovered a murder victim. The acid perfectly preserved his face in the bog, and he looked as though he was sleeping peacefully. The body was reported to the police.

Figure 206: Tollund Man.

The police were stunned by the body's condition and brought in archaeology professor Peter Glob to determine the time of death. In the first examination, Professor Peter Glob suggested that the body was over 2.000 years old and most likely the victim of a sacrifice ceremony.

The Tollund Man was buried about 2 meters under the peat, and his body was in a fetal position. His eyes and mouth were closed. A pointed hat made of leather and wool was held tightly under his chin with a leather thong. He had a leather belt around his waist. In addition, the body had a noose made of animal skin that was pulled tightly around its neck and dragged down its back.

Tollund Man

Apart from these, his body was completely naked. His hair was pretty short. He had a very short beard (1mm length) on his chin and upper lip, suggesting he had not shaved the day he died.

Archaeologists believe that the Tollund Man was a human victim rather than an executed criminal due to the arranged position of his body, no traces of rope on his hands, and his eyes and mouth closed.

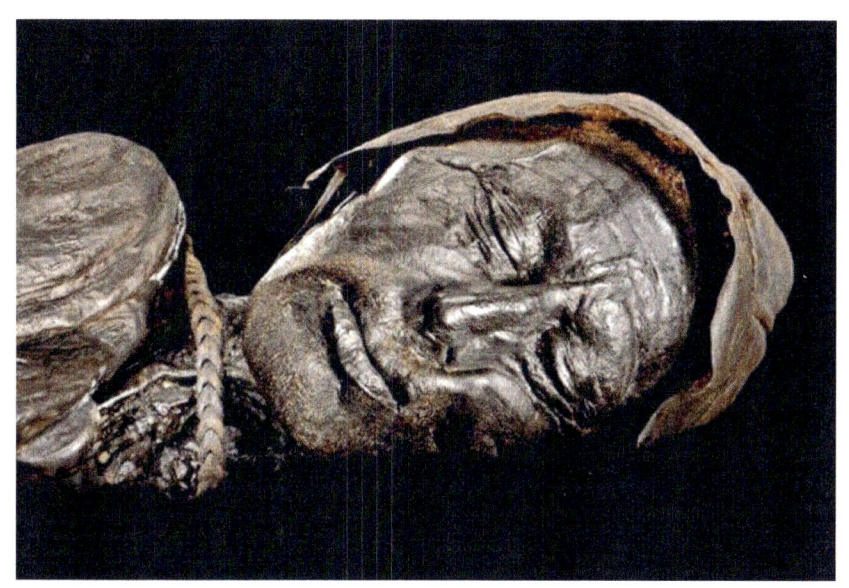

Figure 207

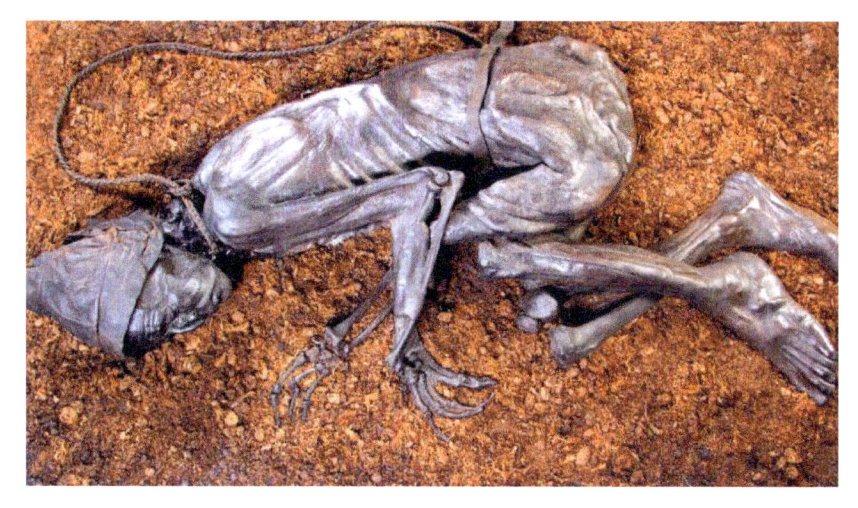

Figure 208

PANAGYURISHTE TREASURE

(Panagyurishte, Bulgaria, c. 4th century BC)

The Thracian treasure of Panagyurishte is one of the most remarkable artifacts of the ancient Thracian civilization. The treasure is composed of 9 objects: a phiale, an amphora, and rithones.

They are all decorated in relief with scenes from the Thracian-Hellenistic pantheon. Its total weight is 6kg and 164gr. The objects are made of gold of the highest quality, without additions. The treasure is dated between the end of the IV century and the beginning of the III century BC.

Figure 209: The Thracian treasure of Panagyurishte.

Working together in the Merul tile factory area near the town of Panagyurishte, brothers Pavel, Petko, and Mihail Deïkovi discovered the nine-piece treasure on December 8, 1949 accidentally. Other workers were also present on-site at the time of the discovery. The three brothers took the treasure, cleaned it, and handed it over to the public authorities, represented for the occasion by the regional governor Stefan Kalpakov.

Panagyurishte Treasure

Figure 210: Deikov Brothers holding the treasure, 1949.

The treasure was exhibited in the bathrobe and towel factory showcase, which was then located on the main street of Panagyurishte. He stayed there for a few days so that all the inhabitants of the town could see it. By chance, a famous archaeologist was working in Panagyurishte at that time - Petar Goranov, who studied in Vienna. He informed the Archaeological Institute and the Museum of History of Plovdiv about the importance of the discovery.

The treasure was then transported to the museum of Plovdiv and exhibited there for a few months. Despite the great displeasure of the Museum of History of Panagyurishte, the museum of Plovdiv registered the treasure in its inventory. Later, on the government's decision, the treasure was moved to the Institute of Archaeology and then to the National Museum of History in Sofia, where it remains until today.

The use of these beautiful gold vessels, richly ornamented, is not clearly established to date. Was it used during festivities or consecration rituals and religious services? It is also possible that such treasures were buried as an offering to the Mother Goddess.

Panagyurishte Treasure

Figure 211: The body of the amphora is decorated with seven figures, five of which are warriors, represented naked and barefoot.

There are diverse interpretations of its meaning. Some scholars assimilate them to the seven kings of the Theban cycle. Others believe it reflects the conquest of the Gate of Persia by Alexander the Great. Others believe that it represents an episode of the Trojan War. A recent interpretation points out that the figures would correspond to Thracian warriors in a ritual dance. The construction that appears on the scene would be the hero (the access to the afterlife). Behind its doors would be the Thracian king walking through the underworld.

Figure 212: Phiale decorated with faces of Ethiopian features. (Plovdiv Museum, 844.7 g, 25 cm diameter)

Panagyurishte Treasure

According to the Greeks, the term Ethiopian indicated the inhabitants of the southernmost part of the known world (oikoumene), identifiable as North Africa. A fragment of a black- figure vase representing the head of an Ethiopian was found near Nesebar.

The presence of Ethiopians in Thrace should not come as a surprise. In the epic poem Ethiopides, which recounts the events of the Trojan War between the death of Hector and the dispute over the arms of Achilles between Ajax Telamonius and Odysseus, there is a story of a contingent of Ethiopian warriors led by Memnon, who came to the aid of the Trojans. The poem (lost and known only by later summaries) is estimated to have been composed in the seventh century BC.

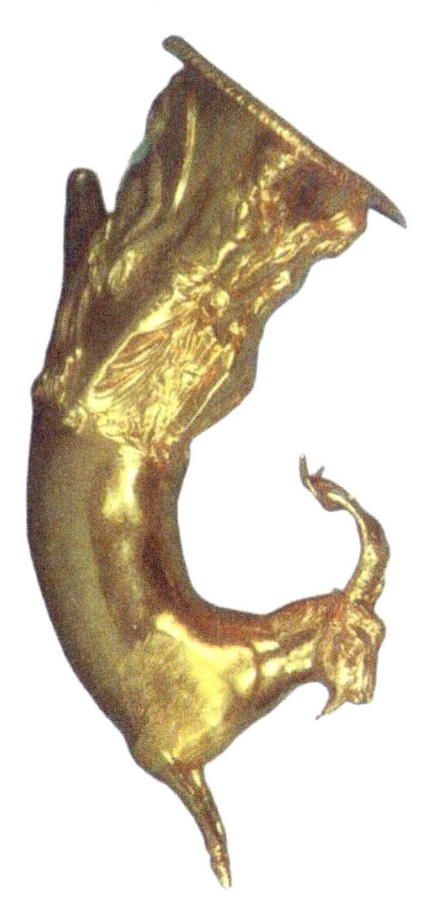

Figure 213: Rhyton with goat protome (Plovdiv Museum, 439.05 g, 14 cm high) This rhyton differs from those in the collection. It has no handle and over half of the animal's body is smooth and undecorated.

LYCURGUS CUP

(Rome or Alexandria c. 4th century AD.)

A precious Roman stained-glass bowl, made roughly 1.600 years ago by an unknown artist, reveals a startling fact: Roman artisans pioneered what we now call nanotechnology.

The ancient goblet, called the Lycurgus Cup, was acquired by the British Museum in the 1950s. It took scientists about 40 years to solve the mystery hidden in the glass of the artifact, which appears green when illuminated from the front, and red when illuminated from the back.

Figure 214: Outer surfaces of Lycurgus Cup.

Lycurgus Cup

The Lycurgus cup in the British Museum is a beautiful 4th-century cup that is thought to have been produced in Alexandria or Rome, probably involving multiple artisans' workshops.

It is a diatreta cup, that is, consisting of a glass goblet set in an outer frame. We do not know if they were two separate vases then joined hot or a magnificent work of engraving.

The Lycurgus Cup takes its name from the myth that tells: King Lycurgus, who had tried to kill the nymph Ambrosia - a follower of Dionysus, is strangled by the nymph transformed into a vine, while the god and his followers watch the scene.

Figure 215

The glass of the cup takes on different colors depending on whether illuminated frontally or backlit; this feature has long remained unexplained. The scientific explanation discovered in the nineties by examining a fragment of the glass is that the artisans of Roman times impregnated the glass with particles of gold and silver as small as 50 nanometers, about one-thousandth of the diameter of a grain of table salt.

The amount of metal present in the glass is so small that the researchers hypothesized accidental contamination of the glass with gold and silver dust, probably unbeknownst to the glassmakers. These tiny elements are responsible for light scattering, so the phenomenon of color change depends on them.

Lycurgus Cup

The interior of the cup is primarily smooth, but behind the main figures, the glass has been hollowed out well beyond the level of the main exterior surface, so that the thickness of the glass is similar across the surface: this shrewdness allows for uniform color when light passes through the glass. Around the torso of Lycurgus is visible an area of a rather different color from the rest of the glass: this feature could be the result of a production accident, or it could have been a shrewdness on the part of the carver to make "the glow of Lycurgus' anger even stronger".

Figure 216

It is impossible that Roman artisans around 1.650 years ago could control all of these technical processes.

Therefore, the Lycurgus Cup is an exceptional example produced before the modern era. Ian Freestone, one of the experts who studied the cup, thinks that the Roman artisans "were highly skilled, but not in nanotechnology. They didn't know they were working at the nanoscale."

Lycurgus Cup

Figure 217

TOMB OF PHILIP II

(Vergina, Greece, 336 BC)

In 1977, a Greek archaeologist, Professor Manolis Andronikos, unearthed a tomb. This tomb remained unlooted and contained an exceptional amount of grave goods. Inside were many objects scattered around on the floor, including a royal headband, a sword, and a solid gold box with a "Vergina Sun" design on its lid. Professor Andronikos knew that the sunburst was the sign of Macedonia, so the tomb must belong to one of its kings. But which one?

Andronikos narrates: "... *Overcoming the inevitable difficulties caused by the organic materials scattered on the floor, we managed to lift the cover. And then we saw something that was impossible to imagine, because never before had such an ossified vessel been found: an all-gold shrine with an imposing star on its cover. We took it out of the sarcophagus, laid it on the floor and opened it. Everyone's eyes were wide open, and our breath was cut short: the burnt bones were clearly placed, placed in a carefully formed pile, still holding the color from the purple that once enveloped them. And in the corner a heavy gold wreath pressed covered them. We closed the precious shrine, covered it carefully and placed it in the inner corner of the cabin...*"

Figure 218: The Golden Larnax contains the remains from the burial of King Philip of Macedon and the royal golden wreath. The larnax was placed in the marble sarcophagus. It was made of 24-carat gold and weighing 11 kg. Inside the golden larnax were Philip's bones and a golden wreath of 313 oak leaves and 68 acorns, weighing 725 grams.

Tomb of Philip II

Researchers announced in 2014 that they succeeded in identifying the people buried in the ancient grave due to anthropological examinations on 350 bone fragments found in the tomb.

Stating that they found "traces of a healed facial trauma" on the facial bones they found, the researchers noted that this finding fits the historical records of Philip's life. II. Philip was shot in the eye during the siege of Methone in 354 before Christ but managed to recover and remained in power for another 18 years. Furthermore, Among the many treasures was a simple pair of bronze leg guards. One leg guard was shorter than the other, and it was recorded that Philip had been lamed in battle.

It was also discovered in the antechamber of Philip's tomb, another golden larnax with a royal crown in a marble sarcophagus, and a wooden mortuary sofa with decoration similar to Philip's. It is thought to contain the ashes of Meda, one of the wives of the Philip, or the daughter of Cleopatra, or the Scythian king Ateas, whom Philip was defeated.

Figure 219

While visiting the city of Aegae, whose modern name is Vergina, Philip II was killed by his guard for still unknown reasons. After that, his 20-year-old son Alexander took his place and was awarded the title of Alexander the Great as one of the best commanders in history.

BOXER AT REST

(Rome, Italy c. 330 BC)

The "Boxer at Rest" (Terme Boxer or Boxer of the Quirinal) is a Hellenistic Greek bronze sculpture of a sitting nude boxer at rest, still wearing his leather hand-wraps. The statue was excavated in Rome in 1885 on the south slope of the Quirinal Hill near the ancient Baths of Constantine, where it is thought to have been displayed.

Was it made by a Greek sculptor in Rome, or was it brought there by ship as many sculptures were? The answer is unknown. And who is the boxer? Some have identified him as the Boxer of Quirinal, who won at Olympia for the first time in 336 BC. following a grueling career of continuous defeats. Others say he is Polydamas, an athlete of legendary strength born in Tessaglia and then called to the court of Persia by Darius II.

The sculpture was buried intentionally in late antiquity, possibly to preserve it against the barbarian invasions that ravaged Rome in the fifth century AD. The Boxer is one of the finest examples of bronze sculptures to have survived from the ancient world.

The sculpture is soldered together from eight segments, separately cast through the lost-wax process. The joins have been filed and finished to be almost invisible.

Figure 220: Boxer at Rest, c. 330 BC, now on display at the National Roman Museum, Rome, Italy.

Boxer at Rest

The boxer's many head wounds are consistent with ancient boxing techniques, in which the head was the main target. The copper inlays, indicating blood, heighten the effect. The artist probably used different tin levels to depict the discoloration from the swelling of blood inside his cheek.

His right eye is swollen, his nose broken, and his ears are swollen from the severity of the blows inflicted, probably causing hearing loss. His scarred lips are sunken, suggesting he also has missing teeth, and there are drops of blood trickling down his right arm and leg. Along with the finely sculpted details of the boxer's facial wounds, the expression and gaze hint at a deeper trauma beneath his bronze façade. Twisting to the side, his face is a mixture of suffering and confusion.

Figure 221-222

DELOS

(South Aegean, Greece, between 800-88 BC)

Situated in the center of the Aegean Sea, Delos was the most important island of antiquity. It was the legendary birthplace of the god Apollo, and about 800 BC it became his holy sanctuary for Ionian Greeks.

Apollo's sanctuary attracted pilgrims from all over Greece, and Delos became a prosperous trading port. The island bears traces of the succeeding civilizations in the Aegean world, from the third millennium B.C. to the Paleo Christian era. The archaeological site is exceptionally extensive and rich and conveys the image of a great cosmopolitan Mediterranean port. Delos was destroyed by Mithridates VI of Pontus in 88 BC and never fully rebuilt.

Today the Sanctuary of Apollo contains remains of the Temple of the Athenians, a fifth-century BC classical temple, a group of treasuries, and the Portico of Antigonus, a Macedonian king. On a terrace are archaic stone lions, symbolic guardians of the sanctuary. At the summit of Mount Kynthos are the Sanctuaries of Zeus and Athena. On the west slope of the mountain are the ruins of the late Hellenistic residential city, which include a Theater and several residences—the Houses of Dionysus, the Trident, and the Masks—which contain exceptionally fine frescoes. The archaeological excavations, which started in 1872 and are still in progress, have unearthed the Sanctuary and a good part of the Hellenistic town. The findings from the archaeological excavations are housed in the Delos Museum. Since 1990 the whole island of Delos has been designated a World Cultural Property and is protected by UNESCO.

Figure 223: The Terrace of the Lions

Delos

Figure 224: Floor mosaic, Dionysos on panther (leopard), Delos, House of the Masks, c. 120—80 BC. Dionysos was the God of wine, festivals, madness, chaos, drunkenness, and drugs. Dionysos' sacred animals were the panther (leopard), tiger, dolphin, donkeys, bull, and serpent. His sacred plants were the grapevine, prickly ivy, and pine tree. Devotees of the god wore wreaths of ivy and carried pine-cone-tipped staffs.

APHRODISIAS

(Karacasu, Asia Minor, Aydın, Turkey c. 300 BC)

Aphrodisias is located on the east of Geyre (Caria) village in Aydın. Aphrodisias is maybe the oldest and the best preserved ancient Greek city in Turkey. The excavation in the area dates to recent times.

Figure 225: With its magnificent hunting scenes of Eros and Nike depicted on the pediments, the tetrapylon was the monumental east gate of the city. The gate leads to the Temple of Aphrodite. "Tetrapylon" means "four gates". Decorated with acanthus leaves, the Corinthian columns were re-erected during the restorations led by Kenan Erim in the '80s.

The discovery of the area was made by the famous photographer, Ara Güler who just discovered it on a business trip. Then, again with the help of him, the ancient city took the attention of an American magazine. The archaeologist Kenan Erim started the first excavations in the area in the 60s. During the rest of his life, he dedicated himself to Aphrodisias. He is buried near the Tetrapylon today. Works in the excavation area continue with the help of New York University. No matter it is known as Aphrodisias for centuries, the first name of the ancient city was 'Lelegonpolis'. Later, it took the names 'Megapolis' and 'Ninoi' , after Ninos – an Asian emperor who settled there in the 7th c. BC.

Figure 226-227: Details from Aphrodisias.

The origin of Aphrodisias

In Mesopotamia, Inanna (Ishtar in Akkadian) was the goddess of love and fertility. When the Assyrians had to flee from their homeland to Caria, they also brought their cult of goddess. Both Inanna and Aphrodite have lots in common. They are both the goddess of love and identified with planet Venus. Both Inanna and Aphrodisias have a 'dying lover'; Tammuz (July) and Adonis. On the other hand, Inanna is symbolized with sun, stars, moon and accompanied with lions like the cult statue of Aphrodite which is on display in the museum now. The Aphrodite statue in the museum is represented as the Mother Goddess here and has similar symbols of Cybele -the Phrygian goddess of fertility and earth. So, Aphrodite has more different features than her portrayals' in modern eras.

Figure 228: The Stadium of Aphrodisias is possibly the largest and the best preserved one of the ancient times. This 1900-year-old-structure had a capacity of 30.000 people. Originally used for athletic events, the stadium was also a place for competitions, animal shows, and competitions of gladiators who were mostly prisoners and slaves. There were two tunnels on the east and west sides of the stadium with reliefs on the arches depicting Hermes and Hercules. The walls of the stadium contributed to the defense of the city as a fortification

MUSEUM HOTEL

(Hatay, Turkey, c. 300 BC)

The Museum Hotel is home to the world's biggest single-piece mosaic, uncovered in 2010. The mosaic rug extends over 1.050 square meters, and it's the world's largest mosaic piece.

The sheer enormity of the mosaic required a different plan of action. Instead of lifting the mosaic, or part of it, or covering it for its protection and building over it, archaeologists and architects worked together to create a hybrid: a museum hotel. The mosaic recovery project started in July 2010 and the construction of the hotel was completed under the supervision of the Hatay Museum officials. No machine has been used because of the fear that it could damage sensitive artifacts.

Figure 229: Mosaic rug contains work from thirteen different civilizations spanning from the Hellenistic period to the Islamic period.

Museum Hotel

The Museum Hotel pays homage to the amazing mosaics, baths, piazzas discovered during the first drills of the site and draws on the tensioned relationship of Archaeology and Architecture by intertwining the ancient and the modern. A raised glass floor shows off the site's history, while prefabricated hotel rooms provide all the modern luxuries in the floors above.

Archaeologists at the site believe the geometric work once decorated the floor of a public building in the previous city of Antioch, one of the most important cities in the Seleucid Empire.

The stone is distinctive due to its curved, rug-like surface, and the mosaic grew curved because of earthquakes in 526 and 528 AD. Despite the quakes, however, somehow the mosaic never broke and made it to the present day intact and unbroken.

Aside from the sheer size of the piece, one of the most remarkable things about the Antakya mosaic is how long it was in progress. Archaeologists and architects who worked hard to restore this priceless mosaic say 13 different ancient civilizations created it. The decorative motifs are from the Hellenistic period until the Islamic period.

Contributions to this mosaic came from cultures as diverse as the Greeks, the Romans, the Byzantines, the Arabs, the Crusaders. The piece was in progress for more than fifteen centuries, from around 300 B.C until the 1200s A.D.

Figure 230: Details from Museum Hotel, Hatay. - themuseumhotelantakya.com

Figure 231-232: Including 35 archaeologists and five restorers, they worked for 18 months to complete the excavation and restoration. The team's work yielded superlative finds, including the world's largest single-piece floor mosaic and the first intact marble statue of the Greek god Eros. All told, the researchers unearthed 35.000 artifacts representing 13 civilizations dating back to the third century

THE LADY OF ELCHE

(Elche, Spain, c. 300 BC)

The Lady of Elche (Dama d'Elx in Valencian, Dama de Elche in Spanish) is a limestone bust of a woman, dated to the 5th or 4th century BC.

The bust was discovered on August 4, 1897, near Elche, Spain, where there is a small mountain that the Arabs called Alcudia (mound), which in ancient times was almost entirely surrounded by a river. It is known that it was an Iberian colony called Helike (Greek) and that the Romans called Illici Augusta Colonia Julia. When the Arabs and the Berbers came in their turn, they established the city lower down on the flat part, keeping however the Roman place name of Illici, which was Arabized in Elche.

The finder was 14-year-old laborer Manuel Campello Esclápez. After only a few weeks, Pierre Paris, a French archaeologist, bought the bust and it was displayed in the Louvre Museum.

Figure 233: The Lady of Elche.

The Lady of Elche

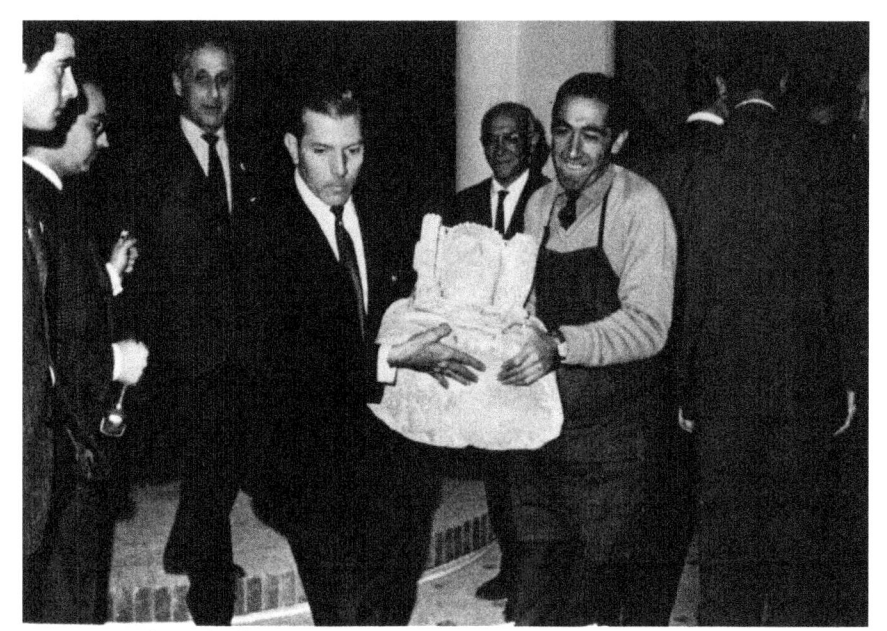

Figure 234: The Lady of Elche in 1941.

Figure 235: The Lady of Elche in 1944.

In 1941, the lady returned to Spain and was exhibited at the Museo del Prado in Madrid. From there, she moved to the city's Museo Arqueológico Nacional, where she remains to this day.

The Lady of Elche

The bust is 56 cm high and has an almost spherical cavity in its back, 18 cm in diameter and 16 cm deep, which may have been used to insert relics, sacred objects, or ashes as offerings to the deceased. Many other Iberian figures of a religious character, located in different places, also have a hollow in their backs, and, like the Lady of Elche, their shoulders are slightly bent forward.

The Lady of Elche represents a richly decorated bust of a woman. Her costume is Iberian. She wears a blue tunic of fine linen, a mantilla supported by a comb (which may be a tiara), which falls across her chest. This mantilla was reddish and even contained remnants of worn paint. A large cloak (mantle) of thick, heavy canvas covered it. It was brown with a red border. The lips also had remnants of red color. The sculpture is made of fine orange limestone, and the face has the natural color of this stone, probably the natural color of her complexion.

The Lady wears jewels characteristic of the Iberians: circles covering her ears where small chains hang from a leather strap that encircles her forehead. Necklaces and crowns with small spheres and filigrees. These are reproductions of jewels that originated in Ionia in the 7th century BC and later arrived in Etruria (Italy). At the last analysis, a small fragment of gold leaf was discovered in one of the back folds. This leads to the assumption that the jewelry of the sculpture was covered with gold leaf.

Figure 236: Reconstruction of the Lady of Elche in original colors.

The Lady of Elche

Artemidorus of Ephesus, a statesman who traveled the coasts of Iberia around the year 100 BC, describes the Iberian woman in a text that has survived and in which the description of the Lady of Elche is clearly recognizable:

"Some Iberian women wore iron necklaces and large armatures on their heads, on which they placed the veil-like an umbrella, which covered their faces. But other women hung a small dulcimer around their necks, which they tightened tightly at the nape of the neck and from the head to the ears, and which they bent upwards at the sides and behind."

The Lady of Elche is exhibited today in the National Archaeological Museum of Madrid. It is the most known and one of the important archaeological remains of the Iberian culture.

Figure 237: The Lady of Elche - side and back views.

BAGHDAT BATTERY

(Khujut Rabu, Baghdat, Iraq, c. 250 BC - 250 AD.)

The group of artifacts known as the 'Baghdad Battery' consisted of a terracotta vessel about 14 cm long, containing a cylinder made of rolled copper plate that fits a single iron rod. During archaeological excavations in the village of "Khujut Rabu", a 2000- year-old settlement near Baghdad in 1936, workers found a strange jar made of yellow clay among the ruins of the ancient city.

The Baghdad Battery caught the attention of archaeologist Wilhelm Koenig, the German curator of the Baghdad Museum, among other works in the National Museum of Iraq in 1938. After careful examination, he suggested that the jar could be a cell used to generate electricity, and that it was produced for the purpose of electroplating precious objects. However, Koenig's discovery and the studies he published were forgotten due to the second world war.

Figure 238

The jars dated to the Parthian period (roughly 250 BC to 250 AD) contained a vertical iron rod surrounded by a copper cylinder. This iron rod was fixed to the asphalt lid at the top of the jar. The rod dropped into the tube and was not in contact with any point. There were also traces of corrosion evidence on the stick, possibly caused by the use of an acidic liquid such as vinegar or wine.

Baghdat Battery

This ancient mechanism began to attract the attention of many researchers in the years that followed the Second World War. Analyzes showed that acidic liquids such as vinegar or wine were placed in the jars, and there were some signs of wear.

After the war, Willard Gray, an American working at the General Electric High Voltage Laboratory in Pittsfield, made replicas and filled them with an electrolyte, proving that the devices could generate 2 volts of electricity. In the '70s, a group of German researchers tested Koenig's claims by making a replica of the setup and succeeded in electroplating a thin layer of silver.

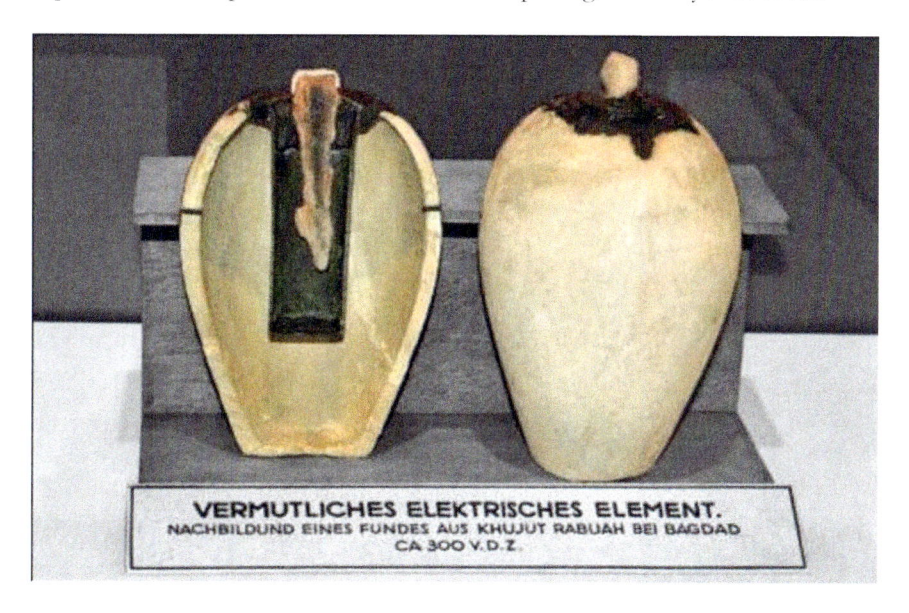

Figure 239

Numerous experiments have been carried out on different replicas of the mechanism, and it is considered a battery because it has been scientifically proven. So how did an ancient culture know about the existence of electricity, and for what reason did it use this battery?

There is more than one theory regarding the usage purpose of the Baghdad battery.

One of the theories says that the Baghdad battery may have been used as a therapeutic method. Because in ancient Greek civilization, it is known that applying electricity relieves pain, for this, electric eels were given to the soles of the patient's feet. This could explain the presence of needle-like objects found in some batteries. However, many researchers have stated that this low-voltage battery cannot produce enough electricity to relieve pain.

Baghdat Battery

Another theory regarding Baghdad batteries is that the batteries are used for religious purposes by hiding them in a statue or idol. People touching religious statues or idols are likely to receive noticeable electric shocks.

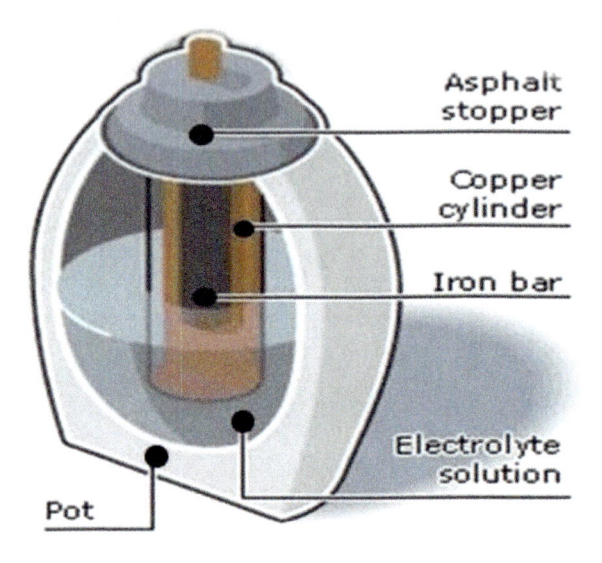

Figure 240

In this view, a parallel-connected battery stack may be hidden inside a metal sculpture or idol.

According to Dr. Paul T Craddock, metallurgical history expert at the British Museum, "A god statue can be tied up and then the priest can ask you questions. If you answer incorrectly, you will touch the statue, and perhaps you will experience a little shock with a small, mysterious flash of blue light. If you get the answer right, the trickster or priest can disconnect the batteries, and no shock comes - he then becomes convinced of the power of the statue, the priest, and religion. "

While there is no theory that archaeologists agree on, the only widely accepted explanation is that it was used for electrolysis coating. You can make you believe copper is gold. For example, if you are producing jewelry, it means that the material in your hand will instantly become valuable.

Baghdad batteries, the exact number of which is unknown, were stolen from the Baghdad Archaeological Museum during the 2003 US invasion of Iraq along with many other important artifacts and are still missing.

DEAD SEA SCROLLS

(Qumran, Judaean Desert, 250 BC - 68 AD)

Seventy-three years ago, in the spring of 1947 when the Judaean desert was still under British mandate, a young Taamire goatherd called Mohammad ed-Dhib set out apparently to look for a lost animal and stumbled on a treasure infinitely more valuable to the world at large - a cave containing jars, broken and others intact, filled with ancient manuscripts. Both original writings and copies of biblical books have been found, some in pottery jars, and they've been dated from between 250 BC to 68 AD.

Between 1947 and 1956, more scrolls were found in 10 caves (4 by Beduin; 6 by archaeologists) on the northwest coast of the Dead Sea. Altogether there were about 900 documents that seem to have formed the library of a Jewish community, called the Essene, who lived in the area over 2.000 years ago.

Figure 241: Two Dead Sea Scrolls Jars at the Jordan Museum, Amman. The Dead Sea Scrolls were stored in jars like this which helped them to survive for over 2.000 years.

The scrolls contain copies of all the Old Testament books of the Bible except Esther. There are also commentaries, psalms, and information about the community they belonged to.

The scrolls are 1.000 years older than any copies of the Old Testament found, and they are valuable examples of the ancient Hebrew and Aramaic scripts. The Essene may have hidden the scrolls away for safekeeping. Their settlement was destroyed by the Romans in AD 66-70.

THE TERRACOTTA ARMY

(Mount Li, China, 210 BC)

In March of 1974, located 1.5 km to the east of Qin Shi Huang Mausoleum mound, the Terracotta Army was discovered in wasteland near Xiyang Village by some local farmers while digging a well.

Shi Huang was a member of the powerful Qin dynasty from western China. A ruthless man, he conquered all the Chinese states and became the first emperor of China. But though the separate states became united under his leadership, barbarian invaders from the north threatened the empire. So Shi Huang built the Great Wall of China. When Shi Huang built the Great Wall of China to keep out his enemies, many workers died in the harsh conditions of mountainous northern China. But they succeeded in building the longest structure on earth and in keeping out the enemies. But, for all his might, the emperor had one great fear- death. According to the writings of court historian Siam Qian, Qin ordered his mausoleum's construction shortly after taking the throne. More than 700.000 laborers worked on the project.

Figure 242: The Terracotta Army.

In 210 BC, the First Emperor of China, Qin Shi Huangdi, was buried in a vast burial mound close to Mount Li. Not far away, hidden underground, were more than 7.500 life-size terracotta soldiers, together with horses and chariots, to guard him after death. They had been sleeping undisturbed for almost 2.200 years.

The Terracotta Army

Archaeologists have found not one but thousands of clay soldiers, each with unique facial expressions and positioned according to rank, in 40 years of excavation.

Since most of the terracotta warriors are look white grey today, it's hard to imagine that they were painted with different colors in the past. In fact, they were originally painted with black hair, beard, and eyebrows like real persons. Their uniforms were also painted in bright colors, including scarlet, green, black, and purple. The moist environment underground was suited to the preservation of the paint. However, when they were unearthed, the terracotta warriors were oxidized, and all colors just turned into white grey in few minutes.

Further excavations have revealed swords, arrow tips, and other weapons, many in pristine condition. Four pits have been partially excavated so far. Three of them are filled with terracotta soldiers, horse carriages and weapons. The fourth pit was found empty, a testament to the original unfinished construction.

Figure 243

VICTORY OF SAMOTHRACE

(Samothrace, Greece, c. 200 BC)

The Winged Victory of Samothrace is among the greatest Hellenistic sculptures in the world. Without a doubt, it is one of the most celebrated works of antiquity.

The statue was excavated in 1863 on Samothrace Island by Charles Champoiseau (head of the French Consulate in Andrinople, now Edirne in Turkey). Having left Samothrace at the beginning of May 1863, the statue arrived in Toulon at the end of August and in Paris on May 11, 1864. Where the statue was discovered were fifteen other large blocks of gray marble, the form, and function of which Charles Champoiseau could not understand. In fact, these gray blocks formed the prow of a ship. He decided to send the statue and the fragments to the Louvre Museum and leave the large grey marble blocks in place. In 1875, the architect of the Austrian archaeological mission working on the Samothrace sanctuary examined the blocks, producing drawings of them. He concluded that they formed the prow of a ship, which formed the basis of the statue. In 1879, they were assembled, together with the statue, at the Louvre Museum.

Figure 244: The Winged Victory of Samothrace.

Victory of Samothrace

The museum also added a plaster wing to the sculpture—an addition that remains today—but did not opt to recreate the head or arms. Later, during the excavation from 1950, Karl Lehman and his team of archaeologists found in the area where the initial discovery had been made the right palm of the statue. These parts were also sent to Louvre Museum. The arms and head of this statue have never been found. It has been speculated she could have held a trumpet or a wreath to commemorate the victory.

The Winged Victory sculpture probably celebrates the victory of a naval battle in the 2nd century BC. The Greeks represented concepts such as Peace, Fortune, Vengeance, and Justice as goddesses at a very early date. The victory was one of the earliest of these incarnations. The statue exemplifies the movement, gesture, and rich texturing of the finest Hellenistic sculpture.

In Greek mythology, the goddess of victory was shown as being a winged figure who would fly down from Mount Olympus. The main characteristics of the goddess were wings and usually a sense of landing or alighting. Winged Victory is shown in the form of a winged woman standing on the prow of a ship, braced against the strong wind blowing through her garments. As wet and wind-blown drapery clings to her body, the winged figure triumphantly steps toward the front of a ship.

During the Hellenistic period, Alexander the Great's successors were constantly fighting to take control over the Aegean Sea. The base of the statue thus recalls the warships typically used in this era.

Figure 245: Wing and metallic frame, detail from the winged victory of Samothrace. Parian marble, ca. 20 BC. Found in Samothrace in 1863.

Victory of Samothrace

Figure 246: The right wing is a symmetric plaster version of the original left one. The arms and head haven't been found.

Figure 247: Greek coin that date between 301 and 292 BC give an idea as to what the Victory of Samothrace might have looked like and demonstrate why the marble blocks were in fact, an integral part of the statue.

THE ROSETTA STONE

(Rashid, Egypt, 196 BC)

The slab of compact black basalt, called for nearly two centuries the Rosetta Stone, stands in the Egyptian Sculpture Gallery of the British Museum in London. It is named from its find place in the Western Delta, a small village called Rashid, better known to Europeans as Rosetta, which lies a few kilometers from the sea on a branch of the Nile.

Napoleon's army invaded Egypt in 1799 and unearthed a black rock slab with inscriptions in three different languages (Hieroglyph, Demotic, and ancient Greek). The stone was an irregularly shaped slab of a dark stone, 112.3 cm tall, 75.7 wide, 28.4 thick, and weighing around 762 kg. The stone was found broken and incomplete. Many of Egypt's temples were destroyed in the 4th century under Roman emperor Theodosius I, and for years afterward, the ruins served as quarries for the country's occupiers. Before the French recovered it in the late 18th century, the immensely valuable Rosetta Stone was part of a wall inside an Ottoman fortress.

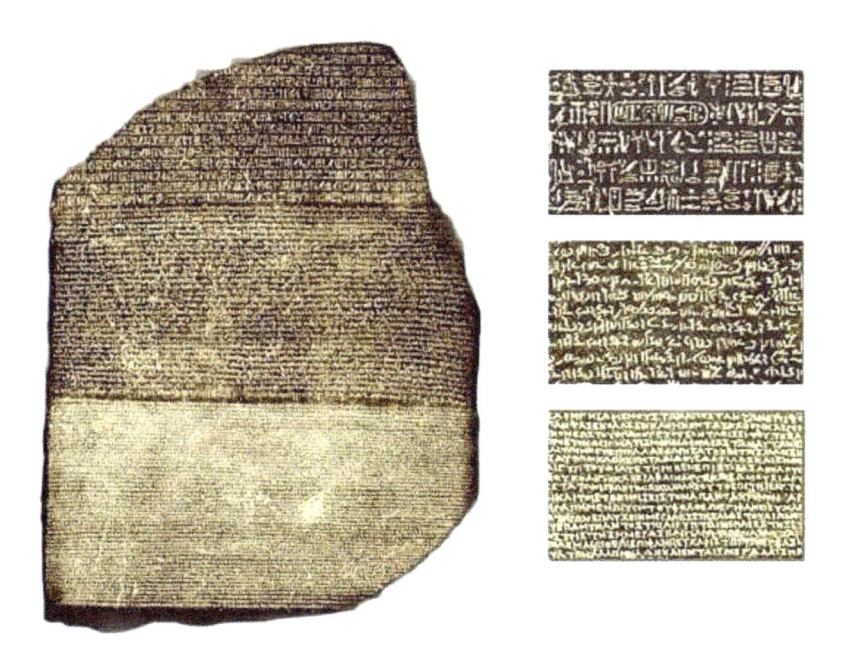

Figure 248: The Rosetta Stone.

The Rosetta Stone

A French scholar of ancient languages, Jean-Paul Champollion, studied the writing and managed to translate the hieroglyphs. After defeating Napoleon's forces at Alexandria in 1801, the British commandeered many of the Egyptian artifacts the French had collected during their occupation, including the Rosetta Stone. So why does Rosetta Stone contain three different languages? In fact, a glance at Egyptian history is sufficient to understand this.

Alexander conquered Egypt in 332 BC. and incorporated it into his empire. After Alexander died in 323 BC., his empire quickly fell apart, and troops commanded by Ptolemy I Soter took control of Egypt. Ptolemaic rulers were actually Greek.

The Rosetta Stone features 14 lines of hieroglyphic, 32 lines in Demotic, and 53 lines of Ancient Greek script. Demotic was an Egyptian script that was more commonly used by the Egyptians by 196 BC., while the Greek language was brought over from Greece by the rulers of the Ptolemaic dynasty and was gradually becoming more widely used in Egypt.

The writing on the Stone is an official message, called a decree, about the king (Ptolemy V, ruled between 204–181 BC). This official message was copied onto large stone slabs called steles that were placed in every temple in ancient Egypt. The Rosetta Stone is one of those replicas, so it's not particularly important on its own. However, the text on the Rosetta Stone states that "the priests of a temple in Memphis (Ancient Egypt) supported the king".

Discovered in 1799, the Rosetta Stone was key to translating hieroglyphs, as it contained the same text in three scripts. The hieroglyphic writing, which has not been used for approximately 1400 years, was deciphered thanks to this stone. The Rosetta Stone is on display at the British Museum today.

MAWANGDUI HAN TOMBS

(Mawangdui, China, c. 186 - 163 BC)

Mawangdui is an archaeological site located in Changsha, Hunan Province. The site consists of two saddle-shaped hills and contains the tombs of three people from the Western Han Dynasty (206 BC - 9 AD). They belonged to the first Marquis of Dai, (Li Cang, Chancellor of Changsha Kingdom), Lady Dai (his wife), and their son.

The archaeological site was excavated for two years, from 1972 to 1974. As a result of archaeological excavations, more than 2,500 artifacts (bamboo objects, lacquerwares, musical instruments, ceramic vessels, wooden figures, silk paintings, garments and manuscripts etc.) were unearthed.

The first Marquis of Dai (Li Cang) died in 186 B.C, and his wife and son both died by 163 B.C. The Li Cang's tomb was not in good condition when it was discovered. But the objects in the son's and wife's tombs were of the great situation and very well preserved.

The most astonishing of all the remains was the corpse of Lady Dai, the wife of the first Marquis of Dai, which was exceptionally well held. She lay at the center of a large wooden chamber covered by a 53-foot mound of earth. She had been dressed in twenty layers of clothing and buried in four coffins, each one smaller than the last.

Hundreds of possessions surrounded her to ensure a happy life in the next world.

Figure 249: Nesting coffins of Lady Dai (Xin Zhui), 2nd century B.C., wood, lacquered exteriors and interiors, 256 x 118 x 114 cm, 230 x 92 x 89 cm and 202 x 69 x 63cm, tomb 1 (Hunan Provincial Museum)

Mawangdui Han Tombs

The Mawangdui tombs provide a striking picture of early Chinese beliefs in the afterlife. The tombs of rulers and nobles give us a picture of how the well-off lived-they believed that they had to take their possessions to the afterlife, so they were buried with everything they might need.

Figure 250: One of world's best-preserved mummy: The Lady of Dai (Hunan Provincial Museum).

Figure 251: Funeral banner of Lady Dai (Xin Zhui), 2nd century B.C., silk, 205 x 92 and 47.7 cm (Hunan Provincial Museum)

Mawangdui Han Tombs

Figure 252: Excavations of Mawangdui Han Tombs.

Figure 253: Excavations of Mawangdui Han Tombs.

VENUS DE MILO

(Melos, Greece, c. 130 BC.)

Venus de Milo was found by a peasant in a field on the Greek island of Milo (or Melos) in 1820. The Marquis de Rivière, then French ambassador to Constantinople (now Istanbul), bought it and offered it to the French king Louis XVIII. The latter gave it to the Louvre Museum in 1821.

The Venus de Milo represents a half-naked female figure. Her bust emerges from the drapery that wraps her hips and legs. A headband holds her hair in a bun. The lack of arms makes her strange and dreamlike. It also fueled endless speculations on what her arms might have originally looked like. It is also known from her fixing holes that the goddess was once adorned with jewels. It was originally wrapped in jewelry, including a bracelet, earrings, and a headband. These embellishments have long since disappeared, but the holes for the attachment to the piece remain in the marble and give clues to the missing accessories.

The Venus de Milo is an original sculpture dating to the Hellenistic period. The sculptor Alexandros is believed to have carved this masterpiece in 130 BC.

Figure 254: Venus de Milo.

Venus de Milo

The plinth that could have helped identify the subject of the sculpture has been lost, as have the arms.

Since the statue is of Greek origin, the correct name is clearly "Aphrodite of Milos", although she became known as "Venus of Milo". Some have suggested the sculpture is not Aphrodite/Venus but Amphitrite, the sea-goddess who was particularly adored on Milos. However, the prevailing view today is that the statue depicts Venus.

The lack of arms also made it hard to identify the statue. Many depictions of Greek gods and goddesses contain clues to their identity in the form of 'attributes' (objects or natural elements) held in their hands. She could have held an apple in her missing hand, and that would identify her as the Venus who received the golden apple from Paris. This vital clue was however lost, and it remains a mystery as to who she really was. Venus de Milo is exhibited today in the Louvre Museum.

Figure 255: Details.

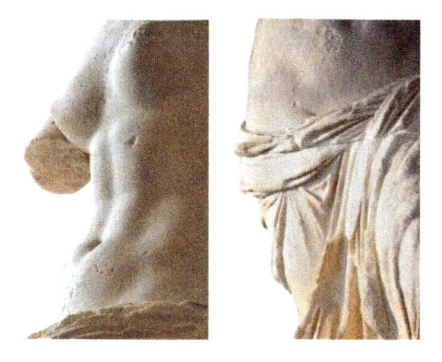

Figure 256: Details.

ANTIKYTHERA MECHANISM

(Cape Artemesion, Greece, c. 100-150 BC)

In April 1900, a group of Greek sponge-divers dived in the Aegean Sea near the island of Antikythera, near Crete. One of the members of this divers-group, Elias Stadiatos, discovered an ancient shipwreck near a small island called Antikythera in Greece. The wreck was 25 meters from the coast, at a depth of about 50 meters. This was a cargo ship that sank in about 87 BC.

The finds included bronze and marble sculptures, as well as clay vases and fragments of furniture. The first object retrieved from the bottom of the sea was the right arm of a bronze statue of the 3rd c. BC depicting a philosopher. The most valuable find among those excavated from the wreck was a wooden box with impellers that had been crushed and intertwined with the effect of saltwater. Inside this box, about the size of a shoebox, there was some mechanical mechanism. In the years of the shipwreck, the box deteriorated and disappeared shortly after it was removed, as there were no methods of preserving the wooden finds.

The Antikythera mechanism was disassembled when it was found. At first glance, the mechanism, which looks like a piece thrown into the corner in any junkyard today, basically consisted of gears made of rusted brass in a wooden box. Some parts were missing, and the existing ones were rusted and covered with sediment. Since then, researchers have been trying to unravel the function of this extraordinary machine and rebuild it.

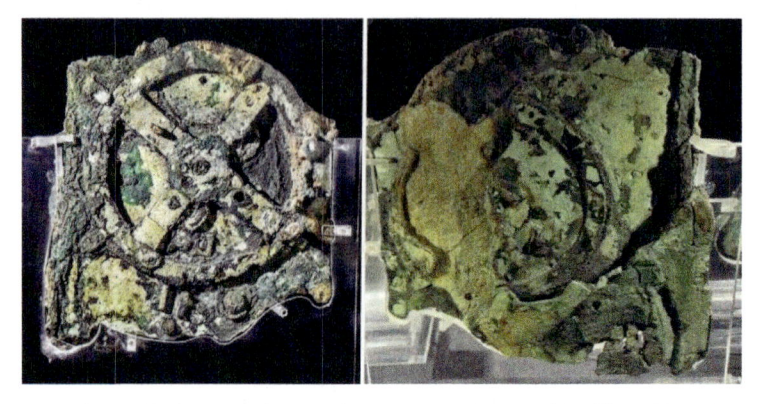

Figure 257: The Antikythera mechanism (Fragment A - front and back); visible is the largest gear in the mechanism, approximately 14 centimeters in diameter. Now on display at the National Archaeological Museum in Athens, Greece.

Antikythera Mechanism

Figure 258: Seven large fragments (A-G) and 75 minor pieces, made of bronze, have survived. It is not certain that the 75 small fragments belong to the mechanism. It contained at least 30 gears, dials, axles, scales, and pointers. The Greek inscriptions on the surface of many fragments refer to astronomical and calendar calculations as well as to instructions for its use. It was contained in a wooden-framed case, probably with a bronze plaque on its front and back.

The Antikythera mechanism indeed has an extremely complex structure. Due to its astrolabe-like appearance, it was thought to be a tool used for navigation in ships, but later it turned out to be a much more complex machine. In fact, after a while it started to be seen as the oldest analog computer. Although the exact date of manufacture of the mechanism is unknown, it is thought to have been produced between 150-100 BC. There are theses that it was produced in Rhodes or Asia Minor as a place of production, but this could not be proven. Many researchers attribute the device to Hipparchus, one of the first thinkers to think that the Earth revolves around the Sun, who died in Rhodes. The reason for this is that Cicero mentions a planetary device made by Posidonius, who took over Hipparchus' school in Rhodes after his death. Cicero Tusculan used the following statements in the 25th chapter of the first book of the Disputations series:

Antikythera Mechanism

"For when Archimedes fastened on a globe the movements of moon, sun and five wandering stars, he, just like Plato's God who built the world in the" Timaeus ", made one revolution of the sphere control several movements utterly unlike in slowness and speed. Now if in this world of our phenomena cannot take place without the act of God, neither could Archimedes have reproduced the same movements upon a globe without divine genius "

Recent research on the mechanism has shown two different people's handwriting in the writings discovered on the mechanism. For this reason, the mechanism is considered to be a "workshop" job.

The mechanism was first interpreted as an astronomical clock in 1902 by archaeologist Valerios Stais, who studied the gear mechanism inside. In 1959, almost half a century after Valerios Stais, Derek J. De Solla Price, a science historian from Yale University, wrote a comprehensive scientific article describing this mechanism. In this article, he also included illustrations of the mechanism.

Examining the gears closely, Price found that the mechanism was useful for predicting the positions of the planets and stars in the sky according to the calendar used at the time.

This is because the main gear was advancing the year, turning the other smaller gears representing the motions of the planets, the sun, and the moon. In other words, you could find out what the position of the planets, the sun, and the moon would be when you set the main gear to that date.

According to Price, this was a computer in its simplest form. An amazing astronomical clock. Or one of today's analog computers that can perform complex calculations. You could see the 12 symbols of the zodiac on the mechanism and make astronomical calculations. Also, the mechanism could show 365 days. It had a structure with a lunar calendar. The reason why Price calls this mechanism a computer is that it presents complex mathematical calculations because of the users of the mechanism inputting some variables.

Today, in modern computers, these inputs are made digitally using the numbers 0 and 1. This mechanism uses the mathematical ratios of its gears. The only thing that uses the Antikythera mechanism is to enter the date with the main gear. In this way, the mechanism rotates the relevant gears; for example, the angle drawn by the sun in the sky can be seen.

Antikythera Mechanism

Figure 259

Price's analysis was, of course, an analysis without today's technologies. However, thanks to new X-ray and 3D modeling technologies, many details about this mechanism would emerge in the 2000s.

In the 90s, Australian computer scientist Allan George Bromley worked with a watchmaker in Sydney to replica the Antikythera assembly. However, it was not fully successful. Because they could not find what some parts of the assembly were for. Later, a British astronomer named John Gleave reconstructed the device parts and assembled them into a working mechanism. On the face of the resulting device, the changing positions of the Sun and Moon in the sky throughout the year were shown. On the back surface, years and months were shown according to the Ancient Greeks' concepts of year and month.

Working with the curator of the Science Museum in London, Michael Wright started working on Antikythera with the help of Allan G. Bromley. The two experts re-examined the setup using a special and sophisticated imaging method called "linear tomography." They obtained very detailed images of the wheels that made up the assembly. Based on this information, Wright made a working replica of the assembly, consisting of 72 parts. This new setup showed the movements of the Moon and the Sun and the movements of Mercury, Venus, Mars, Jupiter, and Saturn. These were all celestial bodies known to the ancient Greeks.

According to Michael Wright: "The Antikythera mechanism could have been an astronomical clock. At that time, measurements had to be made to know the time of agricultural work and religious holidays."

Wright also suggested that distant planets such as Mars, Jupiter, and Saturn could be determined with the Antikythera mechanism.

Antikythera Mechanism

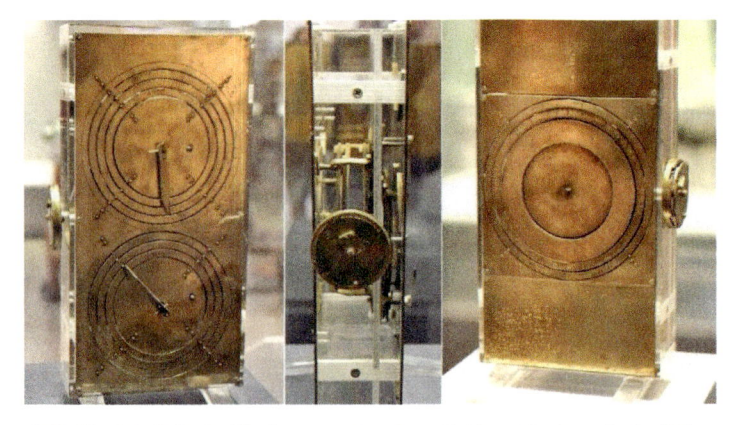

Figure 260: Model of the Antikythera mechanism. National Archaeological Museum in Athens, Greece.

By the 2000s, modern X-ray and 3D mapping technology confirmed Wright's work, and even more. The researchers unearthed the ancient Greek text, a kind of manual written in never-before-seen parts of the mechanism. This text, which can be read about 3.500 characters, contained an inventory of what all the dials on the device mean (estimated to be 20,000 characters in total). Researchers previously suggested that there is a moving image of planets in a zodiac in front of the mechanism, but this was not proven. This thesis has been verified by the help of Greek letters, some of which are less than 1mm, written in the spaces around the dials on the device.

Figure 261: Greek letters on the mechanism.

The mechanism had several dials and clock dials, each with a different function for measuring the movements of the sun, moon, stars, and planets, but were all operated by a single main crank. Small stone or glass spheres were moving on the front of the machine to show the motion of Mercury, Venus, Mars, Saturn, and Jupiter in the sky.

Antikythera Mechanism

The mechanism was able to predict the positions of the sun and moon against the zodiac and had a system that rotated a black-and-white pearl-sized stone that showed the phase of the moon on a given date.

When past or future dates were entered with a crank, the mechanism could calculate other astronomical information such as the position of the Sun, the Moon, or the position of other planets.

SOLAR POINTER

LUNAR POINTER

ZODIAC DIAL: Showed the 12 constellations along the ecliptic, the sun's path in the sky.

EGYPTIAN CALENDAR DIAL: Displayed 365 days of a year.

PLANETERY POINTERS (Mercury, Venus, Mars, Saturn, and Jupiter): May have shown the positions of the planets on the zodiac dial.

FRONT PLATE INSCRIPTIONS

METONIC CALENDAR DIAL: Displayed the month on a 235-lunar-month cycle on a spiral

OLYMPIAD DIAL: Indicated the years of the ancient olympics and other games.

SAROS LUNAR ECLIPSE DIAL: Inscriptions on this spiral indicated the months in which lunar and solar eclipses can occur.

Figure 262-263: Model of the Antikythera mechanism.

Antikythera Mechanism

The mechanism also had dials that count the days according to different calendars. For example, a solar calendar shows 365 days of the year and a lunar calendar that counts a 19-year lunar cycle.

The mechanism's calendar dial could turn the scale back every four years to compensate for the extra quarter of the astronomical year. It's really incredible.

The Antikythera mechanism was not just a scientific tool - it also had social purposes. For example, the ancient Greeks held large athletic competitions (such as the Olympics) in certain periods. A small dial within the Metonic dial showed the dates of these important events. For example, a mark was discovered on the dial giving dates of various athletic events, including an athletic competition held in Rhodes.

The Antikythera Mechanism shows that the Ancient Greeks had the technology to make complex mechanical assemblies. According to some experts, this technology later passed to the Arab world and then moved to Europe. The truth is that something like this would not reappear until the 14th century when the oldest gear clocks began to be built in Europe.

Today, the original Antikythera Mechanism is exhibited in the National Archaeological Museum in Athens, Greece. Next to it is a copy of the works made by experts. Another copy of the mechanism is on display at the American Computer Museum in Montana, USA. Unfortunately, another example of this mechanism has not been found to date.

We do not know how the Greeks developed the technology needed to create such a delicate, perfect mechanism. Still, the truth is that the ancient Greeks came very close to our age in their thinking and their scientific technology.

LION OF KNIDOS

(Knidos, Turkey, c. 2nd century BC)

The Lion of Knidos was found by the British archaeologist Charles Thomas Newton at a tomb within the ancient cemetery of Knidos, near modern Datça, a coastal city in southwest Turkey.

In the 1850s, British researcher Charles Newton actually had no intention of researching Knidos for the first time. His main purpose is to excavate Mausoleum in Halicarnassus, one of the world's seven wonders, and bring the artworks he found here to his country.

On July 2, 1858, he met a Greek named Nicholas Galloni. Galloni mentioned that after looking at the lions found during excavations in Bodrum, he saw a much larger lion statue on a cape in the south of Knidos. As soon as Charles Newton arrived in Knidos, he asked locals questions about the lion, but he could not get any information and find the lion the Greek man was talking about.

However, Charles Newton continued to search for the lion statue. Finally, on a May morning in 1859, a tomb with a lion statue was found on it.

Figure 264: Lion of Knidos and Charles Newton, 1858.

The weight of the lion was about 6 tons. After the scissors and pulleys were carefully adjusted on the lion, the statue was placed on the sleighs, and the sleighs were pulled by 100 Turk villagers in about three days. After the lion was lowered to the edge of the cliff where it was found, it was loaded onto the ship and taken to England. Along with the Lion of Knidos, most of the valuable works which were found during these excavations were taken to the British Museum in London.

Lion of Knidos

"We had never seen his face while he was lying on the ground, so when we sat the lion on his pedestal, our eyes met his calm and majestic gaze for the first time," says Charles Newton in his diaries.

The ancient tomb where the lion was found was a square structure covered with a Doric peristyle with columns, covered in the form of a pyramid. Most likely the Lion pyramid was on the roof, thought to have fallen down as a result of an earthquake.

Figure 265: Lion of Knidos, British Museum. The weight of the lion is about 6 tons, it is 2.89 meters long and 1.82 meters high.

The marble from which the statue was made was brought from Mount Pentelikon near the city of Athens. Pentelikos marble was a very difficult marble to be processed. This marble was known to turn into a "honey" color when it saw the morning and evening rays, and this was preferred as the color of the lion. The lion's lower jaw and his forepaws are missing. The lion's eyes (now empty) were once probably filled with a precious stone or a glass. It is unknown precisely to which period it dates back, and it's believed that it dates to the second century BC.

Since 2000, the Lion of Knidos has been prominently displayed on a plinth under the roof of the Queen Elizabeth II Great Court in the British Museum.

TREASURES OF BEGRAM

(Begram, Afghanistan, c. 100-230 AD)

Afghanistan has been a center of trade and cultural exchange for millennia. At the center of the Silk Road—the routes for the exchange of goods and ideas across Asia—Afghanistan was the historic crossroads linking China and India with ancient Persia, West Asia, and the West.

The Silk Road spanned over 6.440 km and allowed for exchanging goods, ideas, technology, and religions between ancient East and West. The goods carried by the merchants included papers, spices, iron, silks, and bronze objects, all of which were very valuable. In return, merchants from the west sent bronze, coins, and precious stones to the far east.

The cities along the silk road route became very wealthy by demanding a portion of the goods carried by the merchants. In return, the merchants were allowed to pass. Archaeologists have found many treasures which give us a very clear idea of trading at the time.

T This glass goblet from Begram (from room 10), in eastern Afghanistan, depicts figures harvesting dates. It's from the 1st or 2nd centuries AD.

Figure 266: This glass goblet from Begram (from room 10), in eastern Afghanistan, depicts figures harvesting dates. It's from the 1st or 2nd centuries AD.

Treasures of Begram

One of the most famous finds was at the city of Begram in Afghanistan, which stood at the junction of three main trade routes. The archaeological site of Begram is found at the confluence of Silk Road trade routes and the juncture of two major rivers, only about 64 km. from the modern capital Kabul. In 1938, Delegation Archaeologique Francaise Afghanistan (DAFA) uncovered two storerooms that were filled with what came to be known as the Begram Treasure. There were ivory plaques and statues from India, bronze statues and glassware from Egypt, lacquerware from China and much more. The treasure had lain there, hidden away, for nearly 2,000 years. The most recent datable object was a coin of Vasudeva I (191-230 AD).

Figure 267: View of the Begram site, 1930-40's.

THRONE OF GODS: MOUNT NEMRUT

(Adiyaman, Turkey, 62 BC)

In what is now the Turkish-Syrian border region once lay the empire of Kommagene, which had come into being after the collapse of the Diadochi (The Diadochi were the rival generals, families, and friends of Alexander the Great who fought for control over his empire after his death in 323 BC).

Antiochos I ruled there from 69 to 34 BC. He had chosen a place "in heaven" as his place of worship and burial: the summit plateau of the 2150-meter-high Nemrut Daği. The monumental burial site consisted of an artificially raised, terraced plateau of over 50 m and was framed with statues of the gods.

... "I believed that piety was not only the most secure possession for us humans among all goods but also the sweetest joy. (...) When I decided to lay the foundations of this hierothesion near the heavenly thrones, so that there the outer shell of my body, well preserved until old age, might rest until infinite times, (...) I also resolved to declare this sacred place the throne seat common to all the gods. " .. Thus begins the large inscription on the back of the monumental statues of the gods on the east terrace of the cult sanctuary on Nemrut Daği. At an altitude of 2.150 meters, the massive stone monuments with their broken and weathered sculptures and reliefs bear witness to a great past. Here was the center of the Hellenistic kingdom of Kommagene, in the 2nd century BC a buffer state between Roman rule in the west and the Parthian empire in the east.

Figure 268: Western Terrace at Mount Nemrut and Tumulus.

Throne of Gods: Mount Nemrut

Its most important ruler was Antiochos I, who made himself equal to the gods, had the top of the mountain transformed into a gigantic tomb complex and erected the "thrones of the gods" on two terraces to the east and west. He had the top of the mountain removed, the rock crushed to gravel, and heaped up again to form an artificial cone 50 meters high. Thus, a huge burial mound was created, in the depths of which the still- intact tomb of the deified king rests, unmolested by the grave robbers of earlier times and still inaccessible to the archaeologists of our time.

For many centuries the stone witnesses remained hidden from the world. It was only at the end of the 19th century that the sanctuary was rediscovered, and since then, it has been systematically researched and restored. Since 1987, attempts have been made to survey the interior of the burial mound using modern geophysical methods to explore the cavities present in the rock and also to find Antiochos I's burial chamber.

Five gods are enthroned on each of the two terraces, flanked by lions and eagles. The depictions of the gods form an unusual synthesis of the Greek and Persian world of gods; they show Zeus-Oromasdes, Apollo-Mithras, Heracles-Artagnes, the national goddess Kommagene, as well as the god-king Antiochos himself, who confidently placed himself in the gallery of the gods.

Figure 269: The statues appear to have Greek-style facial features, but Persian clothing and hairstyling.

Antiochos derived his origin equally from Greek and Persian ancestors, on his mother's side via Alexander the Great from Zeus and on his father's side via the Persian kings from the highest Persian god Ahura Mazda. With this ancestral line, he founded his godlike being. In this conviction, he let erect the cult images of the gods "after Persian and Greek tradition according to his double descent", as an inscription testifies.

Throne of Gods: Mount Nemrut

These ancestral lines, on which the ancestors are gathered, beginning with Darius I on one side and Alexander the Great on the other, form a unique "picture book of ancient genealogy".

The conscious equality with the gods manifests itself particularly impressively in the four welcome reliefs. The king is welcomed by Apollo-Mithras, Heracles, and the national goddess Kommagene and recognized as their equal. Greek and Persian influences are also mixed in the depiction of the figures: Heracles is depicted naked according to Greek custom, while the other gods, like the Persian ancestors on the relief slabs, wear Persian costumes: long robes decorated with ornaments and headdresses resembling a cockscomb.

The tomb of Antiochos, I on the top of the mountain, manifests as a widely visible and memorable symbol of the claim to be "near the gods" and equal to them. However, the new cult, which was supposed to be "everlasting," survived its creator by only a few decades.

Figure 270: Illustration of the Mount Nemrut from the Gaziantep Museum of Archaeology.

NAZCA LINES

(Nazca Desert, Peru, c. Between 200 BC and 500 AD)

Between 200 BC and 500 AD, the Nazca Lines, which the pre-Incas indigenous communities began to draw on the desert, is a great mystery for humanity. There are still many who believe that aliens did or that there was some kind of communication between aliens and ancient humans. Science still has no proven answers today; it has theories.

Figure 271: Illustration showing the most famous Nazca Lines together.

It is not known exactly who created the Nazca Lines. Because the people living in this region before the Spanish conquerors did not use writing. Historians believe that most of the lines were made by the thriving Nasca people from 200 BC to 600 AD.

This coast of South America has been inhabited for many thousands of years, beginning perhaps 15.000 years ago when the climate of the nearby Andes was cooler and wetter. The people lived very simply by hunting wild animals and gathering edible plants. Traces of an ancient meal were found in a mountain cave due north of Nazca and dated by the radio-carbon method to approximately 13.000 BC.

In the area close to Nazca, the most striking development began about 500 BC with an artistic innovation of designs on simple ceramics. These were the earliest days of the so- called 'Nazca Style'.

Nazca Lines

The view that the Nazca Lines are a kind of astronomical calendar has been a common view until the 1970s.

The indigenous people of the Paracas and Nazca cultures living in the region called Pampa Colorada (Red Flat) drew over 800 straight lines and 300 geometric figures over 1000 years and 70 animal figures, especially concentrated in a single region, in a 500 square kilometer rocky, arid area. Some straight lines approach almost 50 km in length. Animal and plant motifs vary in size between 15 and 365 meters. So, some are as big as the Empire State building!

Figure 272: Nazca Lines, Human Figure.

The most striking patterns are animal patterns. In particular, the spiral-tailed monkey, the 180-meter giant lizard, and the South American vulture, with its wingspan of 130 meters, are the most famous.

In addition, the owl-headed man figure, which many people compare to the astronaut, is among the most famous figures. Some say this man was a mystical clergyman with an owl mask on his head. The arid climate of the desert has kept the figures intact for almost
2.000 years.

Toribio Mejia, a Peruvian archaeologist, started researching the Nazca Lines for the first time in 1926. However, the figures are so large that the motifs can only be understood when seen from the air.

Therefore, the motifs were not understood until an airplane flew over it for the first time in the 1930s. When Paul Kosok, a pilot in 1941, coincidentally went to examine the Nazca Lines the day after the winter turn, he noticed that the sun was aligned with the lines at sunset, and the Nazca Lines became world-famous.

The view that the Nazca Lines are a kind of astronomical calendar has been a common view until the 1970s. This was the common view until a group of American researchers arrived in the 1970s. The American Johan Reinhard suggested looking at these lines from a broader perspective, including sociology, geography, anthropology, and ethnography: While alignments in winter and midsummer are not accidental, not all lines point to celestial things, trapezoids and most straight lines are made in the desert for water and agriculture. He claimed that it was related to rituals.

Figure 273: Nazca Lines, Spider Figure (47 m length) and Monkey Figure (93 by 58 m).

The researchers found that the giant drawings were depictions of exotic birds not found in the area, living in remote rainforests and coastal coasts. According to the researchers, these drawings were made in honor of creatures thought to bring rain. The peoples of the region had a great need for rain to survive. One of the things that reinforces this claim is that archaeological research in Peru revealed that the spider symbolizes rain, the hummingbird symbolizes fertility, and the monkey symbolizes the abundance of water.

In 2019, the article prepared by researchers from Hokkaido University in Japan was included in the Journal of Archaeological Science Reports. According to the researchers, the birds in the depictions have been misnamed so far, and some of these drawings represent bird species that are now extinct. According to this article, the Nazca lines are simply depictions of exotic birds drawn to please the gods during the rain dance.

According to the researchers, the rainy periods in these plateaus coincided with the migration period of seabirds. If the migratory birds were not visible, the locals feared that it would not rain and drought.

Nazca Lines

These lines were made in honor of the birds, and the people living in this area may have hoped that the birds would come back. Perhaps the native people worshiped these birds as signs of the gods. We don't know this exactly.

Although there are those who associate aliens with the ability to draw such large drawings so perfectly without seeing the total, it has been proven by a research team that this was within the human capacity at the time. A team of fewer than ten people, using only ropes and stakes, was able to complete the exact reproduction of these complex figures in about one week. The research team used a fairly simple drawing technique: digging out the sun-tanned rock surface to reveal the lighter underlying sunless layer.

Figure 274: Nazca Lines, Hummingbird Figure (about 97 m. Long and 65 m. wide).

Figure 275: Nazca Lines, Whale Figure and Pelican Figure.

LAOCOÖN AND HIS SONS

(Rome, Italy, c. 40 AD)

This sculpture group was found in a vineyard in Rome in 1506 on Esquiline Hill near the palace of Emperor Nero. It is said that the Pope himself visited the excavation. The sculpture, which was moved to the Vatican after the work was restored, was highly appreciated during the period. Michelangelo himself discovered this work, then examined it and was inspired by the nude figures he used in the Sistine Chapel.

Figure 276: Laocoön and His Sons.

The statue is based on the theme of the murder of Laokoon (Laocoön), who warned the people of Troy against the Greeks who tried to enter Troy with a wooden horse and told them not to take the wooden horse on the beach, by being punished with two snakes sent from the sea by the Greek god Athena.

Laocoön and His Sons

Laocoön, a priest, has two sons with him. While the priest's older son struggles to get rid of the snake, his younger son has an expression of the pain of the snake bit. Priest Laocoön, on the other hand, held the snake that was about to bite him.

The statue depicts the intense expressions of effort and pain on the faces of Laocoön and his sons, and the dramatic, desperate attempts of these three protagonists to free themselves from fatal realization.

According to the Roman writer and philosopher Plinus (died AD 79), this statue was made by three sculptors from Rhodes; It was located in the palace of the emperor. Although there are discussions about the date of the statue's construction, the dominant opinion and the inscriptions found are that the work was made in the 1st century BC (between 40-30 years).

This work was stolen from the Vatican by Napoleon during the invasion of Italy, taken to the Louvre Museum, but returned to the Vatican after Napoleon's defeat. The right arm of the work was mounted incorrectly & restored. The original right arm of the statue was found in 1905, experts confirmed the originality of the arm in 1960. In the 1980s, it gained its current appearance with the replacement of the arm.

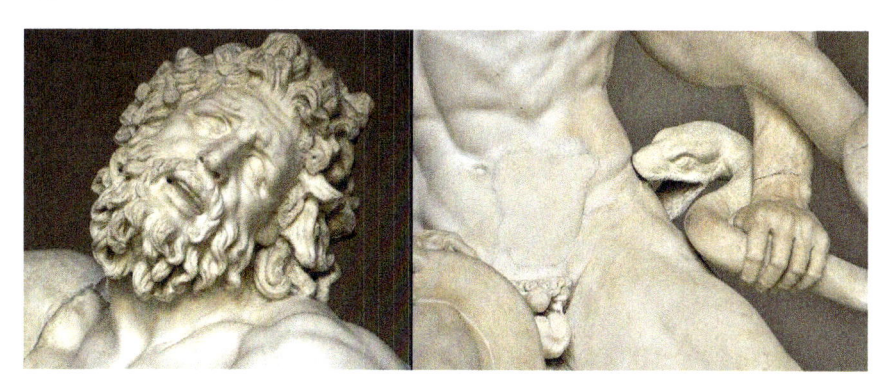

Figure 277: The statue of Laocoön and His Sons, details.

BROKEN POT MOUNTAIN

(Rome, Italy, c. 40-300 AD)

Monte Testaccio, also popularly known as Monte dei Cocci (literally meaning "Mount of Shards"), is an artificial hill located in the port area of ancient Rome and near the warehouses (horrea).

Figure 278: Aerial view of the Monte Testaccio.

Fifty-four meters high and with a circumference of about 1 kilometer, the mountain is formed by testae, shards, mostly fragments of amphorae used for the transport of goods, which were systematically unloaded and accumulated after being emptied in the nearby river port.

At first glance, it might appear to be simply a hill, much like the other seven in Rome that surrounds the city. But when you walk through the gates of Via Zabaglia, you quickly realize that this is no ordinary mound; it is entirely human- made from the remains of some 53 million crushed olive oil amphorae. The huge numbers of broken amphorae at Monte Testaccio illustrate the enormous demand for olive oil of imperial Rome, which was at the time the world's largest city with a population of at least one million people. Monte Testaccio is one of the largest and best-preserved ancient dump sites.

According to the latest studies, this activity was carried out between the Augustan period and the middle of the third century AD. Most of the jars examined date from 140-250 AD, but it is possible that the earliest layers date back much earlier, possibly to the first century.

Unlike the amphorae used for the transportation of agricultural products, the oil amphorae coming mostly from Betica (present Andalusia, Spain) were not reusable because of the rapid alteration of the olive-oil residues. There is a reason for this: because of the clay used to make the amphorae not coated with a glaze, after the olive oil was transported, the amphorae could not be reused because the oil created a rancid smell within the fabric of the clay.

Figure 279

Figure 280

The reason of why those amphora fragments is found in the same place is the site was located on the Tiber where the Empire's state warehouses of food, wine, grain and building stocks were supplied. When the ships from abroad came, the supplies used in the transportation amphorae were thrown away after they into smaller storage boxes.

Broken Pot Mountain

Archaeological excavations in the 1990s showed that the hill was created carefully and intentionally, not merely as a dump. Empty amphorae were probably carried up the mound intact on the backs of donkeys or mules and then broken up on the spot, with the shards laid out in a stable pattern. Lime appears to have been sprinkled over the broken pots to neutralize the smell of rancid oil.

Olive oil was an essential staple in the cuisine of the Romans. In Greece, Italy and Spain, olive has been cultivated in the farms for ages. Monte Testaccio in Rome is one of the best-known reminders of the olive oil commerce.

Figure 281: Aerial view of the Monte Testaccio.

ARCHAEOLOGICAL PARK OF BAIA

(Bacoli, Naples, Italy, c. 1st century AD)

The name Baia easily translates into "Bay", but the legend goes it comes from Baios. He was Ulysses's helmsman, who died and was buried there by the Greek hero. Some of the most famous emperors and figures of the Roman Empire, such as Caesar, Augustus, Cicero, Agrippina, Septimius Severus, and Nero, at one point or another visited the ancient town of Baia. Back then, Baia was the resort town for ultra-wealthy Romans. Today, it's a small seaside town just a few kilometers from Napoli.

Baia is home to the most spectacular submerged treasure in the Mediterranean; its ruins have slowly sunk into the Bay of Napoli over the centuries because of the region's frequent earthquakes. The archaeological park of Baia includes baths and ruins, taking you from uphill down to the sea resorts and harbor of Bacoli.

The ancient Baia's port was a delimited lagoon with an entrance channel, which ruins are visible nowadays and the ruins of ancient shops and thermal buildings.

Figure 282

The Romans came here for the same reasons we do: the sparkling Mediterranean, the balmy weather, the lush vegetation. They were also drawn to the area's thermal springs – the result, of course, of the volcanic activity beneath their feet.

Archaeological Park of Baia

The city, which was located over natural volcanic vents, was famous for its healing medicinal hot springs, which occurred all around the city and were quite easy to build spas over.

Even as the Western Roman Empire declined, Romans, and then Visigoths (western tribes of Goths) and Vandals, continued to use the baths at ancient Baiae. But by the time Giovanni Boccaccio described it in a 1344 novel – "no sight under the sun is more beautiful or more pleasant than this." he wrote – Baiae's great baths and villas had fallen into ruin.

Because of bradyseism (from the Greek bradus=slowandsism =movement), many were also undersea. Over the last 2.000 years, much of the site has sunk between 5 - 6m; in some places, it's up to 11m. About 45-50% of built-up area is now thought to be under the water.

Today, the depths of Baia give us a clear idea of the ancient structure density of this stretch of coast. A few meters below sea level, you can swim among the remains of taverns and deposits that were once teeming with life and ready to pick up goods from around the whole of the Mediterranean, used to supply Rome. Imperial baths, precious mosaics, statues, and marble floors have been found underwater. In the 2000s, the Archaeological Marine Park of Baia was created with an incomparable historical and cultural value to protect all this.

There are five underwater sites, ranging from 5 to a maximum of 13 meters of depth, therefore suitable both for snorkeling, for scuba diving and, for try scuba diving for beginners. (More info: subaia.com)

Figure 283: Underwater Archaeological Park of Baia.

NERO'S GOLDEN PALACE

(Rome, Italy, c. 64 AD)

Immediately after the fire of 64 AD, which destroyed most of the center of Rome, Nero built a new imperial residence: Domus Aurea. This was far bigger and more luxurious than the previous one, the Domus Transitoria.

Nero employed Severus as an architect and Fabullus as a painter and produced what has been called the first expression of the Roman revolution in architecture. The new palace was immense: it covered the Palatine, Velia, and Oppian hills and the valley where the Colosseum was later built. Domus Aurea consisted of countless pavilions scattered over an immense park and was adorned with works of art taken from cities and temples in Greece. Completed in AD 68 and it seemed more like a town than a palace. Its walls were decked with gold and precious stones, giving it the name the Domus Aurea or Golden House.

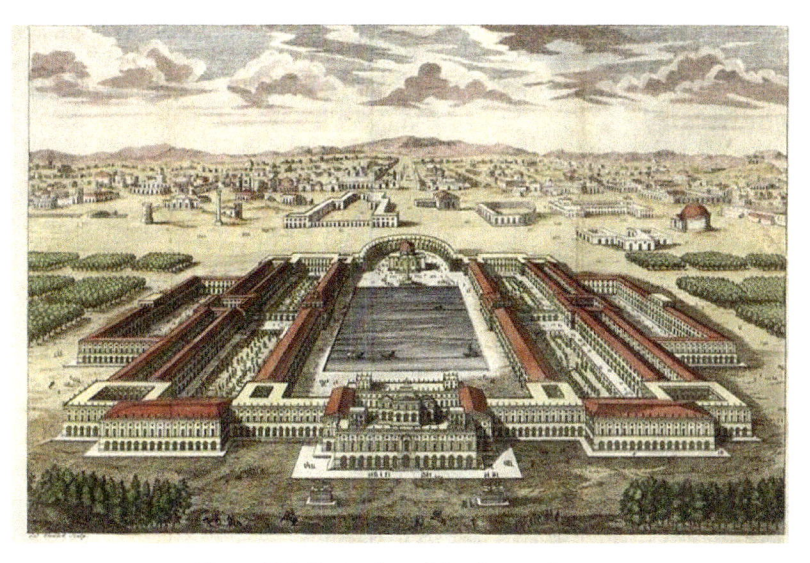

Figure 284: Illustration of the Domus Aurea.

This grandiose edifice did not survive the tyrant's death in 68 AD, as succeeding emperors demolished or covered up his buildings. In 72 AD, Vespasian obliterated the lake to build the Colosseum; Domitian (81-96 AD) buried the constructions on the Palatine to make room for the Flavian palaces.

Nero's Golden Palace

Trajan (98-117 AD) destroyed the houses on the Oppian to build his baths, and Hadrian (117-78 AD) built his Temple of Venus and Roma on the site of the atrium and moved the statue. The gloomy chambers of the ruins of Nero's palace are mostly underground today.

13 centuries later some of the rooms in the palace were rediscovered and the painted decorations caused an artistic sensation - it was the first time in over a thousand years that anyone had cast their eyes on the style that later became known as "Pompeian". Raffaello Sanzio used the decorations as his model in the Vatican Loggie without knowing he had been copying wall paintings from Nero's Golden Palace. The famous Greek sculpture of Laocoön now in the Vatican Museums was discovered here in pieces in 1506. It most likely formed part of Nero's splendid collection.

Figure 285: Laocoön and His Sons, Vatican Museums, Rome, Italy (left) - Reconstruction of the great hall of the Domus Aurea with the Laocoön, in a painting by G. Chedanne (nineteenth century). Musée des Beaux-Arts, Rouen. (right)

Today visitors can view the labyrinthine but well-lit subterranean palace only by booking a tour lasting approximately 45 minutes in Italian or English or in other languages with an audio guide. A passage system consisting of a corridor and cryptoporticus with adjacent rooms, some of which are decorated with frescoes and stucco with garlands, birds, mythological scenes, and landscape views, leads to the Octagonal Hall.

Nero's Golden Palace

Domus Aurea's most significant room is the Octagonal Hall, largely intact despite Trajan's rebuilding efforts. The Octagonal Hall represented a breakthrough in design and aesthetics. Concrete allowed Nero's architects to use myriad shapes -- prisms, cubes, octagons, and semi-cylinders. The Octagonal Room also had a revolving or rotating floor, mimicking the movement of celestial bodies. Four spherical mechanisms beneath the floor rotated the structure. Ancient sources tell us that the Octagonal Hall was served as a banquet hall, very luxurious and scenic as well.

Figure 286: Octagonal Hall of the Domus Aurea, Rome. The rectangular openings between the supports serve as alcoves and entrances and terminate in horizontal lintels to provide additional support for the semi-dome, which has an oculus (a round opening) at the highest point to admit sunlight.

Figure 287: Octagonal Hall of the Domus Aurea, Rome.

Nero's Golden Palace

The luxury of the 80ha (c. 800.000 m²) palace, of which 150 rooms have been made accessible to date, was recorded by the emperor's biographer Suetonius (c. 70-130 AD):

"A huge statue of himself, 120 feet high, stood in the entrance hall; and the pillared arcade ran for a whole mile. An enormous pool, more like a sea than a pool, was surrounded by buildings made to resemble cities, and by a landscape garden consisting of plowed fields, vineyards, pastures, and woodlands — where every variety of domestic and wild animal roamed about. Parts of the house were overlaid with gold and studded with precious stones and nacre. All the dining rooms had ceilings of fretted ivory, the panels of which could slide back and let a rain of flowers, or of perfume from hidden sprinklers, shower upon his guests. The main dining room was circular, and its roof revolved slowly, day and night, in time with the sky. Seawater, or sulfur water, was always on tap in the baths. When the palace had been completely decorated in this lavish style, Nero dedicated it and condescended to remark: "Good, now I can at last begin to live like a human being " **(Suetonius, Lives of the Caesars)**

Figure 288: Details, Domus Aurea, Rome.

Nero's Golden Palace

Figure 289: Details, Domus Aurea, Rome.

Figure 290: Details, Domus Aurea, Rome.

Figure 291: Details, Domus Aurea, Rome.

TEMPLE OF GARNI

(Garni, Armenia, c. 77 AD)

4.000 km from Rome and 2.500 km from Athens, in a remote corner of the South Caucasus, stands an enormous Hellenic temple: the Garni Temple.

The Garni Temple is the only pagan Hellenistic and Greco-Roman structure that has survived in Armenia and the Caucasus. It was built in honor of the ancient Armenian god Mythra (Mihr in Armenian), God of the sun, light and purity. The name "Mythra" is synonymous with the Greek "Helios" meaning sun or sun god.

The exact construction date of the temple is unknown. The dominant view is that the temple was built in the eleventh year of the reign of the Armenian King Tiridates I, in 77 AD.

Figure 292: Temple of Garni.

In 1945, Armenian painter Martiros Saryan discovered a Greek inscription near the temple. Although the inscription was damaged, the words "... the undisputed king of the great Armenia, the Sun God Tiridates, built the temple and the impregnable fortress ... in the eleventh year of his reign" can be read.

Temple of Garni

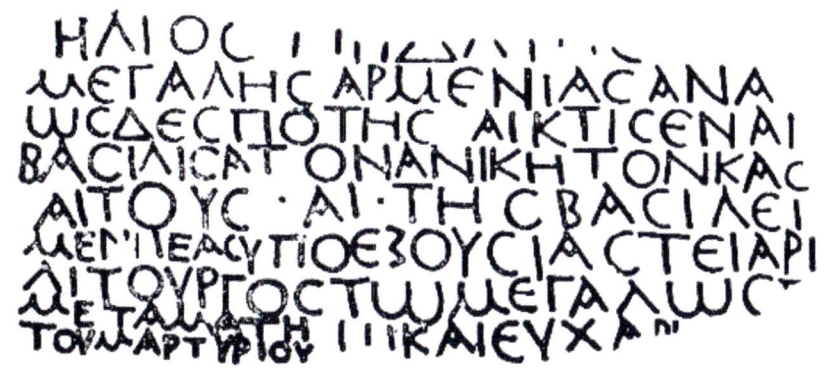

Figure 293: Greek inscription of Tiridates I.

The Armenian king Tiridates I visited Rome in 66 AD to be crowned by Emperor Nero (54-68 AD). After Tiridates I was crowned by Nero, he returned with a large amount of money to rebuild Armenia. Tiridates' visit to Rome reinforces the thesis that this temple was built during Tiridates I.

The Garni Temple is part of a complex at the tip of a high cliff that includes a Roman bathhouse, a royal summer palace, and a 7th-century church. The temple was built in gray basalt over an ancient Urartian temple. The temple was originally an Ionian-style Greco-Roman peripetero (enclosed chamber) on a 3-meter-high podium. On the north side of the temple, a wide (8 meter) staircase with nine steps leads to the inner sanctuary. It is supported by a total of twenty-four 6.54-meter-high columns of the ionic layout: there are a total of 24 columns, six in the front and six in the back, and eight on the sides.

Garni's architecture is richly decorated with numerous ornaments typical of Armenian architecture, unlike such temples found in other countries. Various ornaments typical of Armenian art, such as grape and walnut leaves, were carved into the temple.

Temple of Garni

When the Armenian King Tiridates III adopted Christianity as the state religion in 301 AD, all pagan places of worship were destroyed, except for the Garni Temple. It is believed that the Garni Temple was saved thanks to the efforts of the sister of Tiridates the Great, Princess Khosrovdoukht.

The area surrounding the Garni Temple was used as a royal garrison and military headquarters in ancient and medieval times. This area was surrounded by Roman baths in the 4th century, a church with four apses, and a church with a single nave in the 7th century. Debate continues over whether Garni was used as a summer palace in late antiquity. Due to its strategic importance, the area around the Garni Temple was subjected to numerous invasions by Persians, Arabs, Byzantines, Turks, and Mongols. Today, Arabic graffiti dating to the 9-10th centuries AD can be seen on the walls of the Garni Temple.

Figure 294: Arabic Graffiti, Temple of Garni.

The temple remained almost flawless until the earthquake of 1679 near the village of Garni. However, this earthquake destroyed the temple completely and turned it into the wreckage and scattered the columns and stones of the temple in all directions over the Azat River and the surrounding valley.

Temple of Garni

It took about ten years for the archaeologists to piece together the temple. The reconstruction was completed in 1975, about 300 years after it collapsed in the earthquake.

Soviet rule was biased towards religious structures but also valued classical forms. So, the Garni Temple was an inspiring place for the Soviet regime. Today, the Garni temple is a symbol of Armenia's deep historical ties with the Roman and Greek civilizations and the richness of the culture standing between east and west and welcomes hundreds of thousands of visitors each year.

Figure 295: Temple of Garni in 1918. Photographer: Strzygowski, Josef.

Figure 296: Temple of Garni, details.

POMPEII

(Naples, Italy, 79 AD)

The first settlements in the Ancient City of Pompeii date back to the 9th century BC. The city grew with the settlement of the Ancient Greeks in the 8th century BC. Pompeii, which was under Rome's influence after the 2nd century BC, was where wealthy Roman citizens settled, especially due to the beautiful Mediterranean climate. The settlement of wealthy Roman citizens continued until Pompeii disappeared. Romans built beautiful villas, paved roads, and wide avenues in Pompeii.

Pompeii was located at the foot of Mount Vesuvius. Its proximity to the island of Capri, and the prevalence of Roman pomp made the city one of the favorite centers. As a result of the Vesuvius Volcano eruption in 79 AD, it was buried under ashes with the ancient city's inhabitants. Perhaps this was Vesuvius's most violent eruption, which exploded more than 50 times.

Figure 297: Pompeii, General view.

It is thought that ash and lava rained from the sky for 18 hours. Although some can act quickly and escape by ships, about 2 thousand people have been trapped under a layer of ash and lava.

Pompeii

The bodies of approximately 1.150 of them have been reached. (It is estimated that there were 12.000 people in Pompeii at the time of the explosion. This reveals that the number of people who acted fast and escaped, contrary to what is believed) The reason for the high disaster is that the people are accustomed to earthquakes and that day is a festival. Also, those who remained under the collapsed structures or those who were injured during the earthquake that took place simultaneously as the explosion died because they could not escape.

The day after the volcanic eruption, the cone of the Vesuvius Volcano collapsed. As a result of this collapse, the giant clay landslide (archaeologists speak of a landslide with a speed of 160 kilometers hr.), Pompeii, and Herculaneum village disappeared. It was this clay landslide that completely wiped-out Pompeii from the earth. Vesuvius last erupted in 1944; It still threatens millions of people living in Naples 23 miles away.

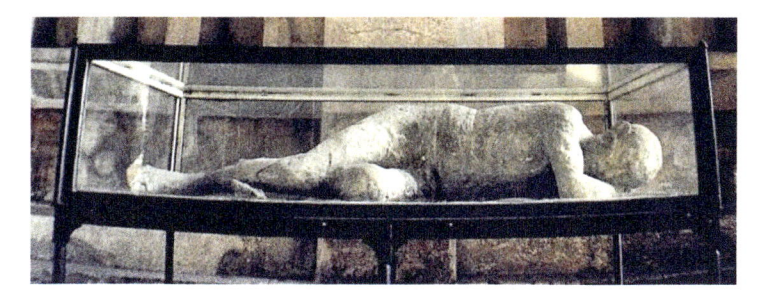

Figure 298

For about 2000, the ancient city of Pompeii waited to be found in its original form, untouched by human hands. Although there are hints that excavations were made during the Roman Empire period, the first known excavations in Pompeii were carried out between 1594-1600. However, these studies ended due to the earthquake in 1631.

After the 1631 earthquake, the first excavations started in 1748 under the leadership of Carlo Borbone. Because Borbone intended to find treasure, Giuseppe Fiorelli took over the excavation work in 1861. Fiorelli systematically excavated and sprayed liquid plaster into the cavities around petrified human corpses and molded them.

Fiorelli unearthed the streets, squares, grand bazaars, temples, markets, and courtrooms of Pompeii. In Pompeii, a UNESCO world cultural heritage located in 165 decares, approximately 75% of the ancient city has been unearthed in the works still ongoing today.

Pompeii

After the Pompeii excavations began systematically under the supervision of Fiorelli, archaeologists discovered that human bodies had decayed but were surrounded by voids in the trapped ash.

Thanks to these gaps, the details of the bodies of many victims have been almost completely revealed. With a special plaster-like mixture (like liquid clay) filled into this space, the final state of the bodies before they died was unearthed.

Figure 299

Figure 300: Pompeii Amphitheater is one of the oldest known theaters of the Roman period. It is estimated to have been built in 70 BC. It has a capacity of 20 thousand viewers. It has stairs with two exits from the outside and one pass from the inside.

Pompeii

Figure 301: Thermopolium, Pompeii. Thermopolium means "the place where hot food and drinks are eaten fast" in Greek. The beverage service area is an ancient restaurant with its counter and has survived perfectly. In the area where Mercury, the god of trade, and Dionysus, the god of wine, were found and served hot food and drinks in jars on the benches on the wall. The hob is used to heat the food.

Figure 302: Casa dei Vetti is one of Pompei's richest and most luxurious houses. The god of welfare Priapus is depicted on the right side of the door to show the welfare of the landlord. As in all houses, there is a courtyard and a pool in the middle of the living room. The garden was enlarged, and fountains and sculptures were placed. Since the frescoes were made after the earthquake that occurred in 62 AD, they are almost completely preserved. When you enter the kitchen area, you encounter erotic frescoes.

Pompeii

Figure 303: The forum, 157 meters long and 38 meters wide, was the center of life in Pompeii. It was the open space in the center of the city and opened to the Basilica, the Temple of Apollo, and other important buildings of the city. The lower row consists of dor-style columns, and the upper row consists of ion columns. It is estimated that there were many statues adorning the forum, but they were destroyed in the earthquake of 62 AD. The only thing that has survived is the pedestals of these sculptures.

Figure 304: House of the Small Fountain, Pompeii. It is estimated that this house, which has a very rich decoration, was built in the 1st century BC. It has been discovered that there is a system that collects rainwater on the roof and recycles it for wine production. Its frescoes are eye-catching. The fountain that gives the house its name is believed to be popular in houses in Pompeii in the 1st century AD. As you can see from the picture below, the water flows from the gutters in the fountain with a triangular roof and spreads from the area where the bronze figurines are located.

Pompeii

Figure 305: Temple of Apollo, Pompeii. Excavations in this building, one of the oldest places of worship in Pompeii, showed that the first temple was established in the 6th century BC. In the center of this temple, which was renovated in the 3rd and 2nd centuries BC, there is a courtyard with an altar. Many sculptures extracted from this area are on display at the Naples Archaeological Museum, and the sculptures in the temple are copies of those in the museum. We recommend that you do not leave without examining the sundial on the column next to the altar in the courtyard.

Figure 306: The Basilica, Pompeii's most magnificent building, is one of the oldest examples in the Roman world and dates back to the 120s BC. The city was run from here. The courts were also located here. Access to the building is provided through 5 doors. The building is divided into three sections by columns. On the west side, there is a richly furnished tribune where the judges provide justice. There are horse-drawn statues and marble blocks in the place.

THRACIAN CHARIOT OF KARANOVO

(Karanovo, Nova Zagora, Bulgaria, c. 1st Century AD)

The Thracians were Indo-European nomadic people who settled in the central Balkans about 5.000 years ago. They established a powerful kingdom in the fifth century BC. Over the centuries, the Thracian territory was subjected to numerous invasions by everyone, from the ancient Macedonians to the Huns. They were conquered by Rome in the 1st century and assimilated by Slav peoples in the 6th century. For almost 1.400 years, Thracian culture was then largely forgotten.

However, in the 20th-century, archaeologists began excavating sites located where the ancient people had once roamed, mostly in Bulgaria's south.

In November 2008, a team of archaeologists led by Veselin Ignatov discovered the 2.000-year-old wooden chariot. The chariot was covered in bronze. Its exact age is uncertain and maybe closer to 1.900 years old. In 2009, Veselin Ignatov also discovered a brick tomb containing the remains of a man dressed in what appears to be armor near the wooden chariot. He was buried with various items, including gold rings, coins, and a cup showing a depiction of the Greek god Eros (in Roman Times called Cupid). This man was probably a nobleman or ruler living in ancient Thrace, now Bulgaria.

Figure 307: Thracian Chariot of Karanovo.

Thracian Chariot of Karanovo

The four-wheeled wooden chariot, its carved bronze plating and fittings, and the skeletal remains of two horses and a dog have been preserved in situ instead of being transferred to a museum.

This chariot is decorated with scenes from Thracian mythology –the god Eros, a jumping panther, and a mythological animal with the body of a panther and the tail of a dolphin. It has wheels 1.20 meters in diameter. Four-wheeled chariots are an extraordinary find, and this one is particularly notable because of the large diameter of its wheels.

Ceramics, glass objects, well-preserved wooden and leather objects, some of which may have been horse harnesses were discovered at the burial mound. All artifacts were used for the funeral of a wealthy nobleman or a ruler.

Figure 308: A team led by Bulgarian archeologists Vesselin Ignatov and restoration expert Silvia Borisova made a reconstruction of the chariot in 2009, The National Archeological Museum in Sofia, Bulgaria.

CARVILIO'S RING

(Grottaferrata, Italy, c. 1st century AD)

In 2000, an intact Roman tomb of the Flavius era was found in Grottaferrata, southeast of Rome. The tomb contained two marble sarcophagi, each with an elegant garland decoration and on the front a tabula with the name of the deceased. One belonged to Aebutia Quarta, mother of Antestia Balbina and Carvilio Gemellus, which allows us to know that the woman had two children, Balbina and Carvilio, from two different husbands, the other belonged to Tiberius Carvilio Gemellus, son of Tiberius who lived 18 years and three months. The young man died before his mother; Aebutia Quarta later died at the age of 40-45, and her second husband's daughter, Antestia Balbina, buried her.

Flower garlands for both consisted of roses, violets, and lilies. They died in the summer. Although they were Roman, they were not cremated. Inside the sarcophagi were found traces of myrrh and rosin, substances used to preserve the bodies of the deceased for their long exposure and embalming.

Figure 309

Carvilio's Ring

The skeleton of Aebutia Quarta was covered almost entirely by a layer of well- preserved vegetal elements.

The only element of the personal belongings was a gold ring with a rock crystal bezel covering a portrait, probably identifiable with that of his young son Carvilius. A mini bust of Carvilio, who died early at the age of 18, is embedded in a rare rock crystal.

The bust is a lost-wax cast and represents a shirtless young man with curly hair, thin lips, and an aquiline nose. The convex surface of the rock crystal adds a mysterious depth to the image of the deceased, evoking the closeness of his soul to his mother's love.

Aebutia must have said to her daughter Balbina: "See this ring? You must put it on my finger when I die." Italian archaeologists found this exceptional ring almost as it was on the first day 2.000 years later. Carvilio's ring is exhibited today in Palestrina Archaeological Museum, Italy.

Figure 310

OXYRHYNCHUS PAPYRI

(Al-Bahnasa, Egypt, c. 305 BC-c. AD 200)

Papyrus means the paper-like sheets made from the cross-laid fibrous self- adhesive strips from the stalk of the papyrus plant, indigenous to Egypt, which could be pasted in series to form rolls (books, etc.).

Egypt came under Persian rule in 525 BC. In 332 BC, Persia surrendered to Alexander the Great, and Egypt became part of the Greek empire. After Alexander the Great's conquest of Egypt by the Persians in 322 BC, more than a quarter of a million Greeks settled in Egypt. For millennia until the Arab conquest in 641 AD, Greek was the main language of the Ptolemaic, Roman, and Byzantine governments, literature and private documents, and the people.

The Oxyrhynchus Papyri first came to light in the 1890s. Most of the papyri come from the excavations of Bernard Grenfell and Arthur Hunt on behalf of the Graeco-Roman Branch of the Egypt Exploration Society between 1896 and 1907.

Figure 311

Oxyrhynchus Papyri

In 1896, two British Egyptologists, Bernard Pyne Grenfell and Arthur Surridge Hunt chose to excavate at Al-Bahnasa. One factor that influenced the two men to choose this city as their excavation site was its reputation as a key Christian center in ancient times.

The two Egyptologists were hoping that they would be able to find some interesting pieces of early Christian literature there.

They began work in 1896. They didn't find anything until January 1897. Then a leaf of the Gospel of Matthew was found, and in the following three months, enough papyrus to fill almost 300 boxes.

Figure 312: One of the oldest surviving fragments of Euclid's Elements, found at Oxyrhynchus and dated to circa AD 100.

The papyri included legal documents, letters, petitions, and receipts, which all gave important information about the Greek and Roman way of life. There were also copies of lost works by classical authors and scholars, such as Plato, Sophocles, and Aristotle. All in all, the papers provided a unique insight into this period in Egyptian history. Housed at the University of Oxford, the collection comprises over 500,000 fragments of literary and documentary texts dating from the third century BC to the seventh century AD. The texts are written in Greek, ancient Egyptian (hieroglyphic, hieratic, demotic), Coptic, Latin, Arabic, Hebrew, Aramaic, Syriac, and Pahlavi.

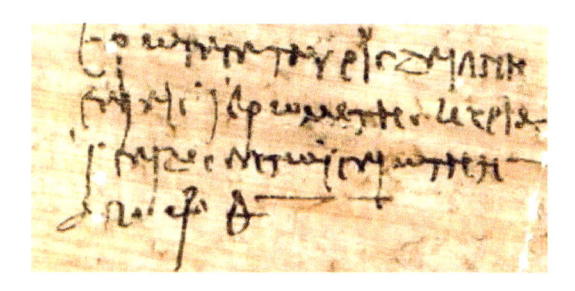

Figure 313: Social life at Oxyrhynchus: "Tayris asks you to dinner for the offering to our Lady Isis, in the Iseum, on the 8th, from the 9th hour" (2nd/3rd cent. AD.)

ANTINOUS AT DELPHI

(Delphi, Greece, c. 130 AD)

Antinous was a young Greek of extraordinary beauty from Bithynia (modern-day Bolu in Turkey), who became the lover of the Roman emperor Hadrian but later died in the Nile.

Stricken by the death of Antinous, Hadrian ordered that the statues of the beautiful young man, whom he had loved so passionately, be erected in all temples and cities of the Roman Empire. A statue of Antinous was accordingly erected within the sanctuary of Delphi after his death in 130 AD. It is universally recognized as one of the most beautiful and impressive cult statues of all time. During the archaeological excavations in the year of 1894, the statue was found upright on its pedestal, next to the wall of a brick chamber, alongside the holy Temple.

If you take a closer look at the Antinous's statue, the head of Antinous is tilted to the side like he is in a position of a reflection. Archaeologists say that Antinous's long hair was once crowned by a wreath since there are indications of a band with leaves made of a different material. His body is carved in a way that gives it the beautiful nudity which characterized the statues of gods and heroes of classical antiquity. Its melancholy beauty, the graceful angle of the head, and the high polish of the marble surface embodied the spirit of the Roman Imperial age when there was a tendency to revive ancient Greek ideals.

Figure 314: Statue of Antinous (Delphi Archaeological Museum, Delphi, Greece) and discovery of statue in 1894.

MITHRAEUM

(Basilica di San Clemente, Rome, Italy, c. AD 200-300)

Basilica di San Clemente, with its relics of the martyr, its thousand-year-old history, and its famous frescoes, creates a strong impression, which is also felt in the Mithraeum. This church is one of the oldest places of Christian worship in Rome and was the home of St. Clement, the disciple of St Peter and the fourth Bishop of Rome (88-97).

In the 1860s, Mithraeum was discovered in a notable Roman house situated under the Basilica S. Clemente. As the flow of water made further investigations impossible in the beginning, the excavations could only be continued in 1914 after the construction of a water tunnel.

Ancient residence, far below the current street level, housed a sanctuary of Mithras in the 2nd century; in 385 AD, a church dedicated to St. Clement, the third bishop of Rome after St. Peter, was constructed above it. After the Normans destroyed this church in 1084, construction of a basilica began in the 12th century.

Figure 315: Mithraeum, Basilica di San Clemente, Rome, Italy.

Mithraism began in ancient Persia (now Iran) in the fifteenth century BC and spread to Europe about a hundred years before the birth of Christ.

Centuries later, an arcane cult that changed in character in time developed and became very influential, particularly on Rome's army officers and legionaries. Mithraeum in Basilica di San Clemente was a place where the Romans worshipped the god Mithras. He was a very popular god: a sun god and the god of love.

Mithraeum

The altar in the center of Mithraeum has a relief of Mithras slaying a bull (an animal is often seen as a symbol of strength and fertility) Apollo commanded Mithras, a god born of a rock, to slay the bull to ensure fertility and renew life. Rebirth was an essential idea in the myth of Mithraic Mithraism. After the acceptance of Christianity by the emperor Constantine in the early 4th century AD, Mithraism rapidly declined.

Figure 316

Figure 317

APOLLO BELVEDERE

(Vatican Museums, c. 2nd century AD)

This statue, dated to the 2nd century AD, is thought to be a copy of the original bronze statue in the Halicarnassus Mausoleum in Bodrum (330-320 BC), one of seven wonders of the ancient period.

This depiction, which was highly appreciated in ancient times, has been found in many ancient cities. The provenance exactly is unknown, yet the excellent condition of the statue suggests that it was never buried. At the end of the fifteenth century, it stood in the garden of San Pietro in Vincoli; early in the sixteenth century, after the beginning of Pope Julius's pontificate (1503), but, at the latest, before 1509, it was placed in the sculpture court of the Belvedere in the Vatican, on the very spot where it customarily stands today.

Figure 318: Apollo Belvedere.

Apollo is the sun god, the god of music and art, the god of prophecy in mythology. He is also known as the archer god and is often depicted with an arrow in his hand.

There is no same finding as to which mythological story this 224 cm tall statue depicts. However, it is claimed that Apollo, an "archer god", initially left an arrow with the bow he held in his left hand.

Apollo Belvedere

Apollo is depicted here as a mature man. Apollo's left arm is extended forward, and his head is turned at right angles to the direction of his movement. The empty quiver filled with arrows indicates that Apollo once carried a bow in his left hand and an arrow in the other. The composition of the sculpture combines the movement and torsion of the sculpture. The weight of the body is on the right foot, only the toes of the left foot touch the ground. The flow of movement is restricted by the position of the left arm. As in the classical style, the free leg corresponds to the active arm.

The Apollo Belvedere embodies the Apollonian ideal of the Greeks. Since the sixteenth century, it has lived on in countless copies, imitations, variations, quotations, parodies, and caricatures, as well as in illustrations and reproductions. This statue was also the symbol of the Apollo-17 team of the USA, who landed on the moon in 1972. You can see this statue today in the Vatican Museums.

Figure 319: Symbol of the Apollo-17 team

FAYUM MUMMY PORTRAITS

(Egypt, c. 200 AD)

Fayum mummy portraits are also known as Faiyum mummy portraits or mummy portraits. They belong to the tradition of wood painting. They are faces of men, women, young people, and children, painted mostly on boards, fixed with the bandages of their mummies on their faces.

In ancient Egyptian and Coptic language "Fayum" meant "the lake" or "the sea. The Greeks called this lake Moeris, and the ancient Egyptians called it "mer-wer" or "great lake". In Roman times this site was known as Antinoopolis. In prehistoric times it was fresh water and had about 1,500 km^2; now it is only 202 km^2. It is located 35 km from the left bank of the Nile River, there is the necropolis, where the first faces were found in 1615 (well preserved due to the dry climate of the area). These portraits receive their name from the Fayum necropolis (located in Hawara, Egypt), since it was in this location that the greatest number of portraits have been found.

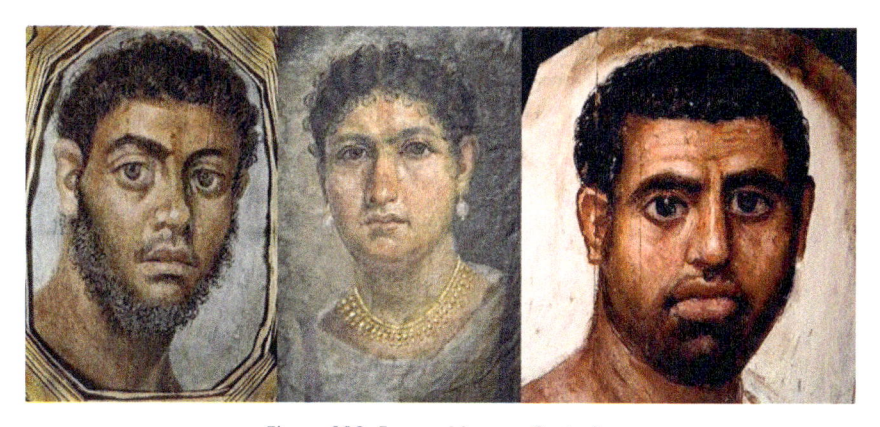

Figure 320: Fayum Mummy Portraits.

Although most of them come from the Fayum region (nowadays, around 900 mummy portraits have been found), these types of portraits have also been found all over Egypt. Nowadays, they can be found in the Egyptian Museum in Cairo (Egypt), in the Louvre Museum in Paris (France), and in the British Museum in London (England).

Pietro della Valle found the first two funerary portraits in 1615. He was an Italian explorer from a noble family who traveled through Egypt and the Orient.

Fayum Mummy Portraits

However, they did not make much of an impression, or at least not as much as the cuneiform writing bricks from Mesopotamia that he brought with him; or the Persian cat, which he also seems to have introduced into the West. We will have to wait a few more centuries until from 1887 Theodor Graff began to get an important collection that surely came from the current Er- Rubayat or Kerka. He bought some of the panel paintings from the dealers and showed them to the Egyptologist and writer Georg Ebers. In the 1880s, portraits were displayed at exhibitions in all major European capitals. The portraits aroused the public's interest.

We owe the great advance in the knowledge of these portraits to British archaeologist Flinders Petrie, who was excavating in Arsínoe and Hawara until the beginning of the 20th century. He discovered there a necropolis that yielded 81 to 90 portrait mummies. Petrie's excavations were the first example of a systematic study of these ancient masterpieces for subsequent researchers.

The Egyptian society of the first centuries shows a multicultural structure. Fayum Mummy Portraits are a mixture between Greek and encaustic (wax) painting, Roman realism, and Egyptian funeral rites. The mummy was a complex Egyptian ritual that tried to prevent the rotting of the body. It was done because, according to Egyptian belief, it was necessary for life in the afterlife. Most of the portraits were made between the first and third centuries. Their production declined at the end of the third century, probably due to the diffusion of Christianity. In these years, mummification was a highly industrialized process in which bodies were not treated with the care and affection of previous times.

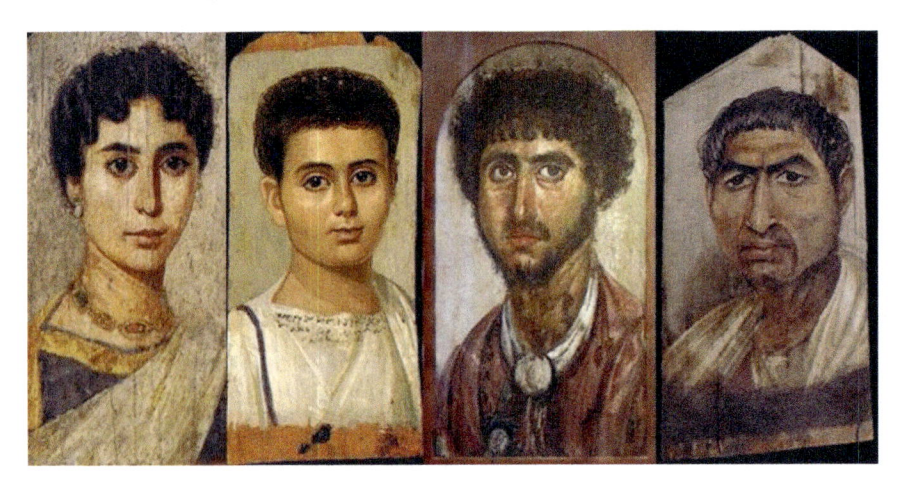

Figure 321

Fayum Mummy Portraits

At the beginning of the first century A.D., a painted portrait of the deceased began to be placed on the mummies.

The traditional was a funerary mask, but later it gave way to this new fashion. It was painted on wood, many of them imported. The oak, cedar, sycamore, and cypress stand out. A bright attribute of Fayum mummy portraits is gold leaf.

Sometimes, jewels and hair ornaments were made with gold. The portrait was fixed on the deceased's face, either through a network of bandages or by gluing it with stucco. Due to Egypt's hot and dry climate, some portraits were well preserved and have not lost their bright color.

As for the painting technique, tempera (pigments mixed with some organic substance) or encaustic (pigments mixed with wax) was used. The first and best portraits were rendered in wax paint. Over time, tempera completely replaced wax paint. As a result, the technique and the style of painting became simpler: having lost its former volume, it became schematic and less realistic.

An important question, who were the depicted?

According to the portraits found, it can be said that the people portrayed had a high purchasing power, because they could afford the religious service. In some portraits have inscriptions on the portrayed (for example, the age of the deceased to die, their family affiliation), also appears the name of the author, although mostly are anonymous works.

Figure 322

Fayum Mummy Portraits

These people belong to the military or religious elites; they could be descendants of settlers or the settlers themselves. In general, the portraits correspond to young people; there are also many portraits of young women. At first, it was explained by the short lifespan.

In the Greco-Roman period in Egypt, the region of El Fayum presented a very cosmopolitan area, but the average life span was less than 35 years.

But later, there appeared a theory that people got their portraits done at the age of 15 to 25 years since they were intended "for future use". With the help of computed tomography, researchers have confirmed this assumption and have come to a conclusion that, according to ancient Greek tradition, mummy portraits used to decorate their rooms before becoming a ritual attribute.

Fayum portraits show real people. Therefore, each portrait reflects the character of a different individual. Faces in portraits are asymmetrical and eyes are larger than they are. The reason why the eyes are depicted large is the ancient Egyptian belief. According to the beliefs of the ancient Egyptians, the soul leaves the body in the mouth and returns from the eyes.

In addition, when observing the individual traits of the people portrayed, different ethnic types (corresponding to different origins) can be appreciated. The population of the El Fayum area grew largely due to a wave of Greek immigrants during the Hellenistic period (initially by veteran soldiers who settled in the area). Greeks, Macedonians, individuals from other parts of Europe, Syrians and Indians are recognized.

The portraits of El Fayum are a rich painting sample of the deceased. In any case, historians realized that those portraits were much more than an antique or a work of art: they are the largest collection of faces from a distant world.

THE ROYAL TOMBS OF SILLA

(Gyeongju, South Korea, c. 250 AD)

Today's Korea was once an isolated country made up of small farming communities. Both the developments in ironworking in the 4th century BC and the rule of the Han Dynasty contributed touch to better trading opportunities, creating a wealthier Korea.

As Korea's prosperity grew, separate states began to form and develop into strongly organized communities. In the fifth and sixth centuries, the Korean peninsula was divided between three rivaling kingdoms. The most powerful of these was the Silla kingdom in the southeast of the peninsula. In the ancient world, the Korean kingdom of Silla (57 BC–AD 935) was renowned as a country of gold. The Silla elite's desire for gold ornaments originally arose from contacts with various kingdoms of China and the northeast's nomadic cultures. The raw material was initially imported but eventually produced within the Silla territories to satisfy the enormous demand.

Ancient Koreans used to practice shamanism in which a shaman-a kind of priest intercede to solve the problems of the community before they adopted Buddhism. In the northern steppe cultures, they practiced shamanism however the Silla royalty would use the customs of the Chinese and bury their elite in mounded tombs. The important things that they used while they were alive were put in the grave.

Figure 323

The Royal Tombs of Silla

Excellent tomb goods have been discovered in the graves at Shilla because they were hard to rob. A wooden construction containing the coffin was covered over with stones and earth.

Gyeongju, the capital of the kingdoms of Old Silla (57 BC–676 AD) and Unified Silla (676–935), is dotted with impressive mounds of royal tombs. Monumental tombs that remain in downtown Gyeongju belong to the kings, queens, and aristocrats of the Maripgan-ruled Silla.

Maripgan means the supreme leader, which is a combination of the word "gan," the equivalent of khan, a common Northeast Asian term for a ruler, and the word "marip," referring to supreme status. The Maripgan and his clans showed off their status by wearing a gold crown and various ornaments made of splendidly crafted gold, silver, and gilt bronze. Gold was a symbol of supreme power.

Figure 324: Crown, Silla kingdom, second half of 5th century, gold and jade, excavated from the north mound of Hwangnam Daechong Tomb, 10 34 in. 27.3 cm high Gyeongju National Museum, Korea, National Treasure 191)

The Royal Tombs of Silla

Figure 325: Conical Cap, Silla kingdom, 5th–6th century, gold, found in the Cheonmachong (Flying Horse) Tomb, National Treasure #189 (Gyeongju National Museum, Korea)

Figure 326: Diadem Ornament from Silla. The diadem ornament of Silla is shaped into a bird flying with fully extended wings.

ROMAN VOODOO DOLL

(Egypt, c. 300 AD)

Voodoo Doll is a doll type made to resemble a person to cast spells on them or to harm them by harming the doll.

In ancient times voodoo dolls were placed especially in tombs, homes, holy places and wetlands. The Athenian philosopher Plato mentioned that dolls were displayed at points where three roads met, on doors and on graves. Dolls were often associated with curse tablets in that they were often inscribed with the name of the curse victim. They are often represented as bound and twisted into violent positions. Also, some voodoo dolls were crafted specifically for erotic attraction shells depicting a male and female in an erotic position.

The below image is of a Greco-Roman Nude female voodoo doll in a kneeling position, bound and pierced with thirteen pins. The effigy was placed in the clay pot with a lead scroll containing a 'binding spell', a kind of love spell written in Greek. It was discovered in Egypt and purchased by the Louvre Museum in 1911. It is dated to the 4th century.

Figure 327: Roman "Voodoo Doll", showing a nude female bound and stabbed with 13 pins. Date: 2nd-3rd century AD, Louvre Museum.

The spell invoked all the spirits of the dead and the gods of the underworld to bind a woman (Ptolemais) to an infatuated man (Sarapommôn). It prevented her from eating, sleeping, having sex, or even leaving her house and dragging her by the hair to Sarapommôn, whom she would fall in love with.

GIRLS IN BIKINI MOSAIC

(Piazza Armerina, Italy, c 3rd. century AD)

Villa Romana del Casale is a magnificent example of a Roman country house of the late Empire (3rd-4th c. A D.; occupied until about 1.200), baths, a peristyle, and a basilica. The villa is particularly notable for its splendid series of ' mosaics, covering 3.535 square meters, which are among the largest and best of their kind. It has been excavated since it was rediscovered early in the nineteenth century, and the first professional archaeological excavations were carried out in 1929. In the vicinity of the Piazza Armerina are other excavations of the ancient city of Morgantina, with Greek theatre, extensive Agora, and remains of a shrine. The Roman Villa was declared a UNESCO World Heritage site in 1997.

Figure 328: General view of "Girls in Bikini" Mosaic.

"Bikini Girls" are featured in a mosaic in the Villa Romana del Casale in Sicily, a large agricultural estate that was probably owned by a member of the Roman Senate or, possibly, Emperor Maximian (was Roman emperor from 286 to 305).

The room is named after the mosaic and is referred to as the Sala delle Dieci Ragazze ("Room of the Ten Maidens").

Girls in Bikini Mosaic

Of the ten women depicted in the mosaic, nine wear what look like two-piece bathing suits. The girls in the mosaic are engaged in sports; the "bikinis" are clearly intended as sportswear, not swimwear. The girls in ancient Roman villa are engaged in a number of activities, such as long jumping with weights in their hands, throwing discus, running, and playing a form of handball.

Contrary to popular belief, women in the Roman Empire participated in sports shows. Upper-class women in the Roman empire were granted some personal freedoms in the realms of entertainment and leisure, often frequenting bathhouses, racetracks, theaters, and even gladiator stadia with their husbands. However, there were some rules. For example, women were not allowed to compete with men. Female public nudity was not welcome. The ancient "bikini" allowed women to exercise comfortably.

The bikini-style bottom was a wrapped loincloth made of cloth or leather. In Ancient Rome, it was called a subligaculum. The top part of the "bikini" worn by these girls consists of a breastband (called strophium). Those breastbands were often made of linen. These ancient breast bands may have been used to flatten big breasts and, sometimes, also padded to make them similar to contemporary push-up bras. Those bands had to be wrapped several times around the breasts, largely to flatten them.

Figure 329: One corner of the bikini mosaic is broken, so you can see the previous one underneath it. We know that this mosaic laid over a perfectly good one underneath so, this was made to commemorate an important sporting festival held at or near the villa. It is unclear what the girl at the top, the far left, was doing, but the girl next to her was carrying weight in her hand. These are not dumbbells used to increase muscle building; instead, they are used to prolong the long jump: swinging the backward arms increases the person's acceleration, making it possible to jump farther.

Girls in Bikini Mosaic

Figure 330: The girl in the middle is about to throw a disc; two girls on the right half of this panel are depicted running.

Figure 331: At the bottom, the two girls on the right are busy with a ball game. The ball they play is colorful.

Girls in Bikini Mosaic

Figure 332: At the bottom and to the left, a young woman in a transparent yellow dress carries a rose crown and a palm: these were prizes awarded to the winners in athletic competitions. They were the equivalent of cups or medals in the ancient world. Mature women were generally responsible for female athletic events; she may represent an older woman.

Figure 333: The girl in the middle of the panel was given a palm and about to put the winner's crown on her head. The girl between the winner and the yellow woman holds what looks like a stylized flower: it has also been interpreted as a kind of umbrella or perhaps a stylized a wheel.

MOGAO CAVES

(Dunhuang, China, c. 366 AD)

Mogao Caves are lined for about 2 kilometers from south to north on the eastern slopes of Mount Mingsha around the city of Dunhuang in Gansu province in northwestern China. Mogao Stone Caves, considered to be the world's largest and best-preserved Buddhist art treasure, covers a period of 1.000 years, and was included in the UNESCO's "World Heritage List" in 1987.

According to legend, a Buddhist monk named Yuezun arrived in Dunhuang in 366 AD. Yuezun, who thought that he saw thousands of Buddhas among golden lights while looking at Mingsha Mountain, was inspired by this delusion and created the first cave.

Figure 334

Figure 335

The number of Mogao Caves, whose construction started in 366 AD, has continuously increased with the subsequent expansion. During the Tang dynasty, which reigned in the 7th century AD, Mogao had more than a thousand caves with Buddha statues.

Mogao Caves

For this reason, Mogao Caves are also called "Thousand Buddha Caves". While caves were built here for centuries, many Buddha statues and wall paintings were also made inside. Since Mogao is located at an important point of the "Silk Road" from east to west, it has become a place where Eastern and Western religions, cultures, and knowledge mix.

As a result of the destructions of time and people, approximately 492 caves, and more than two thousand statues have reached today in Mogao. Sculptures in different poses, carved with different ornamentation and art methods, reflect the characteristics of different periods. There are so many murals here that they can create a 30-kilometer-long painting corridor if they are interconnected.

In these murals, which mostly deal with Buddhism, pictures of Buddhas and the God of Sky, the stories told in Buddhism books, and the spread of Buddhism in India, Central Asia and China, and religious stories about the clergy known in history are depicted. Wall paintings made in different periods reflect the social lives of different ethnic elements and different classes of the time. In addition, these caves are very important in creating records of cultural contacts between China and foreign countries. This is why historians call the Mogao murals "the library on the wall".

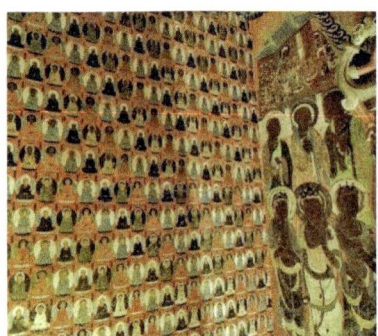

Figure 336

Mogao Caves

In 1900, a cave where books were found was found in Mogao Caves and it was named "Library Cave". Thousands of rare historical artifacts such as Buddhism.

Figure 337

Books, historical books, embroidered fabrics, paintings, and silk fabrics with Buddha figures have been discovered in this cave. Dating between the 4th and 11th centuries, these works contain historical, geographical, political, military, and linguistic works of China, Central Asia, South Asia, and European countries. These works cover almost all fields such as literature, art, religion, and medicine.

After the discovery of the Library Cave, "adventurers" from all over the world flocked here. These people stole approximately 40 thousand volumes of Buddhism books, many valuable murals, and sculptures from Mogao Caves in about 20 years.

Today, Mogao historical artifacts are found in England, France, Russia, India, Germany, Denmark, Sweden, the Republic of Korea, Finland, and the USA. The number of works in these countries accounts for two-thirds of all.

Figure 338: Paul Pelliot examining manuscripts in the Library Cave, 1908.

Mogao Caves

In recent years, the Chinese government has established the Dunhuang Artworks Exhibition Center at the foot of the Sanwei Mountain opposite Mogao Caves. Imitation caves have been created here for visitors.

In addition, the Chinese government has allocated 200 million yuan for the establishment of "Virtual Mogao Caves" with digital technology. With these virtual caves, it is aimed that visitors who enter Mogao caves feel as if they have entered the original Mogao Caves and clearly see the structures, colorfully painted sculptures, and wall paintings in the caves.

Today, only 6.000 visitors are allowed per day to help preserve the caves, and each guided group can tour eight caves on average.

Figure 339

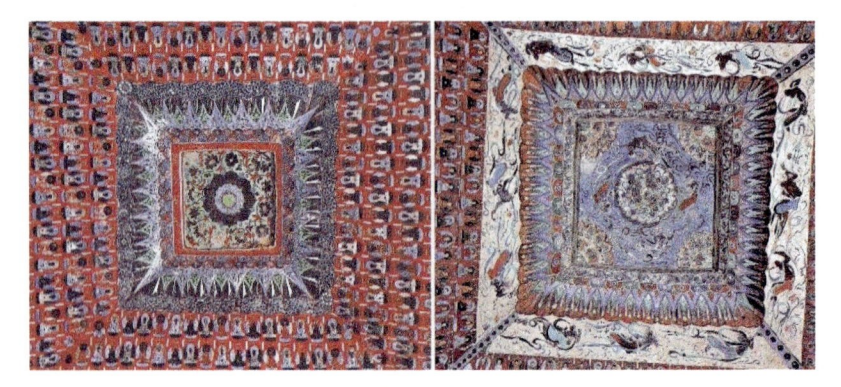

Figure 340

PYRAMID OF THE SUN

(Teotihuacan, Mexico, 445 AD)

Eight hundred years ago, the Aztecs built their capital city, Tenochtitlan, "place of prickly pear cactus," in the swamps of Lake Texcoco, where Mexico City now stands. Tenochtitlan was one of the largest cities in the world, about the same size London was at that time. Two hundred thousand people lived there. All kinds of foods and services could be obtained from its markets. The Aztecs were skilled architects, and Tenochtitlan's magnificent palaces and temples made it one of the most beautiful cities in the world before it was conquered by Cortez in 1519.

Figure 341: Pyramid of the Sun.

Unlike the Maya, with whom they traded, the Teotihuacanos did not have a written language. Nonetheless, their ceremonial and religious center became the largest pre-Columbian site in the Americas and one of the world's great cities. The pyramids of the Sun and Moon, which stand in the center of the city, are two of the most impressive man-made monuments in the Americas.

The pyramid rises 216 feet (65 meters) above ground level, and each side at the base is longer than two football fields.

Pyramid of the Sun

Homes for the priests surrounded the ceremonial center, and beyond them were the homes of the craftsmen and farmers. This gigantic structure, which in the whole of Meso-America is only surpassed in size by the Pyramid of Cholula, is laid out so that the sun sets exactly opposite its front side on the summer solstice day. The base area (220x225m) is almost as big as the Egyptian pyramid of Cheops; its height (65m, with the former temple 74m) is less by 70m.

The capacity of its interior, which for the most part is filled with adobe bricks, has been estimated as being a million cubic meters. During ill-fated restoration work at the beginning of this century, a layer of stucco and stone not less than 7m thick was lost from the original covering of the pyramid. Two rows of steps lead across the entrance building, which is divided into three parts, up to the first level section of the pyramid.

From here a wide staircase goes up past several intermediate storeys to the top of the building, which is where the temple once stood. From the top, the visitor has a magnificent view of the whole of the archaeological site of the most beautiful cities in the world before Cortez conquered it in 1519.

In 1971 a shaft 7m deep was discovered by chance at the foot of the main flight of steps. From it, a 103m long passageway leads to a group of four cloverleaf-shaped rooms.

Inside these chambers, which until today have not been open to the public, the remains of ceramic objects and slates have been discovered, presumably left behind after acts of plunder.

Figure 342: A view of the Sun Pyramid from the Moon Pyramid. Teotihuacan, Mexico. Taken in 1905 before major restoration work had taken place.

Pyramid of the Sun

The most wide-ranging speculative theories have been advanced as to the purpose of this cave system, which was probably laid out around AD 250 - these extend from a place of sacrifice or a tomb to a cult chamber dedicated to the rain or maize gods.

Teotihuacan survived until 1.200 years ago. Its impressive pyramids and many of its buildings still stand. When the Spanish came here in 1519 after their defeat at Tenochtitlan After the Conquista (Noche triste), the old city was completely covered over with earth.

The first excavations were undertaken in 1864 by Almaraz and these were followed in the 1880s by those of Desire Charnay and Leopoldo Batres. Reconstructions carried out at the beginning of the 20th c. partially destroyed and falsified the original outlines of some of the main buildings.

Further excavations and restorations carried out under Manuel Gamio, and Ignacio Marquina in the 1920s and other work started in 1962 by the Instituto Nacional de Arqueologia e Historia all resulted in outstanding achievements. The Arizona State University has continued this work. In 1988 UNESCO declared these ruins of Teotihuacan to be cultural heritage sites.

THE MOZU TOMBS

(Sakai, Japan, c. AD 480)

Japan's tumulus culture arose during the middle of the 3rd century AD, the beginning of what became known as the Kofun period (mid-3rd to late 6th centuries). About 1.700 years ago, ancient Japan was divided up into many separate states. One of these states was Yamato in southeast Japan. Yamato was located on the plain around Osaka and was Japan's richest agricultural region.

The Yamato rulers were too strong, and eventually, all the states of Japan were united. This period is commonly called the Tumulus, or Tomb, the period from the presence of large burial mounds (kofun), its most common archaeological feature. Larger tombs and cemeteries began to be constructed as Yamato society prospered. At the cemetery in Mozu, the rulers of Yamato are buried, and the tombs of their nobles surround this magnificent cemetery.

Figure 343: The Mozu Tombs in Sakai.

The Mozu Tombs consist of 44 megalithic tombs located in Sakai city, including Emperor Nintoku (800 m. long and 600 m. wide), one of the three largest tombs in the world. Tombs were created between the 4th and 6th centuries for members of the ruling class.

The Emperor Nintoku Mausoleum is one of the world's three largest tombs, along with the pyramid of King Kufu in Egypt and the Mausoleum of the First Qin Emperor of China. This keyhole-style burial mound is the longest in the world at 486 meters and nearly 36 meters high. The smaller tombs have simpler shapes such as circles or squares. You can find some of these within Daisen Park, which is located between the two large tombs.

SIGIRIYA PALACE

(Sigiriya, Sri Lanka, 480 AD)

Sigiriya is an ancient palace, built-in 480 AD, located in the central Matale District of Sri Lanka. Sigiriya means the Lion's Rock, where you have to climb up 1.200 steps before you reach the Lion Rock Fortress on top of Sigiriya. UNESCO listed Sigiriya rock as a World Heritage in 1982 under the name "Ancient City of Sigiriya Sri Lanka."

Historical research carried out at the site has showed that the origins of Sigiriya date back to pre-historic times. In the 3rd century B.C., a Buddhist monastery was established at Sigiriya rock fortress. Buddhist monasteries began to appear all over the country. The rulers of Ceylon followed the new religion, but they also used it to promote themselves as godlike figure

The palace-fortress at Sigiriya was built by Kassapa (AD 447-495), who had seized power after killing his father through a coup, fearing military threats by Price Moggallana, the rightful heir to the throne, King Kashyapa chose to build his castle on a strategically beneficial position, on the top of 200-meter tall Sigiriya. Kasyapa and his royal family lived their lives within this palace. Kaspaya's brother Moggallana had fled to South India, where he managed to build an army that would help him return and fight for his throne. Kasyapa fought with his brother 18 years after he built his palace castle. He committed suicide by cutting his throat because his elephant got stuck in the mud and his army left him.

Figure 344: Aerial view of the site.

Sigiriya Palace

The ruins of the palace built by King Kassapa I (477-495 AD) lie on the steep slopes and at the summit of a granite peak standing, the 'Lion's Rock,' which dominates the jungle from all sides. A series of galleries and staircases emerging from the mouth of a gigantic lion constructed of bricks and plaster provide access to the site. The palace could only be reached by a walkway up the side of the rock. Once at the top, people were safe from attack as no one could approach without the greatest of difficulty.

Main sightseeings in Sigiriya Palace are Lion's paw entrance, Boulders Garden, Sigiri graffiti, Fresco paintings of female figures (below the second image), Mirror wall, Extensive networks of landscaped garden, Moats, Water gardens, ramparts, and the remains of the palace.

Figure 345: At the Northern end of the rock-palace the pathway emerges to a platform, from which the rock derives its name, the Lion's Rock. At one time, a gigantic brick lion sat at the end of the rock, and the final ascent to the summit was between the lion's paws and into its mouth. Today the lion has disappeared; only the paws and the first steps are visible.

Figure 34

MOSAICS OF HAGIA SOPHIA

(Constantinople, modern-day Istanbul, Turkey, c. 537 - 1.400 AD)

Byzantion was founded by a Greek colony before the Romans conquered it. This little seashore town flourished to a capital of the empire of Constantine the Great, who reunited the West & East Rome under his rule and renamed the city as "Constantinople". Constantine was a pagan before he converted to Christianity. After Constantine died, his successor Constantinus decided that Byzantine needed his own Pantheon. It was Hagia Sophia– Sophia of God, Holy Wisdom; that is the second person of Trinity: Christ.

The first name of the Church was "Megale Ekklesia" which means "the Grand Church". The first Hagia Sophia was built in 360. It was a wooden-roofed basilica built on the site of a pagan temple.

When its roof was burned by a fire in 404 and destroyed mostly in the second fire in 414, a great believer of orthodoxy Theodosius II dedicated another church in under the reign of Justinian, the Byzantine Empire lived its most magnificent years. However, a three-day-long riot created an opportunity to overthrow the Justinian in 532. People who were tired of the high taxes and military pressure revolted against Justinian. With the help of his wife Theodora, Justinian was able to quell the riot which was initiated by the Hippodrome's two fractions -the Blues & the Greens. Justinian decided to resist the rebellion after Theodora's impressive speech. 'Purple is the best winding sheet' is her most famous quote supposedly made by her to her husband acc. to Procopius.

Figure 347: Plan of the Theodosian Hagia Sophia – the Western Facade – 415-532 AD.

Mosaics of Hagia Sophia

Figure 348: Lamb relief of the Theodosian Hagia Sophia.

Figure 349: Byzantine Emperor Justinian and Empress Theodora.

Both Hagia Eirene and Hagia Sophia were burned down by the rebels. Within the same year, the reconstruction of the new church began. And it was completed in five years. The architects of the new church were Isidorus of Miletus & Anthemius of Tralles. Isidorus was a professor of mechanics, and Anthemius was a famous mathematician. And Justinian was also pleased with their previous work: The Church of Hagia Sergios and Bachos.

Despite Justinian's hustle, Anthemius & Isidore invented a new perspective in architecture. Hagia Sophia was unique in many aspects when it was finished. Pendentives and a dome with a square base were some of the examples accomplished by them. Justinian was also so concerned about and involved in the construction process.

Mosaics of Hagia Sophia

He would rarely sleep and often control the building. He is said to have separated the workers equally on each side of the building to make them race.

For the construction of Hagia Sophia, old pagan idols and edifices were plundered. Marbles were brought from distant places such as France, Egypt, Marmara Island. Justinian is remembered as the founder of Hagia Sophia. However, he was named as "the builder of the world" by Procopius for building more than 100 churches in both Constantinople and the provinces of Asia after his conquers in both west and the east.

When Hagia Sophia was inaugurated in 537 AD, Byzantine Emperor Justinian was so impressed and excited that after he thanked God, he is said to have cried "Glory to God who has deemed me worthy of accomplishing such a work! O, Solomon! I have vanquished thee" implying the height of the dome.

Figure 350: Ilustration – Justinian's Hagia Sophia.

Figure 351: Main dome of Hagia Sophia.

Mosaics of Hagia Sophia

The fascinating Mosaics of Hagia Sophia tell us many mysterious things about the history of this 1.500-year-old edifice. Though covered and uncovered more than once throughout history, mosaics outstand on the walls of this masterpiece.

Figure 352: Embellishments from Justinian's Era.

Figure 353: Embellishments from Justinian's Era.

On the contrary to the general view, there were almost no figurative images in Justinian's Hagia Sophia. Geometric embellishments, flower, fruit ornamentations, and crosses were used in the capitals of the columns, the walls, and borders.

In 726 AD, there were many superstitions about the mosaics and icons of Hagia Sophia. People used to come and make a wish or even pray in front of the icons. So, an iconoclast period began with the effects of Muslim belief on the prohibition of image and icon worship. Emperor Leo III destroyed the pictures, mosaics, and icons in the churches.

Iconoclasts mean image breakers. It was maybe the first big harm to the mosaics. They destroyed the mosaics except for the Seraphim. Then Constantine V continued to destruct many images and icons all over the churches in the city.

Mosaics of Hagia Sophia

The end of the reign of Theophilos was an end for this period. As soon as Theophilos (829-849 AD) died, redecoration of the church began, and icons were reinstalled in Hagia Sophia. This final victory of Holy Images in 843 is still celebrated as the "Triumph of Orthodoxy" on the first Sunday of Great Lent.

Figural mosaics dated to Basil I. Until the 14th century, mosaic art reached its peak. After the fall of Constantinople by Mehmed II, the mosaics especially the figurative ones and the ones to reach easily were whitewashed and covered.

In 1931, in the leadership of Thomas Whittemore, the Byzantine Institute took the responsibility of recovering the mosaics of the Hagia Sophia after getting in touch with the founder of the Turkish Republic-Atatürk, who also turned Hagia Sophia into a museum.

In 1932, the arduous works began on the restoration of the mosaics. In 1935, Hagia Sophia reopened as a museum. The project of the Institute continued for about 18 years.

Figure 354: On the North side of the great eastern arch there are remains of standing Virgin and Child dating to 1354. Below her, the traces of a Mosaic of John V and his wife Helena Kantakouzene. This mosaic was discovered in 1989, but has not been completely uncovered.

Mosaics of Hagia Sophia

Figure 355: Around the Pantocrator mosaic from the 9th century which was on the central dome, "the Seraphims" are depicted in red. Their faces were covered with stars in 1609 in the reign of Ottoman Sultan Ahmed and remained so until 2009.

Figure 356: The Virgin and Child mosaic is located in the apse semi-dome. In the mosaic, Mary is enthroned, and she puts her right hand on the shoulder of the Child Christ, who is seated in her lap. It was uncovered in 867 by Photius the Patriarch. And from that time, even after the conquest by Mehmed II, this mosaic was never veiled again. Although all mosaics were made after the iconoclastic period, it is the oldest mosaic of Hagia Sophia.

Mosaics of Hagia Sophia

Figure 357: Deesis Mosaic, which dates back to the 13th century, is thought to occupy the place of an earlier mosaic under it. It is located in the upper south gallery. Deesis Mosaic was depicted in a humanistic style, a production of zenith on mosaic art from the Byzantine times. Due to the open windows left to it, the Virgin part has been damaged for centuries. In the mosaic; the Virgin, St. John the Baptist, and Christ are begging for the salutation of man by showing emotions in a realistic style. The mosaic is accepted as a pioneer of Renaissance Art.

Figure 358: Located over the South door in the vestibule, the mosaic dates to the 10th century. In the mosaic, Justinian is giving a model of Hagia Sophia while Constantine is presenting the city of Constantinople to Mary and Christ. Both of the Emperors are dressed alike.

Mosaics of Hagia Sophia

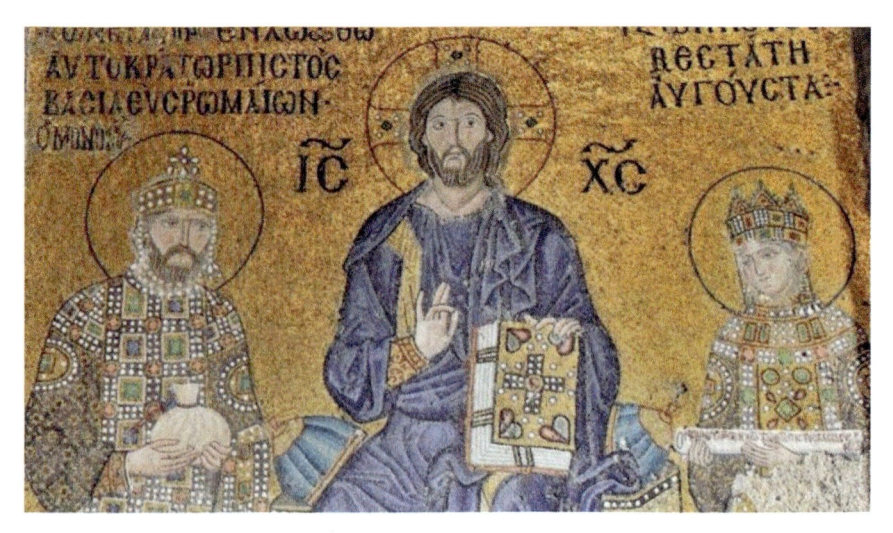

Figure 359: The Empress Zoe Mosaic, Upper Gallery, Hagia Sophia. In the mosaic, Zoe must be 70 years old no matter how she looks like with youthful colors of her skin. She holds an inscripted scroll showing the donations made to the church. The inscription around her says: "Zoe, the most pious Augusta"

Figure 360: Mosaic of John Komnenos – Eirene – Alexios. Situated at the south endpoint, this mosaic panel dates back to the 13th century. This mosaic is similar to Zoe Panel which also depicts the "imperial offering to Mary and Christ".

Mosaics of Hagia Sophia

Figure 361: The Archangel Gabriel Mosaic. Though depiction of a winged angel as a young woman is not an early Christian tradition but a later practice, Gabriel Mosaic is one of the most beautiful mosaics of Hagia Sophia. Located in the bema vault, The Archangel Gabriel has a crystal ball in one hand and a scepter in another.

Figure 362: Mosaic of Leo VI - In this mosaic, we see Leo VI to be performing proskynesis (an act of homage). Christ is enthroned with 2 roundels of Mary and Gabriel. He wears a chiton. Mary's hands are outstretched to Christ to forgive Leo. Christ is holding a script written: "Peace be upon you. I am the light of the world."

SUTTON HOO SHIP BURIAL

(Suffolk, c. 630 AD)

Sutton Hoo is the name of an area along the River Deben opposite the harbor of the small Suffolk town of Woodbridge, about 11 km from the North Sea. The word "hoo" means "spur of a hill." It was an entry point into East Anglia during the early medieval period following the end of Roman imperial rule in the 5th century.

The Sutton Hoo Boat Burial was excavated in the spring of 1939 after a local landowner, Edith Pretty, asked Basil Brown, an archaeologist from the Ipswich Museum, to investigate the burial mounds on her property. Inside, Basil Brown made one of the most spectacular archaeological discoveries of all time. Most burial mounds had been plundered, mostly during the Tudor era (between 1485 and 1603), but a few burial mounds survived untouched. One of the untouched burial mounds held the remains of an Anglo-Saxon ship measuring 27 meters in length that had been used as a burial chamber and contained a substantial number of Anglo-Saxon artifacts.

Figure 363: Illustration of the Sutton Hoo Boat Burial

Sutton Hoo Ship Burial

Archaeologists found within the ship various treasures from across both the British Isles as well as the eastern Roman and Frankish empires — including the famed Sutton Hoo helmet. When the ship was excavated, nobody was found in it.

The body on the ship may have been completely destroyed by acidic soil, or this ship could be a monument to an Anglo-Saxon king who died in the seventh century and was buried elsewhere. As a result, it is unknown who was buried in the ship; however, it is commonly believed that the most likely candidate is King Rædwald, who was an Anglo-Saxon king from approximately 599 to 624 AD.

Figure 364: The Sutton Hoo helmet is a decorated Anglo-Saxon helmet which was discovered during the 1939 excavation of the Sutton Hoo ship burial. It was buried around 625 and is widely believed to have been the helmet of King Rædwald of East Anglia.

King Rædwald (599–624 AD) was an Anglo-Saxon monarch who ruled the kingdom of East Anglia — what is today the counties of Norfolk and Suffolk. King Rædwald was the first king of the East Angles to convert to Christianity, although he continued to practice pagan rites until his death.

The discovery of Sutton Hoo Boat Burial revolutionized historians' understanding of the 7th century and revealed that a time previously seen as dark and insular was in fact cultured, sophisticated and vibrant. Mrs. Edith Pretty donated the finds to the British Museum in 1939.

AMERICA'S POMPEII: JOYA DE CERÉN

(Joya de Cerén, El Salvador, c. 640 AD.)

Joya de Cerén is a small Mayan farming village known as America's Pompeii, which was buried under 14 layers of volcanic ash as a result of the eruption of Loma Caldera Volcano around AD 640. This ancient village is located in the central region of the country, in the Zapotitán Valley, 36 kilometers northwest of the city of San Salvador.

Joya de Cerén was rediscovered during the construction of grain storage silos in 1976, and archaeological excavations began in 1978. Under the volcanic ash layers, including living spaces, warehouses, workshops, kitchens, a communal sauna, and a religious building where a "Shaman" (Mayan spiritual practitioner) performs, which would not have survived until today if it was not covered by volcanic ash and made of mud brick. Many structures have been discovered. All structures are made of earth, and their roofs are made of thatch.

Figure 365: A view of the first excavations at Joya de Cerén (1978). Loma Caldera, a nearby volcano, erupted and buried the village under 14 layers of ash.

America's Pompeii: Joya de Cerén

Archaeological excavations at the Joya de Cerén provided detailed information on the activities of ancient Mesoamerican farmers, revealing a unique example of the daily life of Mayan agriculturalists living in the area.

The fact that no human remains were found in the village shows us that the inhabitants of the village had a chance to escape from the village before the explosion. The villagers left this ancient Maya village suddenly. Although no human remains have been found, Cerén is thought to host around 200 people.

Everyday utensils, ceramics, furniture, and even half-eaten food have been discovered in archaeological excavations. In addition, bean seeds, achiote, corn and yucca seeds were found almost intact in the ceramics used for grain storage thanks to the protective properties of the ash layer.

Figure 366: Structure 9 (Area 2) Sweat house - Its interior, which has only been partially excavated, has a firebox made of river cobbles and earth mortar, surrounded by benches surfaced with pieces of thin stone slabs. A small hole in the ceiling helped for ventilation. (National Foundation of Archaeology of El Salvador)

The archaeological site includes fields with young and mature corn plants, a kitchen garden with various herbs, and a henequen garden. In addition, researchers discovered that the cassava field was harvested and re-planted with cassava stem cuttings just a few days before the volcanic eruption, as a result of examining the ash hollows in the cassava cultivation area in the archaeological site. Joya de Cerén was declared a World Heritage Site by UNESCO in 1993.

America's Pompeii: Joya de Cerén

Figure 367: Carbonized seeds, Joya de Cerén Museum.

Figure 368: Petrified Corn, Joya de Cerén Museum.

America's Pompeii: Joya de Cerén

Figure 369: Structure 11 (Area 1) - A kitchen. This Mayan kitchen is circular and had walls of widely spaced cane which would have helped ventilate its smoky interior. (Description: National Foundation of Archaeology of El Salvador)

Figure 370: Structure 12 (Area 1)- The structure has two rooms, one small with a lattice window and the other smaller yet. Access to the larger room was notably labyrinthine. The principal investigator of the site has proposed that Structure 12 may have been the workplace of a shaman. (Description: National Foundation of Archaeology of El Salvador)

America's Pompeii: Joya de Cerén

Figure 371: Structure 3 was erected on a massive basal platform and has thick walls of modeled earth. It has a rectangular floor plan with a single doorway centered on one of its long sides. Its interior is divided in two rooms, with two benches in the first, and niches and both rooms. (Description: National Foundation of Archaeology of El Salvador)

Figure 372: Structure 2 - Its bed has a niche where two bowls had been stored, one inverted over the other. The interior of one of the bowls had a thin layer of food remains, which still showed streak marks from fingers used to scoop up a last meal. (Description: National Foundation of Archaeology of El Salvador)

TOMB OF THE PAKAL THE GREAT

(Palenque, Chiapas, Mexico c. 683 AD)

The discovery of the tomb of the great Mayan ruler Pakal, deep inside the Temple of Inscriptions in Palenque, is one of archaeology's greatest stories.

Pakal was the son of Lady Sak K'uk, who ruled as Queen of Palenque from 612-615 AD. Lady Sak K'uk ruled for three years until her son reached maturity. Pakal was crowned by his mother's hand on 26 July 615 AD. He was twelve years old when he ascended the throne.

Figure 373: Temple of Inscriptions in Palenque.

Pakal ruled Palanque for 68 years, from AD 615 until his death on March 31, 683. Palenque was a medium-sized site when Pakal became king, but it became one of the largest cities in Mesoamerica and even rivaled Tikal's grandeur by the end of his reign. Palenque began to decline in the middle of the 8th century AD. Around 900 AD, the once-mighty city was largely abandoned, and local vegetation covered all the ruins.

One of Pakal's greatest architectural monuments was the magnificent Temple of the Inscriptions. Like the Great Pyramids of Egypt, this place was designed as the King's final resting place and was completed shortly after Pakal's death.

Tomb of the Pakal the Great

The burial chamber is located below ground level, and the massive sarcophagus was put in place before the temple structure rising above it was built. Pakal was buried here in AD 683, and his tomb remained sealed for 1.265 years.

A century after Palenque was discovered, in 1948, Mexican archaeologist Alberto Ruiz Lhuillier discovered several holes closed by stone plugs in a cobblestone in the center of the floor of the Temple of the Inscriptions and could not find the answer to the question of why these holes were drilled.

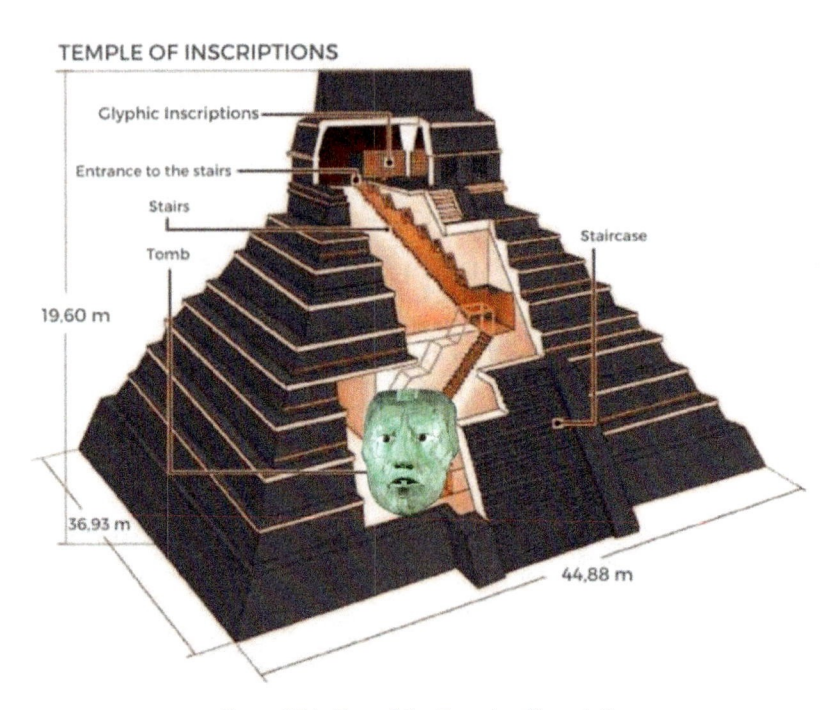

Figure 374: Plan of the Temple of Inscriptions.

After Ruiz noticed that the walls of the Temple of Inscriptions continued underground, he thought there was a tomb under the ground, and archaeological excavations began. Until that day, the Temple of the Inscriptions was thought to be only a religious center. The passage leading down to the grave was covered with debris along the narrow, curved descent towards the burial chamber.

They had been lowered into place with ropes through the last floor boreholes on the temple floor, closing the holes with stone plugs. It took Ruiz and his team four years to remove this fill and rubble.

Tomb of the Pakal the Great

Ruiz reached the burial chamber at the end of the summer of 1952. The elaborately decorated burial chamber was cleaned, and they found the Pakal the Great, along with the richest treasure ever found in Mesoamerica.

Pakal was buried in the jade trim, including a beautiful death mask. Next to Pakal's tomb were the remains of five sacrificed people to accompany him on his journey to the other world. On top of Pakal's tomb was a large sarcophagus lid elaborately carved with the image of Pakal himself being reborn as a god. This sarcophagus lid weighed more than 5 tons and was 3.6 meters long. The entire sarcophagus weighed about 15 tons. It was impossible for such a heavy and large tomb to be placed on the floor of the Temple of Inscriptions later on. So Pakal's tomb was first sealed and then a temple was built around it.

Figure 375: Sarcophagus of Pakal the Great.

The limestone carved stone sarcophagus lid is one of the wonders of Mesoamerican art: it depicts the rebirth of Pakal into eternal life as the god Unen-K'awill, associated with corn, fertility, and abundance.

Pakal emerges from a corn seed held by the Sun Monster in a stance representing rebirth.

The Sun Monster, whose mouth is a live lower skeleton, symbolizes the sign of death, representing the sun's death or sunset, and the sun lies on the horizon, traveling towards the underworld Xibalba.

Tomb of the Pakal the Great

The movement of the sun from east to west represents Pakal's journey from life to death.

In the center, you can see the "Wacah Chan", the world tree (similar to the cross). The top of the tree goes to heaven; its roots are in the underworld. On top of this world tree, you can see a bird-like creature accompanying the god Itzamnaaj. This is 'Itzam-Yeh', the heavenly bird, a symbol of the kingdom of heaven.

Figure 376: Sarcophagus Lid of Pakal the Great.

There has been a lot of discussion about whether the body found in the tomb really belonged to Pakal. Considering the wear on the teeth of the skeleton, the grave does not belong to Pakal; It was claimed to belong to someone who died in his 40s. However, the presence of the teeth of the king, who died at the age of 80 and the good condition of his teeth were later associated with the king's eating habits.

Although the official authorities do not allow the inspection and visit of the remains of Pakal in the Temple of Inscriptions, it is widely believed that the tomb belongs to the Pakal the Great.

Tomb of the Pakal the Great

A reconstruction of Pakal's tomb is exhibited together with other grave goods at the National Anthropology Museum in Mexico City today.

Figure 377: Funerary jade jewelry and mask of Pakal the Great, National Anthropology Museum in Mexico City.

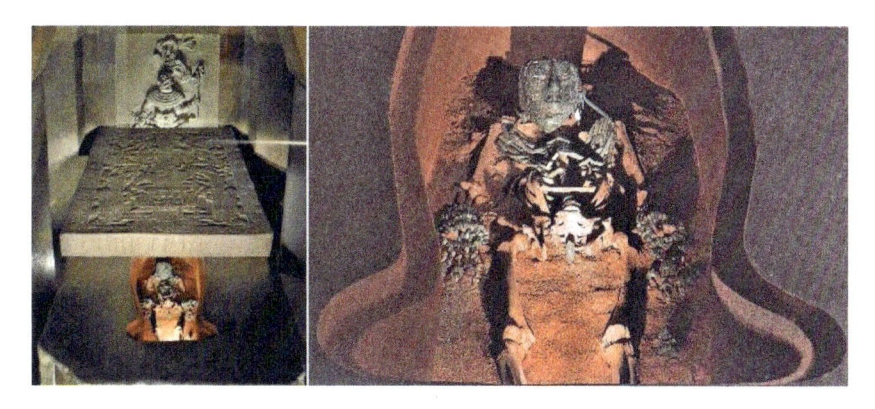

Figure 378: Reconstruction of the tomb of Pakal the Great, National Anthropology Museum in Mexico City.

THE MAYAN CALENDAR

(Palenque and Copan, Central America, c. AD 700)

The Mayans were one of the most advanced civilizations in history. They inhabited southeastern Mexico, Guatemala, and parts of Honduras and El Salvador. They developed a writing system, built great cities, and were excellent astronomers and mathematicians. Ancient Mayans also enjoyed art and architecture. However, the Mayans are best known for their calendar. They calculated the movements of the planets, determined the exact length of a year, and built observatories to study events in the sky.

Figure 379: Mayan Calendar: Haab', Cozumel, Mexico.

The Mayan Calendar

The Mayan Calendar is a hieroglyph-calendar and comprised three interlocking calendars.

First Calendar: Tzolk'in

Tzolk'in (also called sacred calendar), was the first calendar. It is the oldest calendar cycle known in Mesoamerica. Each day has a name and is associated with a number from 1 to 13. Since there are 20-day names and 13-day numbers, the year contains 260 days. The Tzolk'in Calendar was used in various special events such as weddings, religious ceremonies, holidays, to name the individuals, to predict the future, to decide on auspicious dates for battles, marriages, and coronations.

The cycles of 13 and 20 repeated until they came back to the first number, the first name again in 260 days. While some scholars are still searching for an astronomical basis for this cycle, most agree it was based on the nine-month human gestation period.

Second Calendar: Haab'

The Haab' was the second calendar, and it was a solar calendar. It is the one most similar to the Christian calendar. While the calendar contains 365 days, it also had 18 months, and that included 20 days. The remaining five days at the end of the year is an unlucky, dangerous month known as the Wayeb. During this time, people stayed at home and neglected all activities during this time to avoid disaster.

Figure 380

The Mayan Calendar

The Haab' didn't consider the extra quarter-day it takes the Earth to revolve around the sun. It's called the "vague" year because it does not include a leap year.

Other calendars have addressed this issue by including leap years. This calendar was created to be used in conjunction with the Tzolkin.

Third Calendar: Long Count Calendar

The Long Count Calendar was the third and final calendar. Its creation was to keep track of more extended periods.

The Mayans designed the Long Count calendar to last approximately 5.139 years (13 baktuns -1.872.000 Kins), a time period they referred to as the Great Cycle.

The Count counts all the days since the beginning, which the Mayans marked as August 11, 3.114 BC. They identified the beginning of recorded time as the date when they believed the world last came to an end and was recreated a new.

The Long Count calendar is divided into five units:

1 day: Kin
20 days: Uinal / Winal 360 days: Tun
7.200 days: K'atun
144.000 days: B'ak'tun - 144,000 days from the calendar's base date would be called 1.0.0.0.0, for 1 baktun, 0 k'atun, 0 tun, 0 uinal and 0 kin.

Figure 381

The Calendar is cyclical as each period will begin again, but it is also linear. The Long Count Calendar was the calendar causing panic in some people in December 21, 2012. But the world didn't end on Dec. 21, 2012.

TEMPLE OF BOROBUDUR

(Island of Java, Indonesia, c. 825 AD)

In the middle of the Indonesian island of Java, 40 km northeast of Yogjakarta, stands the splendid sanctuary of Borobudur, a marvel that combines sculpture, architecture, and symbolism, as well as the teachings of Hinduism and Buddhism to produce the largest monument in the world dedicated to Buddha.

Borobudur was built between 760 and 825 AD and was mysteriously abandoned in the 14th century during Indonesia's conversion to Islam, resulting in the decline of Buddhism and Hinduism throughout the archipelago.

The temple was rediscovered in 1814 by Sir Thomas Raffles, the British governor of Java, who began some restoration work. The actual restoration was carried out by the Indonesian government and UNESCO in 1975-1982, after which Borobudur was inscribed on the World Heritage List. Borobudur has been classified as a UNESCO World Heritage Site since 1991.

Figure 382: General view - Temple of Borobudur.

This enormous complex is a Buddhist Temple built entirely of volcanic stone. Two million stones from local rivers and streams were used to build the temple on a site of circa 2.500 square meters (123 x 123 meters). In particular, it does not involve any cement or mortar. The architecture and stonework of this temple have no equal.

Temple of Borobudur

Borobudur was built on a hill, following the pattern of a giant mandala, representing Buddhist cosmology. In Buddhism, the mandala represents a landscape of the universe, with the Buddha in the center, and shows the various stages of the process to find the truth.

The main temple consists of nine floors, six of which are square and three are circular, decorated with 2.672 elaborate reliefs and 504 Buddha statues, each with a different appearance:

- The upper three are circular, called Arüpadhãtu, and are oval in shape, slightly curved, consisting of two minor axes aligned with the cardinal points and two major axes aligned with the intermediate directions.
- The lower six platforms are square, called Rüpadhãtu,
- In addition, a base structure was discovered in 1885 that was nameda Kãmadhãtu.

The lowest platform probably also had a structural function to prevent the collapse of the structure. It was added after the temple was finished, as can be seen in one of the corners, where the older reliefs were displayed.

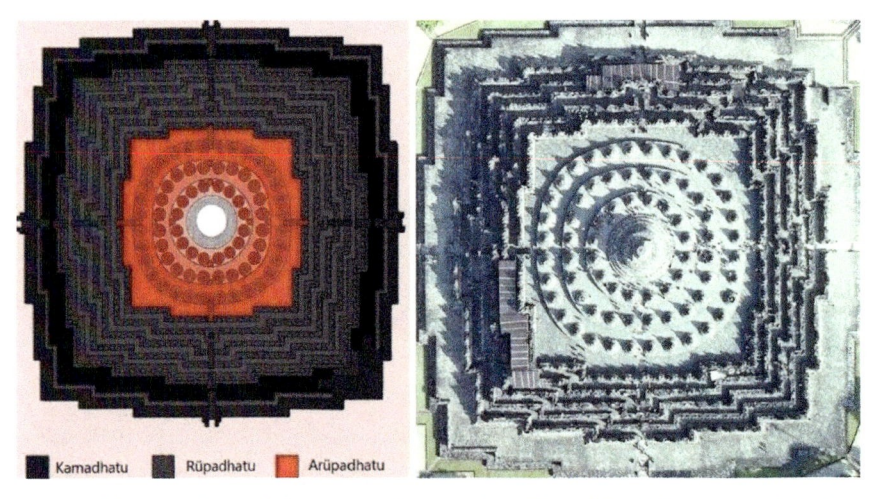

Figure 383: It consists of three ascending realms, Kãmadhãtu (the realm of desire), Rüpadhãtu (the realm of form), and Arüpadhãtu (the realm of formlessness).

Climbing Borobudur-Temple is a pilgrimage in itself, meant to be experienced physically and spiritually according to the tenets of Buddhism. Bas-relief sculptures mediate a physical and spiritual journey that guides pilgrims progressively toward higher states of consciousness.

Temple of Borobudur

As they climb upward from level to level, pilgrims are guided by the stories and wisdom of the reliefs from one symbolic plane of consciousness to the next, higher level on the journey to enlightenment.

Figure 384: Bas-relief sculptures, Temple of Borobudur.

Figure 385

OSEBERG VIKING SHIP

(Tønsberg, Norway, c. 834 AD)

The story of the discovery of the Oseberg begins at the end of the 19th century with a certain Johan Hansen, farmer, and sailor. On the grounds of his farm near the town of Tønsberg in Norway was a mound. One day, Johan Hansen decided to consult a fortune-teller. The woman told him about the mound, and that fortune was waiting for him there. Unfortunately, while digging, the man found only a yellow liquid with a horrible smell.

In 1900, a man named Oskar Rom bought the farm and started digging the mound himself. On Friday, August 7, 1903, he finally discovered a piece of carved wood. To find out more about this piece of wood, Oskar Rom met the Swedish archaeologist Gabriel Gustafson and invited him to excavate the mound. Two days later, Professor Gustafson started his investigations at Lille Oseberg at Slagen in the county of Vestfold. He found several parts of a ship decorated with ornamentation from the Viking era. The archaeologist was certain that the mound was a ship burial from Viking times. But to avoid problems with the autumn weather, the archaeologists waited until the following summer before starting the dig in earnest. The archaeological excavation was conducted between June 13 and 1 November 1904.

Figure 386: Discovery of Oseberg Viking Ship.

Oseberg Viking Ship

Finally, the Oseberg was discovered in 1904. The ship was gigantic: it is 21.5 meters long and 5 meters wide and is made of oak wood.

The ship's interment into its burial mound dates from 834 AD, but parts of the ship date from around 800 AD, and scholars believe that ship itself is older. The ship had 15 oars on each side, so there would be 30 oarsmen on board. The oars are made of pine, and some of them show traces of painted decorations. The oars show no signs of wear, so perhaps they were made especially for the burial. Thanks to the absence of air in the burial site, not only the boat but also the wooden and textile objects were found in a perfect state of preservation.

The archaeologists discover the skeletons of 2 women in the Oseberg. Historians of the time identified these two women as Queen Asa and one of her servants. However, this hypothesis has never been proven. Today's historians still do not know the identity of these two women.

The oldest of those who died was 80 years old, and the youngest was 50 years old. The funeral took place in the autumn of AD 834. The dead women were laid out in a bed made with large down quilts. A magnificent tapestry was placed in the chamber. The two women were buried with many objects, including several sleds and a finely carved wooden cart. Investigations of the skeletons show that the older woman was between 70 and 80 years of age when she died, probably because of cancer. The other woman was younger and a little over 50 years of age.

The analysis of the seeds, present in the mound revealed an interesting piece of information: the funeral took place in two stages. During the first stage, only the rear part of the boat was buried, while the front part where the bodies were positioned remained open for six months to perform religious rituals and place offerings. During the second stage (6 months later), the front part of the ship was finally covered with earth in turn. The seeds of the front part and the back part were indeed from different seasons.

If you want to see the Oseberg, it has been restored and fully reassembled in Oslo's Viking Ship Museum. The New Oseberg Ship Foundation has also rebuilt the Oseberg (including the engravings made by the crew). The replica is called Saga Oseberg.

Figure 387: Discovery of Oseberg Viking Ship.

Figure 388: Discovery of Oseberg Viking Ship - Museum of Cultural History, University of Oslo.

Oseberg Viking Ship

Figure 389

Figure 390: The Oseberg ship (Viking Ship Museum, Norway)

EASTER ISLAND

(Polynesian Islands, Chile, c. 1200-1650 AD)

Easter Island is one of the most remote inhabited islands on earth. It is part of the Polynesian Islands, a group found in the Pacific Ocean. Easter Island lies more than 1.770 kilometers from its nearest neighbor, Pitcairn Island, and 3.701 kilometers from the western coast of South America. Although some still call it Easter Island, those who live there prefer the island's Polynesian name, Rapa Nui.

The eruptions of three undersea volcanoes created Rapa Nui. The volcanoes erupted at different times, but the lava from them joined together to form the island. Rapa Nui is shaped like a triangle, with a volcano at each point. However, the volcanoes have not erupted for thousands of years, and freshwater lakes fill some of the volcanic craters and cones.

Easter Island is named after the day on which it was discovered. It was in the evening on the eve of Easter, 1722, that the Dutch Admiral Jakob Roggeveen anchored off this unknown island. The enormous statues that dotted the island mystified Roggeveen. The statues, called moai by the natives, were so large that they could be seen from his ships. Roggeveen writes: "What the form of worship of these people comprises we were not able to gather any full knowledge of, owing to the shortness of our stay among them; we noticed only that they kindle a fire in front of certain remarkably tall stone figures they set up; and, thereafter squatting on their heels with heads bowed down, they bring the palms of their hands together and alternately raise and lower them."

Figure 391

Easter Island

Sixteen centuries ago, in about AD 400, a small group of seafarers and their families sailed east across the Pacific from their island homes in central Polynesia. Their large double canoes were filled with food, water, tools, and other things they needed to survive.

After many weeks they reached the rocky shores of a small island, later known as Easter Island. There they established homes, planted gardens, and started a new life. They developed a rich and complex culture that lasted for more than a thousand years. Perhaps their most remarkable and unique accomplishment was the carving of giant stone statues called "Moai." They created nearly a thousand of these stone figures, some more than three stories high, and erected hundreds of them on huge stone altars called "Ahu." Even more amazing is that all this was accomplished by people whose only tools were stone, bone, and coral. The moai were venerated and believed to possess powers, but they were not representations of deities. According to tradition, each moai represents an ancestor of the family or clan. They are known generally as "Aringa Ora," which means "living faces."

Figure 392

Although Easter Islanders carved some stone images during their early years on the island, the creation of monumental figures did not begin until they had been there for several hundred years.

Easter Island

The earliest-known statue mounted on an ahu is the sixteen-foot-tall moai located just north of Tahai. It was made in the twelfth century. The last moai to be mounted on a platform is at Hanga Kioe and was placed there about 1650. The sizes of moai vary greatly.

The moai were carved from a type of volcanic rock called tuff. Tuff is formed when volcanic ash hardens and compresses. Tuff is a fairly soft stone, but as it is exposed to weather, it becomes very hard. Some are as short as 2 meters, but the usual size is between 5.5 and 7 meters tall.

In general, the smaller moai represent early periods of carving, while the bigger moai is the most recent. The largest moai ever placed on an ahu was the 10 meters giant at Ahu Te Pito Kura. It is estimated to weigh 82 tons. The tallest moai ever carved remains in the quarry, still attached to its base. That statue is 20 meters long and may weigh up to 270 tons.

The body shapes of the moai vary as well. Some are short and compact. The medium-size moai either have straight cylindrical bodies or triangular-shaped bodies with wide shoulders and narrow hips. The largest moai, including those still in the quarry, all have straight, slender bodies.

Figure 393

The statue carving on Rapa Nui ended hundreds of years ago. However, by studying the moai, the other structures on the island, and the islanders' stories, scholars have pieced together a picture of the island's ancient culture.

ONFIM DRAWINGS

(Novgorod, Russia, c. 1240-1260 AD)

Onfim was a boy who lived in Novgorod (modern-day in Russian Federation) in the 1240's AD. Coincidentally, Onfim created fascinating archaeological records that were discovered 750 years after he lived.

Novgorod is a city in Russia famous for once being one of the largest cities in Medieval Europe. In fact, between the 12th and 15th centuries, it was the capital of the Novgorod Republic.

Figure 394: Medieval Novgorod.

The people of the Novgorod Republic enjoyed an unusually high level of literacy throughout the Middle Ages due to the region's abundant birch trees, a free and easily accessible source of paper. The Novgorodians used these trees as living notebooks, peeled off the paper, and wrote everything about life on it. Called beresty (plural form of beresta - "birch bark"), these birch-bark notes were discarded after use, at which point many would be preserved by the unique mixture of clay and bacteria in the local soil.

Onfim Drawings

Since 1950, by Russian archaeologists, over 900 birch bark manuscripts have been discovered in Novgorod.

The number of birch bark manuscripts found at the end of 2017 reached approximately 1200 pieces, most of which date between the 11th and 15th centuries. It is noteworthy that these items have remained intact for hundreds of years.

Slavs used no special chemicals or methods to preserve these papers (as Ancient Egyptians, Indians, and Jews do with their manuscripts). Softwood, when scratched with metal, wood, or bone, was widely used as writing material before the availability of paper.

Birch Bark Manuscripts of Novgorod are just random papers like letters, notes, or even shopping lists. They are dated from the 11th to 15th centuries and include school exercises, tax returns, wills, marriage proposals, spells, curses, and prayers. However, the most interesting is a series of 13th-century drawings by a boy named "Onfim".

Onfim is estimated to be six or seven years old, depending on the style of the drawings and the type of text.

In 1956, on July 13 and 14, 17 birch bark scrolls were found by Soviet archaeologists, which fell into the ground between 1240 and 1260. Their author is the boy Onfim, who lived in the 13th century. There are 12 birch bark letters with Onfim's handwriting, among which there is a carefully drawn beginning of the alphabet.

Onfim studied the alphabet and knew how to write his name; he was also taught all sorts of standard phrases, such as "Lord help your servant Onfim" (parts from Psalm 6: 2 and 27: 3). Many of his works contain excerpts from the Book of Psalms.

Figure 395: Birch Bark Manuscripts of Novgorod.

Onfim Drawings

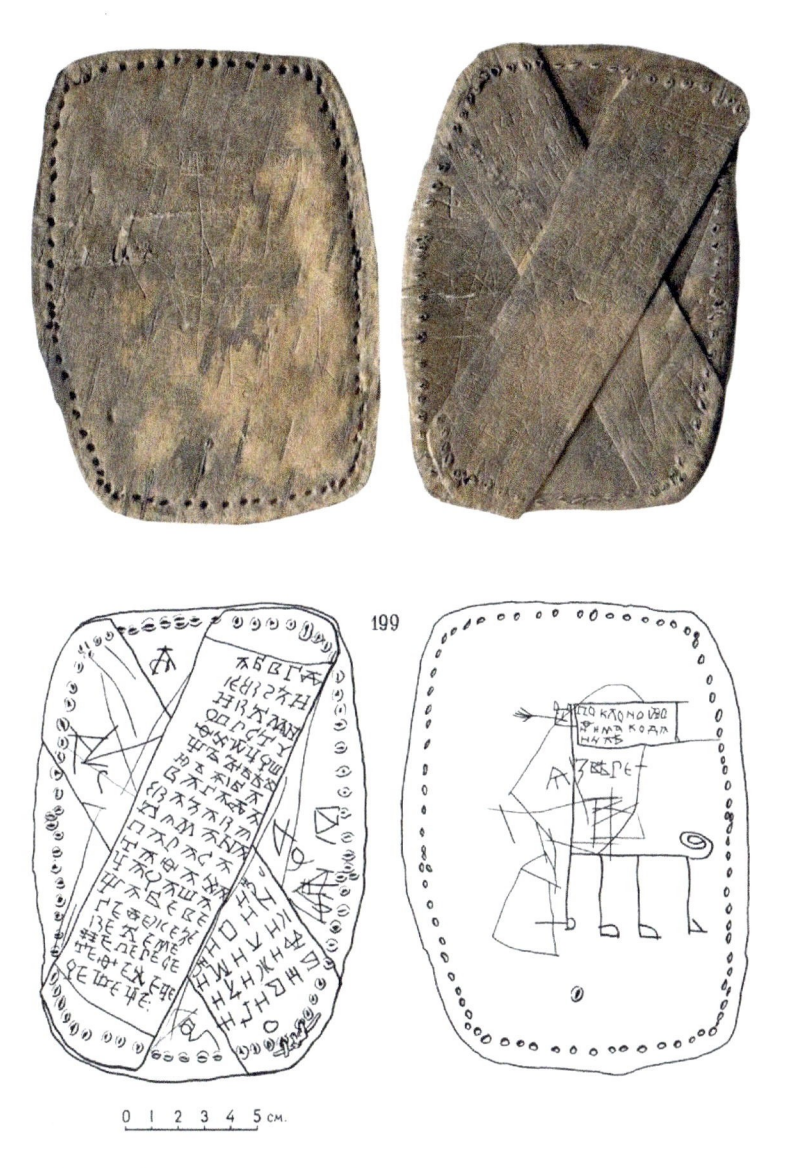

*Figure 396-397: **(Novgorod birch-bank document No. 199 - Source: gramoty.ru)** On this piece of bark, Onfim practiced his alphabet on one side and on the other side drew a picture of himself disguised as a beast over which he wrote: **"I am a beast".** The beast has a long neck, pointy ears, a curly tail, spouting fire from its mouth, or a feathered arrow in it. In the text inside the box next to the beast, we find a dedication: "Greetings from Onfim to Daniel." It is assumed Daniel is a friend or a schoolmate. No. 199 was originally the bottom of a birch bark basket. It was apparently no longer used anymore and the bottom then served as exercise material. Onfim's favorite themes were horses, men, legendary animals and weapons.*

Onfim Drawings

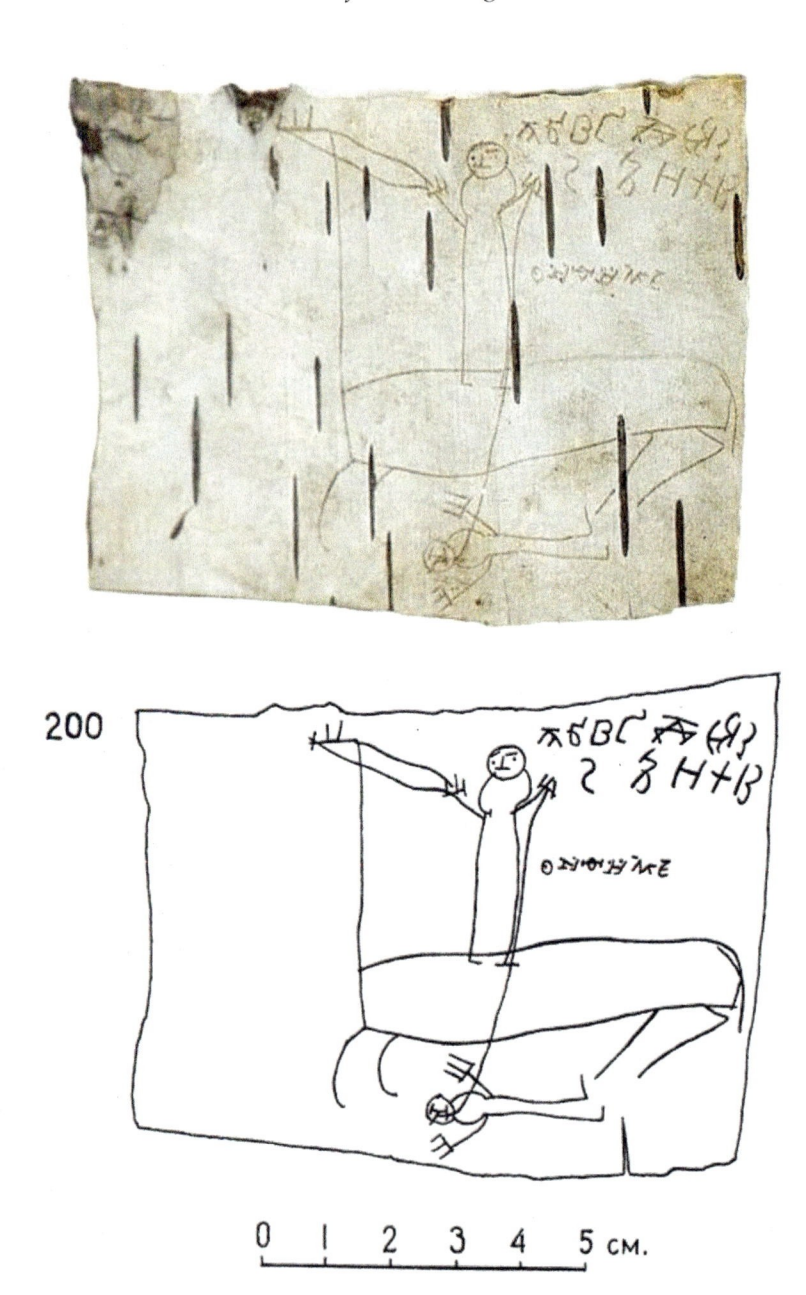

*Figure 398: **(Novgorod birch-bank document No. 200 - Source: gramoty.ru)** Self-portrait of Onfim as a three-fingered horseman, striking the enemy. Onfim fantasized about being a knight and fighting the enemies. Half of the alphabet from A to K is also written out: А Б В Г Д Є Ж. Immediately below these traces of rote exercise, he has written an inflected form of his name: ОНѲИМЄ.*

*Figure 399: **Novgorod birch-bank document No. 202** - Onfim drew his mother and himself. They are not rakes, their hands !*

*Figure 400: **(Novgorod birch-bank document No. 203)** ГИ ПОМОЗИ РАБУ СВОЕМУ ОНѲИМУ - Which is to say: "Lord, help your servant Onfim!" Onfim learned to write not only by practicing with the alphabet but also with small pieces of text. On the left is described as Onfim himself, while the uncertain figure on the right is a boy or a tree with raised hands. Most interestingly, it is seen that the figure on the right is missing, and his drawing was left unfinished because Onfim lost his interest.*

Onfim Drawings

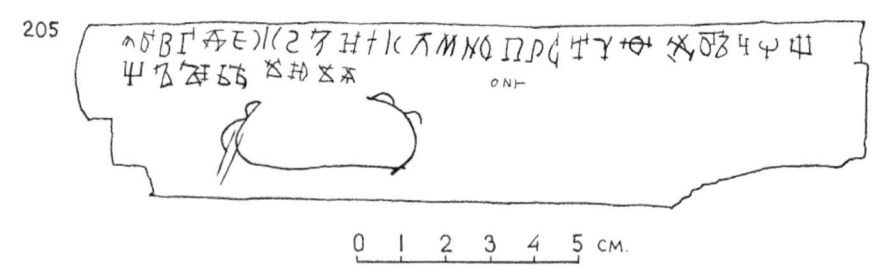

Figure 401: **Novgorod birch-bank document No. 205-** *The letters of the Cyrillic alphabet, followed by On[f] in smaller letters in the middle of the second row. It is clear that 'On' and the unfinished letter 'f' form the beginning of Onfim's name. Below this, some researchers see the outline of a ship with oars.*

Figure 402: **Novgorod birch-bank document No. 206** - *Alphabetic exercises, a series of syllables and "portraits of little Onfim and his friends.*

Figure 403: Battle Scenes.

Onfim Drawings

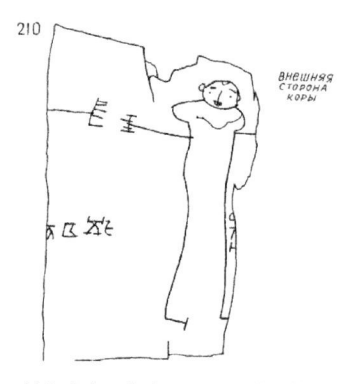

*Figure 404: **Novgorod birch-bank document No. 210** - More Battle Scenes.*

Figure 405: Onfim: "This is my father. My father is a knight. When I grow up, I want to be a warrior like him."

No one yet knows how the boy Onfim lost almost all his letters and drawings. Archaeologists found them during excavations in Novgorod, in the layer of the 13th century. These were various kinds of scraps of birch bark with notes and various drawings. Scientists, as usual, assigned their number to each letter.

Onfim's drawings are highly valued for their childish honesty, which objectively describes the medieval life of Novgorod. Most records of the past are the writings of politicians, theologians, and biased historians; however, children's preserved works are more likely to tell us more about real people's lives.

SACSAYHUAMÁN

(Cusco, Peru, c. 1438-1471 AD)

The Sacsayhuamán archaeological site is located at an altitude of 3,700 meters above sea level, 2 kilometers north of the Main Square of Cusco, the capital of the Inca Empire.

Sacsayhuamán is a fortress built during the reign of Pachacuti (1438-1471 AD), the ninth Sapa Inca of the Kingdom of Cusco and his successors. The word Sacsayhuamán is a Quechua word that can be translated as "Saqsay" - "Satisfy" and "Huaman" - "Hawk". In Quechua, it means "the place where the hawk is satisfied."

Figure 406: General view of Sacsayhuamán, c. 1950's.

The first structure of Sacsayhuamán was built using mud and clay only, as in Inca buildings, then clay bricks were used and replaced with the huge stones seen today. Most of the stones used to build Sacsayhuamán were brought from quarries located 16-32 kilometers (10-20 miles) away in very rough terrain.

These stones are enormous in size, ranging from an average of ten to several hundred tons. The marks on the stone blocks show that they were mostly hammered rather than cut. The blocks were moved using ropes, logs, posts, levers, and earth ramps. The Incas designed the blocks to be interlocked to maximize the resistance of the stone blocks against earthquake damage and built the walls with slopes.

Sacsayhuamán

Built on a rock platform above the capital, the castle is thought to have been built about 50 years and a total of 20.000 people worked.

The walls, which reach 18 meters, are placed in a zigzag manner exceeding 540 meters. There were sections in the walls that allowed defenders to catch attackers in the crossfire. Spanish invaders led by Francisco Pizarro took over Cusco after killing the last Inca Emperor, Inca Atahualpa. After Pizarro captured the city of Cusco, he sent his army to attack Sacsayhuamán. The Spanish invaders used their horses to get closer to the castle and the stairs to climb the walls. The strategy was successful, and the Spaniards captured the castle. The Spaniards attributed Sacsayhuamán to its construction to demons due to its size.

Figure 407: Walls of Sacsayhuamán.

Figure 408

Sacsayhuamán

After the fall of the Inca Empire, Sacsayhuamán was partially dispersed by the Spaniards as they wanted to destroy the idea of Inca revolts. Most of Sacsayhuamán's stones have been reused in the buildings built in Cuzco. The Spanish invaders completely buried the remains of the castle to prevent the castle from being reused. Sacsayhuamán was rediscovered during excavations in 1934.

Only about twenty percent of Sacsayhuamán's original buildings and structures remain intact. Sacsayhuamán is still used mostly today to enact Inca-inspired ceremonies.

Figure 409

MACHU PICCHU

(Andes Mountains, Peru, c. 1450 AD)

Machu Picchu is the site of an ancient Inca city located in the Andes of Peru. Located at the height of 2.430 meters, this site of UNESCO's world heritage is often designated as "The lost city of the Incas".

Machu Picchu was rediscovered in 1911 by the American archaeologist Hiram Bingham, who was led to the site by the local population. Due to its strategic location on the top of a high mountain, there are several theories about what it could have meant for the Incas. Some maintain that it was built as a great mausoleum for the Inca Pachacútec (Reign: 1438–1471), while others claim it was an important administrative and agricultural center whose cultivation areas served sustain its inhabitants. However, it is also considered that it was used as a necessary link between the Andes and the Peruvian Amazon or as a residence for the Inca governor.

The Incas began to build it around the year 1430, but it was abandoned as an official site for the Inca rulers one hundred years later when the Spanish conquest of the Inca Empire. One thing is sure; it was a remarkably well hidden and well-protected place.

Figure 410: General view of Machu Picchu.

Located far in the mountains of Peru, the visitors had to go until long valleys strewn with Inca checkpoints. So well hidden that the Spanish conquistadors missed the site.

Machu Picchu was declared Historic Sanctuary of Peru in 1981 and a World Heritage Site in 1983. As it was not plundered by the Spaniards when they conquered the Incas, it is particularly important as a cultural site and is considered a sacred place.

Machu Picchu was built in the classic Inca style, with dry stone walls. There are about 196 tourist points within the citadel between archaeological complexes, squares, temples, water fountains, monuments, and residences; all intertwined with each other and with the natural environment.

As you walk through Machu Picchu, you can observe two well-marked sectors divided by a wall of approximately 400 meters in length: one oriented to agricultural purposes and the other more urbanistic. The agricultural area is characterized by the presence of terraces or platforms that served for the cultivation of various foods. Very close to this area, some small houses could have been the home of the farmers. At one time, there were not more than 750 people living in Machu Picchu, much less during the rainy season.

On the other hand, in the urban area are located the Royal Palace, which was the finest, most extensive, and best-distributed housing in the place; the Sacred Square, the main ceremonial site of the city, the Intihuatana Pyramid, where the great sundial is located; the Group of the Three Doors, a group of buildings formed by three large portals and the Group of the Condor, which includes temples for ceremonial use.

The truth is that Machu Picchu is one of the greatest symbols behind what was the impressive architecture and engineering of the Inca Empire. Although its origin is still being studied, the value and transcendence it represented in its time, as well as its impressive design, have earned it a place among the new seven wonders of the modern world.

THE GRAVE OF RICHARD III

(Leicester, United Kingdom, 1485 AD)

Richard III, also called (1461–83) Richard Plantagenet, Duke of Gloucester, was born in 1452 and was King of England from 1483 to 1485. He was the younger brother of King Edward IV. When Edward IV died, the king's 12-year-old son was crowned as Edward V, and his uncle Richard, Duke of Gloucester, was made protector of the realm.

In the same year, Richard brought forward evidence that his nephew was, in fact, illegitimate and, therefore, could not be king. Richard III presented himself as a reformer committed to justice and morality who would remedy the supposed misrule of Edward IV's last years and the sexual license of his brother's court.

Parliament, hearing the evidence, decided to declare Edward IV's children illegitimate. Richard was crowned instead. Edward and his younger brother were sent to live in the Tower of London and eventually disappeared.

King III. Richard is one of the most controversial figures in British history. He is blamed for the disappearance of his nephews and was subsequently assumed to be a murderer by the public. It was long rumored but never proven that their uncle, the new king, murdered them. Skeletons found in the London Tower in 1674 are thought to be those of Edward and his brother.

Figure 411: Richard III (1461–83).

The Grave of Richard III

Richard replaced the natural rulers of southern England, who rejected his rule, with those of the north, whom many southerners equated with tyranny. His position was severely weakened by the death of his only son, Prince Edward, in 1484 and his queen in 1485. Across the English Channel in Brittany, Henry Tudor, a descendant of the greatly diminished House of Lancaster, seized on Richard's difficulties and laid claim to the throne.

In 1485 Henry landed at Milford Haven in Wales and advanced toward London. He defeated and slew Richard III at the Battle of Bosworth on August 22, 1485. Richard III was the last monarch to die in battle when he lost against Henry Tudor at the Battle of Bosworth in 1485. Henry Tudor ordered Richard's body to be stripped and draped over a horse and led to the nearest city, where it will be displayed for all to see and believe.

The victor of the Battle of Bosworth, Henry Tudor, did not want to create a pilgrimage site for Richard's supporters. Richard was then buried "without any pomp or solemn funeral" on the floor of the Greyfriars church in the city of Leicester.

Although given a Christian burial, the grave was poorly prepared and remained unmarked. Henry Tudor took the throne as Henry VII, and, little by little, the reputation of the defeated King Richard was destroyed.

Figure 412: Henry Tudor - VII. Henry (1457-1509)

The Grave of Richard III

For centuries Europe had been united under the religious leadership of the Pope, head of the Roman Catholic Church. In the early 1500s, however, a new religious movement known as Protestantism broke within the church. In November of 1538, the Greyfriars abbey and church in Leicester were destroyed.

There was no record from that time describing what happened to Richard's tomb and remains. The popular belief was that his tomb was smashed to bits, and Richard's body was taken by a mob and thrown in the River Soar. The earliest known source for that story comes from mapmaker and historian John Speede, writing seventy years after the purported events. Most historians and writers have accepted this story because there was no evidence to refute this.

Valuable sites of destroyed churches were sold off to swell the royal revenues, and in due course, The Greyfriars site, now named Beaumanor, came into the hands of Alderman Robert Herrick (a mayor of Leicester). A reliable account by the father of the architect Christopher Wren in 1612 records that Herrick had a handsome stone pillar in his garden, marking the spot where the body of King Richard III lays. Inscribed on the pillar was: "Here lies the body of Richard III sometime King of England." Thereafter, in 1711, Herrick's descendants sold the mansion house and garden. Modern buildings rose over the ruins of old ones in the centuries that followed, and the medieval city vanished beneath them. And with it disappeared any certainty about where Richard's final remains might be.

Figure 413: The Grave of Richard III, Leicester City Council Carpark.

The Grave of Richard III

In 2004, the accounts and the map of searching for Richard's grave were perused by an English historian John Ashdown-Hill, he realized the mistake Speede had made by not looking the Greyfriars priory which could be under modern Leicester. University of Leicester experts used map regression analysis (a systematic comparison of different kinds of maps from different eras) to pinpoint the most likely site of the former Greyfriars church. It's a parking lot used by the Leicester City Council.

In August/September 2012 a skeleton was uncovered in a car park in the city of Leicester where the medieval church of the Greyfriars once stood. The University of Leicester confirms that the skeleton is that of Richard III on 4th February 2013.

Following an array of tests including DNA testing, carbon dating, and environmental analysis, the body was finally identified as Richard III and was laid to rest in March 2015 in Leicester Cathedral, closing an important chapter on United Kingdom's history.

Figure 414: Skeleton of Richard III.

The incredible transformation of the former Alderman Newton's School, located right next to the spot where the king's remains were found, was completed in record time and the King Richard III Visitor Centre (official website: https://kriii.com/) opened its doors to the public on 26 July 2014.

The Grave of Richard III

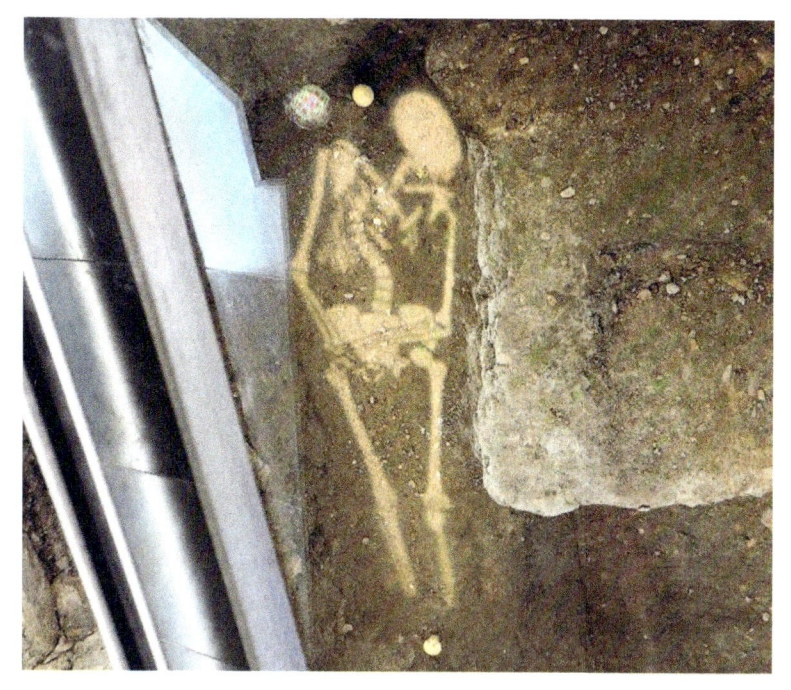

Figure 415: Site of Richard III's grave with a light projection outlining the position of the body was found.

Figure 416: Richard III Tomb and Burial, Leicester Cathedral, United Kingdom.

AZTEC SUN STONE

(Mexico City, Mexico, c. 1500-1521 AD)

The Aztec Sun Stone - also known as the Aztec Calendar Stone - is an enormous circular stone carved from basalt, covered with hieroglyphic carvings, weighing 25 tons, 3.60 meters in diameter and 98 cm thick. It is estimated that it was carved by the Aztecs between 1500 and 1521 AD, before the colonization of the American continent.

The Aztec Sun Stone was found on December 17, 1790, by pavers half a meter below the Zócalo, Mexico City's main square. Researchers believe that the Aztec Sun Stone was first located in the ceremonial site of the Aztec head Tenochtitlán, horizontally and possibly in the area where ritual human sacrifices took place. The stone, which was taken from its location after the Spanish occupation, was buried sometime later by Archbishop Alonso de Montúfar, probably facing down in the late 1550s.

Figure 417: The Aztec Sun Stone.

After the Aztec Sun Stone, which had been buried for nearly 250 years,

Aztec Sun Stone

was discovered by workers, Spanish Colonial and Catholic Church officials planned to use the Calendar Stone as a symbolic expression of Christianity's victory over the pagan as a steppingstone in front of the cathedral where the church community's feet cleared their mud.

However, the Mexican scientist Antonio de León y Gama intervened and convinced the governor-general that the Calendar Stone was not a religious sculpture but rather a chronological and astronomical tool and therefore deserved protection.

Thanks to this, the stone was placed on one of the outer walls of the Metropolitan Cathedral in Mexico City. The Aztec Sun Stone was moved to the Museo Nacional on Moneda Street in 1885 and to the National Anthropology Museum in 1964.

Figure 418: The Aztec Sun Stone on the wall of the Metropolitan Cathedral, Mexico City.

Like other early Mexican societies, the Aztecs' economy was heavily dependent on agriculture (such as growing maize, beans, and squash) and depended on the sun for agriculture. The Aztecs believed that to maintain its movement in the sky and prevent the landing of eternal cosmic darkness and terrible demons on Earth, they had to regularly feed the Sun god with offerings (for example, human sacrifice).

The Aztec Sun Stone's function is thought to be a ceremonial altar. In the center of the Aztec Sun Stone, thought to have been painted in its original form, the sun god Tonatuih sits in the middle holding a human heart in both his claw-shaped hands. Its outstretched tongue means votive knife for sacrificial ceremonies. There are four squares around the center of the stone.

These four squares symbolize the four periods of the eras before the Aztec Sun Stone was made. The Aztecs called these periods "the sun".

The depiction of the sun god Tonatiuh is surrounded by a large ring containing a calendar and cosmological symbols. The ring around the central disc contains 20 signs, which are the basic units of the Aztec calendar. These 20 signs consisted of 13- day units. The 260 days in this holy calendar were divided into twenty periods of 13 days each, making up the 260-day holy "Tonalpohualli" calendar.

The Aztecs used two calendar systems. One of these calendars is a 365-day calendar cycle called Xiuhpohualli, meaning "count of the year", and the other is a 260-day ritual cycle known as Tonalpohualli, meaning "count of days".

The Xiuhpohualli formed the basis of the civic calendar, in which the Aztecs set numerous ceremonies and rituals linked to agricultural cycles. The calendar consisted of 18 months, each lasting 20 days. The months were divided into four five-day weeks. The year was completed to 365 days by adding a five-day period (free days), which is an ominous period marked by the cessation of normal activities and general abstinence.

No dates are repeated for 52 years in these two calendars working together. The Aztecs acknowledged that the universe would be in great danger when the dates in these two calendars were repeated, and they organized sacrificial ceremonies for the survival of their communities.

Figure 419: The sun god Tonatuih sits in the middle holding a human heart in both his claw- shaped hands.

Aztec Sun Stone

The second outer ring, outside the ring of calendar dates, contains a series of boxes containing radiating sun rays and five dots, each representing the five-day Aztec week. The largest of the signs representing the rays of the sun are thought to point to four main directions (north, south, east, and west). The Aztecs believed that the universe consisted of four parts associated with these four main directions. In the third ring of the Aztec Sun Stone, two fire serpents are carved, carrying the sun god in his daily passage from the sky. At the top of the stone, there is an inscription of Aztec history, the fifth and last date marking the beginning of the era.

Figure 420: Colorized Replica of Aztec Sun Stone. Replica was cast from the original in the Museo Nacional de Antropología, Chapultepec Park, Mexico City, Mexico.

ACKNOWLEDGMENTS

Many people and organizations helped us with the research for this guide. For providing pictures we would like to thank:

Airnee Gachet, Ahmet Keskin, Aslam al-Zarnani, Carl Birnbaurn, Classic Stock, Colosseum Rome Tickets Team, Dorninique Bozonnet, Elena Sirnaki, Ernilia Castellanelli, Evie Quin, Firooz Rastkar, Georg Myers, Hagia Sophia Research Team, Hande Gokce, Historic Graphica Collection, Iossif Georgou, Iria Teixidô, Jackie Atkinson, Jahangir Danesh, Julianna Edwards, Khalil Peck, Korchagina Snezhana Vasilievna, Krishan Panikkar, Laurenz Ehrlinger, Leire Monedero, Luciano Salles Melo, Mabel Cooper, Ministry of Culture and Sports of Greece, Muze Biletleri, Naadir al-Bagheri, National Archaeological Museum – Athens (NAMA), Old Paper Studios, Okubo Sae, Olga Blazquez, Pang Seong-Eon, Paulin Larnbert, Paul and Nancy Lapp Collection, Prehistorio Collection, Raya Reid, Robert Schick Collection, Rudy Ball, Sawada al-Naderi, Seth Ortega, Srnith Archive, Shinobu Hirotada, T'ae Si-Yeon, Ted Powell, Tsvetornira Petrova Buneva, Tupoleva Marinka Tirnurovna, Vatican Skip-the-line Tours, World History Archive

BIBLIOGRAPHY

- Alberto Busignani, The Bronzes of Riace, Sansoni, 1981

- Alex Butterworth, Pompeii: The Living City, St. Martin's Press, 2013

- Alexander Jones, A Portable Cosmos: Revealing the Antikythera Mechanism, Scientific Wonder of the Ancient World, Oxford University Press, 2017
- Anastasia Amrhein, A Wonder to Behold: Craftsmanship and the Creation of Babylon's Ishtar Gate, Princeton University Press, 2019
- Anthony F. Aveni, The Lines of Nazca, American Philosophical Society, 1991

- Angela Royston, 100 Greatest Archaeological Discoveries, Belitha Press Ltd, 1997

- Ayse Tatar, Actual Archaeology: Understanding Göbekli Tepe, Iboo Press, 2016

- Barry Cunliffe, Europe Between the Oceans: 9000 BC-AD 1000, Yale University Press, 2011

- Berenice Geoffroy-Schneiter, Fayum Portraits, Assouline Publishing, 2005

- Carl Johan Calleman, Solving The Greatest Mystery of Our Time: The Mayan Calendar, Garev Publishing International, 2010
- Caroline Arnold, Stone Age Farmers Beside the Sea: Scotland's Prehistoric Village of Skara Brae, Clarion Books, 1997
- Charles River Editors, The Antikythera Mechanism: The History and Mystery of the Ancient World's Most Famous Astronomical Device, CreateSpace Independent Publishing Platform, 2015
- Christian Fischer, Tollund Man, The History Press, 2012

- Christos G. Doumas, Thera: Pompeii of the Ancient Aegean: Excavations at Akrotiri 1967-1979 (New aspects of antiquity), Thames & Hudson, 1983
- Clairy Palyvou, Akrotiri, Thera: An Architecture of Affluence 3,500 Years Old (Prehistory Monographs), INSTAP Academic Press (Institute for

Aegean Prehistory), 2016
- Colin Renfrew, Before civilization: The radiocarbon revolution and prehistoric Europe, Knopf, 1974

- Dr. Joann Fletcher, The Search for Nefertiti: The True Story of an Amazing Discovery, William Morrow, 2014
- Euphrosyne Doxiadis, Mysterious Fayum Portraits, Harry N. Abrams, 1995

- Ian Hodder, The Leopard's Tale: Revealing the Mysteries of Catalhoyuk, Thames & Hudson, 2006

- Jean Clottes, The Shamans of Prehistory, Harry N. Abrams Publishers, 1998

- Jean-Pierre Isbouts, Archaeology of the Bible: The Greatest Discoveries From Genesis to the Roman Era, National Geographic, 2016
- Jennifer C. French, Palaeolithic Europe: A Demographic and Social Prehistory, Cambridge University Press, 2021
- Johan Reinhard, The Nazca Lines: A New Perspective on their Origin and Meaning, Editorial Los Pinos, 1986
- Jose Antonio Gonzalez Zarandona, Murujuga: Rock Art, Heritage, and Landscape Iconoclasm, University of Pennsylvania Press, 2019
- Joseph Thomas Rossettie, The Lycurgus Cup, iUniverse, 2000

- JW Bill Copeland, Relic The Copper Ax: The Tragic Story of Otzi the Iceman, PageTurner Press and Media, 2021
- Karl W. Luckert, Stone Age Religion at Goebekli Tepe, Triplehood, 2013

- Kenneth L. Peder, The Past in Perspective: An Introduction to Human Prehistory, Oxford University Press, 2019
- Klaus Schmidt, Göbekli Tepe a Stone Age sanctuary in South-Eastern Anatolia, ArchaeNova, 2012

- Marjorie Caygill, Treasures of the British Museum, British Museum Press, 2009

- Martina Padberg, Louvre (Museum Collections), Koenemann, 2019

- Michael Chazan, World Prehistory and Archaeology: Pathways Through Time, Routledge, 2017

- Naomi Carless Unwin, Caria and Crete in Antiquity, Cambridge University Press, 2011

- Pablo Nerudai, The Heights of Macchu Picchu, Jonathan Cape, 1975

- Paul Bahn, The Story of Archaeology: 100 of the World's Greatest Discoveries, Orion Publishing Co, 1996
- Paul Bahn, Legendary Sites of the Ancient World: An Illustrated Guide to Over 80 Major Archaeological Discoveries, Southwater, 2009
- Paul Wilkinson, Pompeii: An Archaeological Guide, Bloomsbury Academic, 2019

- Roberto Ciarla, The Eternal Army: The Terracotta Soldiers of the First Emperor, White Star Publishers, 2012
- Suetonius, Lives of the Caesars, Oxford University Press, 2009

- T. Douglas Price, Europe before Rome: A Site-by-Site Tour of the Stone, Bronze, and Iron Ages, Oxford University Press, 2013
- Toni Catani, Georgia Lee, Rapa Nui - Storia Dell'isola Di Pasqua, Jaca Book, 1994

- Universitetets Oldsaksamling, The Oseberg Find, 1971
- Vatican Museums, The Vatican Collections: The Papacy and Art, Metropolitan Museum of Art, 2013

Websites

- Alicia Hernandez, Tomb of the Diver at Paestum, Accessed January 10, 2021., https://www.brown.edu/Departments/Joukowsky_Institute/courses/greekpast/ 4716.html
- Ancient Origins, World Famous Shigir Idol is Twice as Old as Stonehenge, Accessed June 25, 2021, https://www.ancient-origins.net/news-history-archaeology/11000-years-old-new-dating-shigir-id ol-reveals-it-oldest-wooden-sculpture-020504
- Denniella Downs and Ava Meyerhoff, Battery of Baghdad, Accessed December 21, 2020., https://www.smith.edu/hsc/museum/ancient_inventions/battery2.html
- Deutsches Archaologisches Institut (DAI), The Tepe Telegrams: Göbekli Tepe, Accessed 2020-2021., https://www.dainst.blog/the-tepe-telegrams/home/
- History.com Editors, Nazca Lines, Accessed May 07, 2021., https:/

/www.history.com/topics/south-america/nazca-lines
- Joseph Hall, The Grave of Richard III, Accessed July 13, 2021., https://www.historic-uk.com/HistoryUK/HistoryofBritain/The-Grave-of-Richard- III/
- Josho Brouwers, Roman girls in "bikinis" A mosaic from the Villa Romana del Casale, Accessed March 22, 2021.,
https://www.ancientworldmagazine.com/articles/ roman-girls-bikinis-mosaic-villa- romana-del-ca sale-sicily/
- Kelly Richman-Abdou, This Armless Sculpture Is üne of the Louvre's Most Treasured Masterpieces, Accessed January 14, 2021.,
https://mymodernmet.com/winged-victory-of-samothrace/
- Khan Academy, Funeral banner of Lady Dai (Xin Zhui), Accessed April 15, 2021.,
https://www.khanacademy.org/humanities/ap-art-history/south-east-se-asia/china-art/ a/funeral- banner-of-lady-dai-xin-zhui
- Khan Academy, Terracotta Warriors from the mausoleum of the first Qin emperor of China, Accessed December 1, 2020.,
https://www.khanacademy.org/humanities/ap-art-history/south-east-se-asia/china-art/ a/terracott a-warriors-from-the-mausoleum-of-the-first-qin-emperor-of-china

- Khan Academy: Dr. Maya Jimenez, Palenque (Classic Period), Accessed July 29, 2020.,
https:/ /www.khanacademy.org/humanities/art-americas/early-cultures/maya/a/palenque-classic- period
- La Stampa, L'ombra d'oro del giovane Carvilio, la Mummia di Roma, Accessed July 29, 2021., https://www.lastampa.it/cultura/2017/11/24/news/l-ombra-d-oro-del-giovane-carvilio-la-mumm ia-di-roma-1.34390857
- Latin American Studies, Matthew Stirling: Olmec Heads, Accessed May 03, 2021, http://www.latinamericanstudies.org/stirling.htm
- Laura Scandiffio, Hidden Majesty: The Lost Grave of Richard III, Accessed July 23, 2021., https:/ /popular-archaeology.com/article/hidden-majesty-the-lost -grave-of-richard-iii/
- Ministere de la Culture (France), Chauvet Cave, Accessed November 7, 2020.,https://archeologie.culture.fr/chauvet/ en
- Ministry of Culture and Sports (Greece), The Archaelogical Site of Delphi, Accessed February 03, 2021., https://delphi.culture.gr/
- Museum of Cultural History, Oseberg Viking Ship, Accessed January 19, 2021, https://www.khm.uio.no/english/visit-us/viking-ship-museum/exhibitions/oseberg/
- Museum Ulm, The lion man, Accessed August 3, 2021., http://www.loewenmensch.de/lion_man.html

- N.S. Gill, Machu Picchu - Peru: Wonder of the World, Accessed July 09, 2021.,https://www.thoughtco.com/about-machu-picchu-119770
- National Foundation of Archaeology of El Salvador, Joya de Ceren, Accessed March 22, 2020.
, http://www.fundar.org.sv/joyadeceren.html
- National Geographic: Jason Golomb, Why the Nasca lines are among Peru's greatest mysteries, Accessed July 02, 2021.,
https://www.nationalgeographic.com/history/article/ nasca-lines
- National Geographic: Kelly Hearn, Teotihuacan, Accessed February 09, 2020.,https://www.nationalgeographic.com/history/article/teotihuacan
- National Research University Higher School of Economics; Institute of Slavic Studies of the Russian Academy of Sciences, Collection of birch bark letters of Novgorod: Onfim Drawings, Accessed 2020- 2021, http://gramoty.ru/
- Omda.bg, Bulgaria's Thracian Heritage: Panagyurishte Treasure, Accessed March 2, 2021., http://www.omda.bg/public/engl/history/panagyurishte_treasure.htm
- Polish Centre of Mediterranean Archaeology, Tell Qaramel, Accessed August 12, 2021., https:/ /pcma.uw.edu.pl/en/2019/01/ 11/tell-qaramel-2/
- Serbia.com, Lepenski Vir, Accessed January 10, 2021.,
http://www.serbia.com/visit-serbia/cultural-attractions/archaeological-sites/lepenski-vir-the-oldest-urban-settlement-in-europe/
- Sigurd Towrie, Skara Brae, Accessed August 25, 2021., http://www.orkneyjar.com/history/skarabrae/
- Silvia Donati, In the Heart of Sicily, the Finest Mosaics of the Roman Wodd, Accessed April 28, 2021.,
https:/ /www.italymagazine.com/featured-story/heart-sicily-finest-mosaics-roman-wodd
- Smithsonian Magazine: Zeeya Merali, This 1,600-Year-Old Goblet Shows that the Romans Were Nanotechnology Pioneers, Accessed August 5, 2021
https:/ /www.smithsonianmag.com/history/this-1600-year-old-goblet-shows-that-the-romans-we re-nanotechnology-pioneers-787224/
- South Tyrol Museum of Archaeology, Ötzi the keman, Accessed June 24, 2020., https:/ /www.iceman.it
- Subaia - Campania Divers, Archaeological Park of Baia, Accessed June 16, 2021, https://subaia.com/
- Staatliche Museen zu Bedin, The Bust of Nefertiti, Accessed January 27, 2021.,
https:/ /www.smb.m useum/en/museums-institutions/aeg_yptisches-museum-und-papyrussammlu ng/collection-research/bust-of-

nefertiti/discovery-and-partage/
- Staatliche Museen zu Bedin, From fragment to Monument, Accessed April 21, 2021., https://www.smb.museum/en/exhibitions/detail/from-fragment-to-monument/
- The History Blog, Lycurgus Cup inspires cool new sensor technology, Accessed July 28, 2021., http://www.thehistoryblog.com/archives/26724
- The Metropolitan Museum of Art, The Boxer: An Ancient Masterpiece, Accessed July 3, 2021., metmuseum.org/exhibitions/listings/2013/the-boxer
- The Museum Hotel Antakya, The Museum, Accessed December 11, 2020., http://www.themuseumhotelantakya.com/the-museum/index-more.php
- The Vintage News: Steve Palace, This Ancient Statue of a Bruised and Beaten Boxer is Almost TOO Realistic, Accessed February 3, 2021., https://www.thevintagenews.com/2020/02/14/boxer-at-rest-statue/

- Turkish Archaeological News: Izabela Sobota-Miszczak ASLAN, Mount Nemrut, Accessed March 12, 2021., https://turkisharchaeonews.net/site/rnount-nernrut
- Vitlycke Museurn, Sweden, Rock Carvings in Tanurn, Accessed July 26, 2020., https://www.vitlyckernuseurn.se/en/
- World History Encyclopedia: Art Rarnos, Early Jericho, Accessed Septernber 13, 2020., https://www.worldhistory.org/article/951/early-jericho/
- World History Encyclopedia: Mark Cartwright, Riace Bronzes, Accessed March 23, 2020., https://www.worldhistory.org/Riace_Bronzes/
- World History Encyclopedia: Mark Cartwright, Sun Stone, Accessed March 2, 2021., https://www.worldhistory.org/Sun_Stone/